Critical Acclaim for *Travelers' Tales*

"The *Travelers' Tales* series is altogether remarkable."
—Jan Morris, author of *Journeys*, *Locations*, and *Hong Kong*

"For the thoughtful traveler, these books are an invaluable resource. There's nothing like them on the market."
—Pico Iyer, author of *Video Night in Kathmandu*

"This is the stuff memories can be duplicated from."
—Karen Krebsbach, *Foreign Service Journal*

"I can't think of a better way to get comfortable with a destination than by delving into *Travelers' Tales*...before reading a guidebook, before seeing a travel agent. The series helps visitors refine their interests and readies them to communicate with the peoples they come in contact with...."
—Paul Glassman, Society of American Travel Writers

"*Travelers' Tales* is a valuable addition to any predeparture reading list."
—Tony Wheeler, publisher, Lonely Planet Publications

"*Travelers' Tales* delivers something most guidebooks only promise: a real sense of what a country is all about...."
—Steve Silk, *Hartford Courant*

"The *Travelers' Tales* series should become required reading for anyone visiting a foreign country who wants to truly step off the tourist track and experience another culture, another place, firsthand."
—Nancy Paradis, *St. Petersburg Times*

"Like having been there, done it, seen it. If there's one thing traditional guidebooks lack, it's the really juicy travel information, the personal stories about back alleys and brief encounters. The *Travelers' Tales* series fills this gap with an approach that's all anecdotes, no directions."
—Jim Gullo, *Diversion*

Travelers' Tales Books

Country and Regional Guides

America, Australia, Brazil, Central America, Cuba, France, Greece, India, Ireland, Italy, Japan, Mexico, Nepal, Spain, Thailand; American Southwest, Grand Canyon, Hawai'i, Hong Kong, Paris, San Francisco, Tuscany

Women's Travel

Her Fork in the Road, A Woman's Path, A Woman's Passion for Travel, A Woman's World, Women in the Wild, A Mother's World, Safety and Security for Women Who Travel, Gutsy Women, Gutsy Mamas

Body & Soul

The Spiritual Gifts of Travel, The Road Within, Love & Romance, Food, The Fearless Diner, The Adventure of Food, The Ultimate Journey, Pilgrimage

Special Interest

Not So Funny When It Happened, The Gift of Rivers, Shitting Pretty, Testosterone Planet, Danger!, The Fearless Shopper, The Penny Pincher's Passport to Luxury Travel, The Gift of Birds, Family Travel, A Dog's World, There's No Toilet Paper on the Road Less Traveled, The Gift of Travel, 365 Travel

Footsteps

Kite Strings of the Southern Cross, The Sword of Heaven, Storm, Take Me With You, Last Trout in Venice, The Way of the Wanderer, One Year Off, The Fire Never Dies

Classics

The Royal Road to Romance, Unbeaten Tracks in Japan, The Rivers Ran East

TRAVELERS' TALES

Central America

Belize, Costa Rica, El Salvador, Guatemala, Honduras, Nicaragua, Panama

TRUE STORIES

TRAVELERS' TALES

Central America

Belize, Costa Rica, El Salvador, Guatemala, Honduras, Nicaragua, Panama

TRUE STORIES

Edited by

LARRY HABEGGER AND NATANYA PEARLMAN

Series Editors

JAMES O'REILLY AND LARRY HABEGGER

TRAVELERS' TALES
SAN FRANCISCO

Cover design: Michele Wetherbee
Interior design: Kathryn Heflin and Susan Bailey
Cover photograph: © Robert Leon (robertleon.com). Lago Atitlan, Guatemala
Illustrations: Courtesy of San Francisco Public Library archives
Map: Keith Granger
Page layout: Patty Holden, using the fonts Bembo and Boulevard

Distributed by: Publishers Group West, 1700 Fourth Street, Berkeley, California 94710

Library of Congress Cataloging-in-Publication Data
Available upon request

First Edition
Printed in the United States of America
10 9 8 7 6 5 4 3 2 1

Peace is the generous, tranquil contribution of all to the good of all. Peace is dynamism. Peace is generosity. It is right and it is duty.

—OSCAR ARNULFO ROMERO,
ARCHBISHOP OF SAN SALVADOR

Table of Contents

Central America: An Introduction

Many images come to mind when one thinks of Central America, that seismically active spine of mountains that snakes between two vast continents: the flash of a toucan against the lush jungle canopy; volcanoes piercing a ring of clouds; tropical islands far removed from the world's cares; temples of a lost civilization emerging from the rain forest; indigenous Maya in clothing as bright as a quetzal's plumage; architecture redolent of old Spain; the unfathomable depths of a pristine volcanic lake.

For these and other reasons, Central America has always exerted a draw on travelers. It is a place to study Spanish, to live out political inclinations, to lose oneself in a foreign culture close to home, and increasingly, to discover the joys of a natural world preserved against all odds. It is also a place to escape the cold northern climes and indulge in tropical exotica through an inexpensive beach vacation, a rain forest adventure, or a dive into a magical undersea world. Archaeological sites pull anyone with an interest in ancient civilizations, but equally engaging are the people here, who collectively have suffered tremendously, but who remain warm, spirited, and open to anyone who responds in kind.

Central America has a history troubled by colonization, military dictatorships, guerrilla conflicts, and interference from that colossus to the north, the United States. The great Mayan cities fell of their own accord, mysteriously, perhaps through environmental mismanagement. Centuries later, when the Spanish arrived, the indigenous people were ravaged by disease and overwhelmed by raw power. Later, the United States used the region at its whim, either through abusive business dealings or overt political pressure. The very concept of a "Banana Republic," for instance, emerged from the United Fruit Company's actions in Guatemala in the early twentieth century. Around the same time the U.S. military continued a series of interventions begun in 1850 that affected El Salvador, Honduras, Nicaragua, and Panama well into the twentieth century. The CIA's role in Guatemala's military coup in 1954 has been clearly documented, and perhaps the most blatant symbol of U.S. meddling is the saga of Panamanian strongman Manuel Noriega, who for years was on the U.S. payroll for drug interdiction but was ousted by the U.S. in a full scale military invasion in 1989 when he became uncooperative. Further notorious U.S. efforts in the region were the funding of El Salvador's vicious regimes of the 1980s and of the Nicaraguan contras around the same time.

But for all of this troubled history, Central America today is an area in the process of healing. Civil wars have ended and representative government is on the rise. Former guerrillas now have a voice in the governments of El Salvador, Guatemala, and Nicaragua. Costa Rica continues to make its way in the world without an army. Panama has avoided the scandals of Noriega's regime since his departure. Honduras is no longer the base for a proxy war against its neighbors. Belize continues to be a magnet for travelers with its luxurious rain forests and pristine cayes along the world's second longest barrier reef.

Central America is still an impoverished place, with a painful disparity between rich and poor, but it is also a place of unremitting hope and inspiration, which is evident in the stories that follow. Nobel Peace Prize winner Rigoberta Menchú finds the strength to imagine wonderful things for her hometown again when she returns to her birthplace in Guatemala after twelve years of exile. Paul Berman proves that one person can indeed make a difference as he delves into the story of Ben Linder, an idealist from the U.S. who lived in Nicaragua during the height of the revolution's optimism and gave his life doing the right thing. Henry Shukman tries to live like the indigenous Cunas of Panama's San Blas Islands and discovers the vital role the shaman plays in the community's well being. Paul Theroux revels in the magic realism of Costa Rica's landscape while trying to escape his fellow travelers, and Tim Cahill explores one of Honduras's numerous national parks. Victoria Schlesinger delves into the spirit world and is guided along her way by a healer in Belize. Kevin Naughton, after an absence of nearly thirty years, rediscovers that Central America's best surfing is still in El Salvador.

All seven Central American countries are revealed here, both in their determination to overcome past and present challenges and their optimism for the future. For those who have visited Central America, these places continue to tug on their hearts; for those who haven't, the stories that follow are a compelling introduction. For both, these stories will create a yearning for that volcanic land between two continents, so close but so far removed from our own daily lives. And make us plan to return.

—LARRY HABEGGER AND NATANYA PEARLMAN

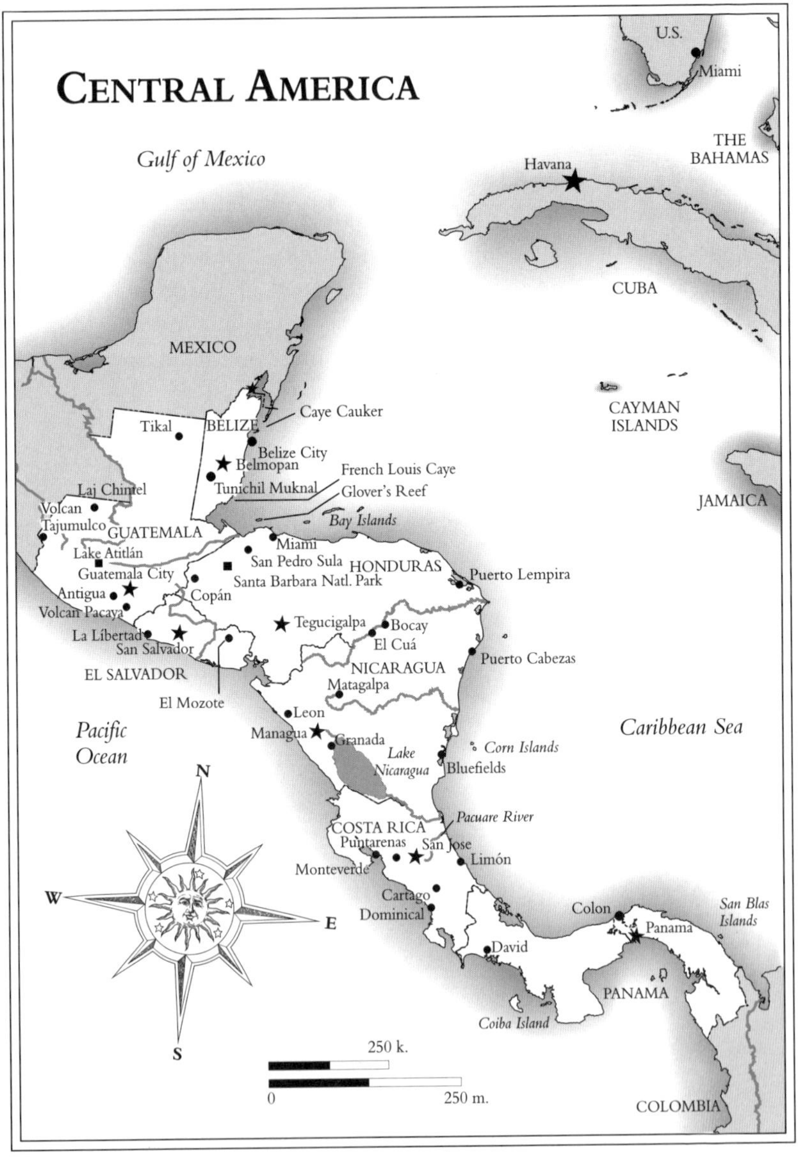
CENTRAL AMERICA
Gulf of Mexico
U.S.
Miami
THE BAHAMAS
Havana
CUBA
CAYMAN ISLANDS
JAMAICA
MEXICO
Caye Cauker
Tikal
BELIZE
Belize City
Belmopan
French Louis Caye
Tunichil Muknal
Glover's Reef
Laj Chimel
Volcan Tajumulco
GUATEMALA
Bay Islands
Miami
Lake Atitlán
San Pedro Sula
HONDURAS
Puerto Lempira
Guatemala City
Santa Barbara Natl. Park
Antigua
Copán
Volcan Pacaya
Tegucigalpa
Bocay
La Líbertad
El Cuá
San Salvador
Puerto Cabezas
NICARAGUA
EL SALVADOR
Matagalpa
El Mozote
Leon
Caribbean Sea
Pacific Ocean
Managua
Granada
Corn Islands
Lake Nicaragua
Bluefields
N
Pacuare River
COSTA RICA
Puntarenas
San Jose
Limón
Monteverde
W
Cartago
E
Colon
San Blas Islands
Dominical
Panama
David
PANAMA
Coiba Island
S
250 k.
0
250 m.
COLOMBIA

PART ONE

Essence of Central America

BUCKY McMAHON

The Moon and Danzel Cabral

On a tiny island eight miles off the coast of Belize, the hermit of French Louis Caye watches the world through his radio.

ONE SATURDAY NIGHT, AFTER A CERTAIN AMOUNT HAD BEEN drunk, I walked a little ways into the backyard to look at the moon, which was full again, a big, orange harvest moon. I was indulging in a little blessing counting, I confess, under the piney woods of Tallahassee, Florida, with a loving wife, good company I could rejoin in a moment, and the comforts of music, wine, and abundant food, a lifestyle granted to me by vast historical forces and sheer blind luck ("You Americans have all the money," you once said) and I heard your voice, Danzel, the castaway caretaker cook of French Louis Caye, reciting a tone poem of resonating pathos. "For tea," I heard you say, "we have fry fish, fry plantain, and johnnycake, and that is all. That is tea. For dessert, we have nothing, and that is because Ranny too damn cheap, he."

The contagious Creole accent, the surprising emphases, the way you seemed to seize upon words and savor the character of them, the sauce of the sound and the soup-bone sense of them—it all sang out so clearly in my mind that it jolted me back to that other Saturday night, my last night on the island. I was eight miles off the Caribbean coast of Belize again, in the dark of the cookhouse, with its smoke and fish smells and the empty bottle of rum on the old, beat-up table, at the moment when you rose to your feet and, struggling to master your emotions, said, "I am not an educated man; I do not know how to express myself to you properly." How properly you pronounced that needless disclaimer, when in fact it was I who failed to address myself to you with the wisdom I must have missed getting at school.

As I write this several months after the fact, it occurs to me that you might not remember me at all, precisely because of that failure, but that doesn't matter much. I came out to the island in the last week of August, intending to stay a week, though I lasted only six days. The heat, you know, the isolation. Hell, yes, you know. But I wasn't the usual tourist, or I would've had a mate, a help-meet, someone to help me meet the heat, bruddahman. I was on a solo mission, there to write about you, a man alone, on a spit of land at the end of the millennium, tethered to the world only through his radio. Your job was interesting to me, the outstanding badness of it, the peculiar combination of innocence and punishment, which is the caretaker's lot. I came at the height of the off-season, when things would be their worst—my muse commanded it—and I was there when you quit.

You said, "Take these job and shove eet! I no work on these islan' no more."

In retrospect, I can see that you were working yourself up to escape velocity the whole time. I saw the seeds of conflict while I was riding out to the island in Ranny's boat. The sight of French Louis Caye, like a floating shrub on the horizon, made me anxious, and I shouted back over the growl of the outboard, "So how does the caretaker like his job?" Fucking fool, me.

"He doesn't have to like it," that seafaring entrepreneur Ranny Villanueva said. He'd worked his ass off setting up the guesthouse out there, and you'd taken the job of cooking for the tourists and guarding his property when no one else was around. And right there you have the futility of your dispute with Ranny. He didn't have to call you every day on the radio, as you would have liked, and you didn't have to like it. "What else is he going to do?" Ranny went on, a tough, practical, imperturbable person in the Belizean business suit of faded swim trunks and shades. "Danzel's too quarrelsome to work on the mainland. But you don't have to worry about that. He'll get along with you because he doesn't know you."

Well, we did get to know each other a little in the days that followed, and we did have us a small quarrel on the last day, about proportionate to our acquaintance. Ranny knew his shit, but my sympathies were immediately on your side. I remember the first thing you said to me. I'd just gotten off the boat—taken in the whole island, really, at a glance. At the foot of the dock, almost in the hooped roots of the mangroves, was the little caretaker's hut. Through the open door, I caught a glimpse of white sheets, a night table with a stack of books lit by a shaft of sunlight—a real monk's cell. In the middle of the island, the rough-hewn guesthouse stood on stilts, with the cookhouse slung underneath it. The dogs—your daggies—came pounding down the planks of the dock to greet us as if they held tickets for the next boat back to the mainland, which they didn't. Then you stepped out of the cookhouse, wiping flour from your hands on a rag, a shortish, plumpish, fiftyish fellow, barefoot in shorts and a Yamaha t-shirt, with wild, wavy hair shot with gray and a grizzled beard and the haunted, harrowed look of a burned-out professor of cosmology. You'd been on the island ten months.

"How you doing, Danzel?" I asked.

"I'm going crazy, man. It too damn lonely. I talk to myself out here. I say, it's O.K. you talk to yourself—just don't answer back."

I said, "That sounds like an answer to me," and you said, "Yes, it does," and you laughed—heh heh heh. Then you showed me around the rest of the island, which you could pretty much do by turning in a circle and pointing. On a precarious little peninsula straggling south were a rain-barrel shower and three wooden outhouses of the shake-and-bake organic-compost sort. Seven hammocks were strategically placed for admiring the sea or dodging the sun. "They're not as comfortable as they look," you warned me in a classic Shakespearean aside. There was a wheelbarrow without wheels beside a compost pile of coconut husks and fruit rinds and fish bones in which five ducks foraged—a female and a male with warty red faces and three buckskin-colored ducklings. They wiped their bills in the mud, lifted up their feet like baseball players digging into the batter's box, and then waggled their asses in unison a half dozen times the way ducks do.

"The first time in history a duck lives on an island and plays in saltwater. The first time in history," you assured me. "You come to French Louis Caye, and you see it with your own eyes, bruddahman. What we want is to raise a whole fleet of them. Boy, that would be so nice!"

And that was it, that was all, that was French Louis Caye—an escape for me from the blinders of luxury, a place of profit for Ranny, and for you, you fantastical person, a dream of a fleet of saltwater ducks.

"Was the island always like this?" I asked Ranny, my third stupid question in a row. I didn't mean the guesthouse and other obvious improvements but the little half-acre of shaded sand between the mangrove muck on the mainland side and the gritty coral edge looking out toward the barrier reef and open sea—the geography of the place. Ranny just chuckled ruefully. He had thrown a foam pad on top of the picnic table in front of the cookhouse and was lying on it, wrapped in a sheet against the nipping of the sand flies.

I am never happier than when deserted on a desert island. Any island will do as long as it is unoccupied, and I am forced to forage for myself. I figure I have contentedly wasted nearly a year of my life on such islands: the wild islets of Baja's Sea of Cortés, the High Arctic islands of northern Canada, and the archipelagoes of coastal British Columbia. This indulgence is less the reflection of an adventurous spirit than it is the product of limited social skills: When my mood sours and I find myself lousy company to the human world, island solitude is the perfect antidote.

Which explains why I decided on a solo outing off the coast of southern Belize where, though more popular with divers and eco-tourists than a decade ago, it was still possible to get off by myself.

—Doug Peacock, "Easy in the Cayes," *Islands*

"No, it had been different," he said with enormous patience. He'd started clearing the island eighteen years ago, he told me. As he described it, you couldn't walk from one side to the other but had to climb through the branches horizontally like a monkey.

I remarked that there seemed to be no hermit crabs on French Louis Caye, which struck me as strange, since I'd been on other islands in Belize where there were multitudes. "This island produces no shells, so there are no crabs," Ranny said, which reminded him of the time back when he was lobster diving for a living and waiting out bad weather on an island much like this one. "That island had too many crabs and not enough shells—a housing shortage. You'd throw a peanut shell to the ground and a crab would move into it. You ever see a crab change shells?" Ranny asked. That thought was vaguely shocking; it seemed to represent a lot of time spent watching crabs.

On the island of too many crabs, Ranny had spent some idle, rainy hours fashioning shells out of tinfoil, and pretty soon there were tin crabs crawling all over the place. "Maybe they are still there, though when the sun hit them maybe it wasn't so good."

Was he speaking in parables, Danzel? I think so. I'd brought along a single bottle of rum in case of emergency, and it seemed to me an emergency had just arrived with the thought of tin crabs cooking in the sun. I fetched the bottle and poured us all a round. That was noon of the first day.

The next morning, Ranny was up before dawn and gone, and we began to find our routine. There were early pelicans circling the island like the delicate parts of some elaborate timepiece, and you philosophized upon them. "After I die, I'd like to turn into a pelican," you mused. "He no have to worry about clothes or money, only to find fish. Though sometimes they miss their aim and break their necks. Then the dogs get them."

I kicked around the reefs surrounding the island, the first of many laps, and hid under the dock during the hottest part of the day, up to my eyes with a mask and snorkel, orchestrating a school of silversides that would part and converge with the motions of my waving hands. And I watched you. Watched you pace the sand and scour the horizon for rescue.

When it was cool enough in the cookhouse, we would turn on the radio, your old boombox with the antenna bent to near breaking by your whipping of the still air, hoping to bring down some message of significance from the world. Music you didn't want; sports was nothing to you: "Give me news!" you said. "The news!" I never met anyone who loved news so much. I remember you were very much concerned about the potato. You'd heard a report on *The Voice of America* that a virus had infected the potato, and then you never heard anything about it again. "Shit, man, now the potato sick." Where did that leave you? Where did that leave mankind? I couldn't tell you how those things were like sunspots, mere academic flare-ups that wink in the general-interest atmosphere and fade as soon as seen. People like me have learned to discard reams of the stuff. Not so for Danzel Cabral. After more than forty years of fishing, you were hungry to learn.

That was the week when Swissair Flight 111 crashed into the sea. You were all over that story. Not a sparrow falls, eh, Danzel? "See! I tell you this happen!" you said, having first heard the story while I was swimming my circles. Divers were searching for the black box. "How they do that?" you wondered. "What the hell is it?" Why did the plane dump fuel before it crashed? Was that acceptable practice? Who? What? Where? Why? And it was the same for every story that followed. You seized the nuggets of knowledge that came your way and vigorously questioned the vague void surrounding them. Clinton and Lewinsky? "Eet between the man and he wife," you said. "Let it go already!" Saddam? "The man fierce. He will be hard to beat." Famine in North Korea? "Where the fokk is that country?" The worst year ever for violent storms? "It because of the oil," you said. "You cannot take out the oil. The earth needs its grease. You can fill up the holes with water, but water not belong there. That's why we have these hurricanes and landslides and such sheet."

You were mostly right, I'd say, a pretty fair pundit, all things considered. Remember when I wrote down your name in my notebook, in big block letters: D-E-N-Z-E-L. (I got it wrong, and that is because I'm a fuckup.) "Yes," you said, "that is it, that is

Danzel. I know my letters, but I cannot tell swiftly all the ways they can meet." Nor can I, my friend. Nor can I.

By then, you'd told me a few facts of your life, and, bruddahman, you never caught a break. A sickly child abandoned by your mother to a Belizean state institution, you lost most of your teeth to bad medication, which has given you your wry, lopsided grin. Lost your childhood, next, when you were adopted, Oliver Twist-style, by a fisherman Fagin and put to work as soon as you could hold a line, filling up the live well of a sailing ship with snapper and jack and yellowtail. He robbed you of your education, but he kept you fed. "And I thank him for that," you said. Next, you were beaned in the head by a random pop bottle hurled by a careless teenager in a rowboat, which nearly killed you. You showed me the long, pale scar under your grizzled beard. The kid never went to trial—too many connections in the town. You endured long years fishing the diminishing local stocks. "Fishing hard work, man. You bust a brain or two in your head. But the money good, the money good." A better job cooking on a banana boat, with Christmas bonuses, but you were plagued by false friends—"bad crows," you called them. A few harrowing years in Belize City, hounded by Bloods and Crips, more bad crows. So you came back to Placencia and started working for Ranny. And he was already cheap."

"Ranny work hard for what he have," you said, always fair-minded. "He earn it. But he cheap, man." He was cheap, and he wouldn't call you on the radio, but as soon as he did we ordered us another bottle of rum. You insisted on buying. I said no, no, no, let me—I'll expense it. "You bought the first one," you said, and I'd already lost too many of those arguments in my past to start winning now. So when we had our Saturday-night party and toasted the moon, you were the proper host.

Remember? The moon was where our conversation started. Hardly surprising, with it shining through the rough-hewn window of the cookhouse like God's own flashlight. A great white stripe of light was slathered across the sea in front of us, and the sky fell down in lucent waves, as if the Milky Way were blowing perfect smoke rings that broke across our brows, wave upon wave. Few have ever enjoyed a better view of space or had to make do with less turf to ride into it. You were an astronaut, my friend, and the cookhouse was your command module, with the tangled roots and limbs of the mangrove fringe behind you a leafy burst of exhaust and the hard, coral, windward edge of the island in front of you cutting a significant swath to wherever the universe was going.

"The man smart who went to the moon. He fokking smart, he," you said. "How he do eet? How far eet?"

It looked close that night, the old, pocked rock. I thought, Jesus, I used to know that. Then I thought how it would be on the Net. Or how, if we had a phone, I could call my wife, who would know. But on French Louis Caye, there's no Net, no phone, nobody to ask. So I took a guess: "Maybe a hundred thousand miles?"

"What!" you thundered, rocking back in your chair in shock. "That far, man, that fokking far!" And then you chortled—heh heh heh—you positively cackled like a miser up to your elbows in a pot of gold. There we were, there was the moon, and we had this, um, fact to contemplate, this marvelous amount of distance. "Boyee!" you said, and you beamed again, like a sports fan glorying in the fabulous stats of a favorite player. It was some moon, the moon.

"Where I would most like to go, in all the world," you told me as we poured ourselves another round of rum and lime juice, "is to Florida, to the Kennedy Space Center. I would like to go there and look into space at the moon. But!" you protested gravely, reconsidering. "I think God will lash the man for flying up in He face. If God had meant man to be on the moon, he would have put man there."

Then you reconsidered again. "I'm not saying we shouldn't go." And you know, I felt an absurd little jolt of rum-fueled optimism at your change of heart, as if we might just go there if we could get off the island. "I say it's all in the manner in which we go," you said. "We must go gentle, with respect."

Everything was silent then, the island bathed in cemetery moonlight, palm fronds drooping like icicles, the vast nimbus of the moon feathered and furred with infinite darkness. Everything still, except me swatting at the flies, the no-see-ums you stoically endured. A single plane described a slow arc south across the sky, a comet full of earnest citizens bound for Tegucigalpa, maybe.

"Why don't you get married, Danzel?" I asked, the obvious intrusive question considering that was what French Louis Caye was all about, what it was for, when you got right down to it. I mean, come on—who was French Louis if not some legendary Lothario of the islands? Guests came from all over the world, you told me, from the First World, and nearly always couples, to spend a night or two naked to the annihilating sky. They would lean out of the guesthouse windows, bare feet on the plank floors right above the cookhouse, and watch the silent heat lightning flare above the Maya Mountains on the mainland, which resemble the teeth of a dragon. We are living right in the teeth of a dragon. You see that clearly on French Louis Caye.

What about a wife, then, a flesh-and-blood woman instead of your cruel lover, the moon? "The happy man is the man alone," you said many times, meaning that a man without a woman has at least a chance at peace of mind. But was your mind at peace? I saw how you lit up with pleasure the day a fishing

> The most developed cayes (keys) are Ambergris, where you'll find the lazy, colorful town of San Pedro at the end of the Yucatán Peninsula; Caye Caulker just south of Ambergris; St. George's Caye, about a mile offshore from Belize City; and the Turneffe Islands, the largest of the three atolls. Other cayes, some hardly high enough to keep their heads above high tide, have imaginative names like Laughing Bird Caye, Tobacco Caye, West Snake Caye, and Glover's Reef. Most visitors stay on the islands because of their beautiful beaches and indolent atmosphere and the hotels are operated by people who treat their customers as genuine guests; you can learn the name of every child on the island, and most dogs, and hear as much local gossip as you choose.
>
> —Archie Satterfield, "Belize: Music, Tin Roofs, and Progress"

boat tied up to the dock and you could chat and gossip in Creole, a social creature if ever there was one. So why not give in, court and marry, accept the usual compromise between exile and community?

"A woman do me bad," you said. "I blame all woman. It a long time I no want to live with woman."

Why? What? Where? When? What did she do to you? I asked, and you told me the saddest tale of woman and liquor I ever heard. She wiped your shot glass on her what? I said. My turn to rock back in my chair, shocked.

"I tell you, I smell it, man!"

You smelled it, but you hadn't seen her reach down the front of her skirt to do it, so you brought the glass to your lips, and the bad crows, raucous, squawking, roared with laughter.

That's when you stood up. "I am not an educated man; I do not know how to express myself to you properly." And what did I say? Such bad behavior, who can account for it? Forgive and forget. Let it go, for God's sake. Some platitude I don't remember. I remember that it was late, and I dragged a foam pad out to the end of the dock and tried to sleep, watching the moon march across the sky, hour by hour. And it only occurred to me months later, in light of the events that followed, that the rest of that night might have been your agony in the garden, and I was the sleeping apostle.

The next morning, you seemed happy. I was happy—I'd decided it was time for me to go home. I had my story. All that was left was to take your picture. You posed in the cookhouse, looking out the window to the sea. Then you got up and wanted me to follow you outside. "You got to take the ducks!" And I shot the ducks. "You got to have a picture of the dogs!" I shot the dogs. "And the beans!" you said. You hustled back into the cookhouse and stirred the pot, lifting up a spoonful of beans to the camera's lens, laughing. Were you making fun of me? I think maybe you were.

"When you write these book about the island," you said, "maybe good things come." It's just a magazine article; you can't expect much, I told you. "Maybe this magazine article help me to find a wife." I said I hoped it would, and would you call Ranny and tell him I'm ready to leave? "He should call me," you said. "I work for him; he not work for me. He should call me. I could be lying down dead here and nobody know." You're right, I said, but would you give him a call?

While I waited, I decided to take a kayak and paddle to Laughing Bird Caye, which I'd been meaning to do all week, though you'd told me not to—"Eet too far, man!" You were right again. It took all afternoon, and it crushed me. I oozed toward the horizon in the little plastic boat; I crawled, melting, like a paramecium on a microscope slide. When I finally pulled into the shade of the mangroves on Laughing Bird Caye, I looked up and saw a pelican hanging in a crook in the branches, its bill open wide in final derision. Some last laugh that was—some joke. I thought, man, I got to go home.

I made it back to French Louis, barely, all burned up, and you were in the cookhouse, sending out an SOS of existential urgency. "Kitty's Place, Kitty's Place, this is French Louis Caye, do you copy? Kitty's Place, Kitty's Place, this is French Louis Caye, do you copy?" Over and over, until finally somebody broke in and said, "Shut up, you bloody ass!" You came storming out of the cookhouse, furious. "You hear that?" you said. "That man call me a big, bad word! He lucky I not know who he are."

"What would you do?" I asked mercilessly.

"Why, I tell him not to call me that, not on Channel 16. That is a public channel, man. You not supposed to curse. And where you go?" you asked me. "I tell you eet too far, but you not listen."

Back into the cookhouse you stormed, back to the radio.

Next thing I knew, Ranny showed up with two new tourists—a young couple this time, the usual thing, backpackers, badly sunburned but full of play and fun—and a new caretaker, this one tall and slim and quiet but looking decidedly nervous as he began to stow away their food. Ranny put you off the boat on the beach at Placencia with all your belongings, which seemed to consist of just your radio and two big bundles of refundable soda bottles. You hadn't said a word the whole way back, and I couldn't think what to say. The last I saw of you was your back as you trudged up the sand under your burden into a very uncertain future.

Which is why I'm writing this the way I'm writing it, making the letters meet this way and not in some other, and not very swiftly, either, I assure you. It's in the hope that someday somebody might read it to you, maybe some tourist if you go back to French Louis Caye or, far better and my fondest hope for you, a good woman who has seen your picture in a magazine and wonders, "Who the heck is this Danzel Cabral?" I'd say he was the cosmic Maytag repairman, ma'am, sitting on an island and doing the heavy mental lifting of moving the moon across the sky. A thinking man and a Christian. "I obey the Commandments and treat people good, and that is a Christian," you once said. Let that be your introduction; I could never write a better one. There's this groovy theory, Danzel, of the cognoscenti—obscure men, wise and good and true, who keep the earth rolling on its appointed rounds. Oil where the oil belongs, water where water goes.

Those things you know. Possibly nobody has told you this before, but you are a great man and, at the very least, an all right guy. Not cracked, not fucked, and not finished. Just don't move into any tin shells, and look out for things falling from the sky, and maybe you'll be all right. I hope so. "If you cook, you're going to get burned (and I just did)," you once said, and said it with a grin, that Danzel grin that takes a stubborn sidelong bite at the world and veers to the side with it like a front end with bad alignment, but always toward something kind and good. And that is the whole point of Danzel Cabral—de hool fokking pint, man!

Bucky McMahon's stories have appeared in many national magazines. A longtime Floridian, he has traveled extensively throughout the warmer parts of the world, scuba diving, surfing, and meeting amazing people. He is a contributing editor for Esquire, *and lives outside Tallahassee, Florida with his wife, fellow world traveler Heather Montanye.*

TIM CAHILL

The Lone Ranger

In his hands rests the well-being of an entire mountain preserve.

THE HIGHEST, THE MOST REMOTE MOUNTAINS ON THE MAINLAND of Honduras form the nucleus of several national parks. We were driving along a network of bad dirt roads, looking for a way to enter the newly established Santa Barbara Park. It was steep country, very green, and the mountains were closely spaced. The land, to my eye, possessed the logic of a sheet of paper crumpled in the hand and dropped on a table.

There were cattle grazing in vertical pastures, moving under strange knobby green peaks. Pineapples grew in adjacent fields, and clear-cuts wound their way up the slopes of the higher mountains, which marched off into the distance, purple against the rising smoke of the agricultural fires burning everywhere.

The roads lacked signage of any sort and branched off to various tiny villages, where we saw horses, saddled Western-style, laden with bananas or pineapples and tied to hitching posts in front of the cantinas. Men in straw cowboy hats and Western-cut shirts pointed off in several different directions at once when we inquired about a route into the mountains above.

The road dropped back down to the country's major north-south highway, which fronted the west side of Lake Yojoa, 100 square miles of clear waters, fringed with coffee plantations, a few resorts, and dozens of prosperous-looking farms. The lake, a seriously picturesque affair, was stocked with large and apparently exceedingly dumb bass. There were at least thirty restaurants lining the highway, each of them selling bass and only bass. We stopped at one of the upscale places, redundantly named Only Bass. They served bass with devil sauce, with tartar sauce, with garlic butter; we could have our bass fried, grilled, or baked. Everything was delicious except for the only beer on the menu, a sour imported American brand whose uniquely honest sales pitch is, "It doesn't get any better than this."

Later that night, we stopped in the town of Santa Barbara and tried to get a fix on the national park rising all around in the darkness. Since the directions given in the town square all smacked of misinformation and Casablanca, we counted ourselves fortunate to run into a man named Martine Rodriguez, of the Green Heart Ecological Association, who trotted us off to his nearby office, showed us some maps, and told us that we could get into the park via the village of San José de Los Andes. The village was set about a mile high and was one of the highest settlements in Honduras. Could we get up there in a two-wheel-drive car without much clearance? Not in the rainy season, Martine said, but since it had been pretty dry lately, hey, no problem.

Which is how, the next day, we came to be irremediably stuck on a cruel boulder-strewn joke of a road at an elevation of about five thousand feet and two miles short of San José. Men from the village, returning from work in the fields, stopped and gave us a hand, as a matter of course. It was necessary to unload the van: twelve big bags, including four backpacks, three tents, and two disassembled kayaks weighing over one hundred pounds apiece. The men literally lifted the van out of some ruts and helped us push it the rest of the way to San José. While they seemed shy, it was clear that we were a source of some quiet amusement to these friendly men.

The town was set out along a sloping dusty street lined mostly by one- and two-room wooden houses. The people were mestizo, which is to say, of mixed European and American Indian heritage:

Almost 90 percent of all Hondurans are mestizo. They directed us to the home of Peggy Chui, a young American Peace Corps volunteer, who lived in a small wooden house with a bucket-flush toilet, a kerosene stove, and a battery-driven shortwave radio.

We cooked dinner for Peggy and ended up talking on her porch, under a sky studded with van Gogh stars, while the lights of various fishing resorts twinkled on the shores of Lake Yojoa far below.

Peggy was working with the village farmers, developing better methods of hillside agriculture. The people of San José, she said, got bad seeds, which they sowed in poor soil. The year before, when the bean crop had come in sparse, some people had gone hungry for a time. Sixty percent of the country lived like this, Peggy said, whole villages existing hand to mouth on subsistence agriculture.

But—and this was hard for her to express exactly—the people in San José seemed...well, content. Happy. *Pero como* was the stoic motto: What can you do? It had taken Peggy a year to feel at home in the village, and now it was a part of her. There were evenings, she said, when a cool fog rolled up out of Yojoa and enveloped her, times when she felt as if she were living inside a glittering cloud, and the whole place felt mystical.

She introduced us to her neighbor, a man named Octivilo Ramos, who had been the chief (and only) ranger for Santa Barbara National Park since it was established in 1987. It was an unpaid position. He was also the only guide in the area, and offered to take us into the forest for a fair price. We bargained in the Honduran fashion, which is to say, when Octivilo named a figure, forty lempira a day apiece, we were struck speechless with an agony of grief and stared hopelessly at the ground. Octivilo let us live in the silence of our unbearable pain for all of thirty seconds, then suggested thirty-five a day. Thirty-five? We stared at one another in shocked delight. Our joy was uncontainable. He couldn't possibly mean it. Thirty-five? Why, it was a miracle. We shook hands on the deal and agreed to start off into the forest at dawn the next day.

Later, after Octivilo went home, Peggy said thirty-five lemps was, in fact, his usual price, which was damn good money in San José. When people worked for others—picking coffee, for instance—

the average wage in the area came to about ten lempira (about a dollar) a day. On our two-day trek, Octivilo would earn the equivalent of twenty-eight days of average wages.

Not many people came to San José to visit the forest, Peggy said. There had been five parties her first year, ten the next.

I suggested that while the numbers were small, visitation had doubled. Since people sometimes went hungry in the village, was it possible that some sort of trekking tourism could make up the slack?

Peggy was torn on the issue. In the best of all worlds the people of San José would improve their farming methods, feed themselves, and live as they always had. You only had to go to Copán, the country's major tourist destination, to see what San José could become. The people there, in Peggy's view, were aggressive, fixated on profit. Most of all, they didn't seem happy.

And yet…the poverty in San José could make your heart ache in dozens of small ways every day. Look at the children, Peggy said. There was no dentist anywhere nearby, no money to get one up to the village, and no real

---

The girls were waiting when I left. We walked from my budget hotel to the new luxury resort where the package tourists were boarding their coach. For three days the girls had waited patiently for a sale, and now the time had come. I looked over the choices they offered me, and it was immediately clear that I wouldn't get away with buying just one. I stood before the girls like Paris before Athena, Aphrodite, and Hera: an impossible choice. I selected one from each and said goodbye.

On board, the elderly package tourists asked me how much I had paid for the idols.

"Did you hear that, George? That's pretty cheap, and we've got to use up our Honduras money."

Before the bus departed, half the group descended to buy the girls' masks and statuettes. The three of them grinned and waved, their stock sold out.

—Stephen Benz, *Green Dreams: Travels in Central America*

---

understanding of the techniques of oral hygiene. When the children, these beautiful children, smiled up at you, their mouths were full of rotting black stumps. So, yes, Peggy supposed, you could put in a visitors' center, charge a small fee of each trekker, and pay for monthly visits from a dentist. Thing was: Where did something like that end?

The next morning, Octivilo marched us through town, out over the coffee plantations, and up through an area of clear-cut that ran smack into the boundaries of the national park. An hour or so into the park we came upon a small canyon that had been slashed and burned.

Octivilo was a "Spaniard" Verne Hyde would have loved. [Verne Hyde was a septuagenarian native of the island of Guanaja who blamed "Spaniards," Spanish-speaking immigrants from the mainland, for despoiling the island.] He stopped there to give us a quick lecture on ecology. Whoever burned the area was planning on planting a crop, using water that would naturally flow into the area. The problem, Octivilo said, was that heavy rains later in the year would erode the gully and cause mudslides to destroy cropland below. Worse, the forest floor, littered with over a foot of fallen vegetation, acted as a giant sponge, storing rainwater that fell during the wet season and releasing it slowly during the dry. Cut the forest, he said, and the rivers—like the one on Verne Hyde's place—would begin to dry up. All the crops below, all the way to Yojoa, would die of thirst.

Octivilo said he'd known about the burn and was investigating. He was an honest, knowledgeable man but essentially a volunteer. Could he really turn in one of his neighbors. In a town of five hundred people?

The cloud forest above the burn was thick—you couldn't really see more than ten feet in any direction—and the trail was narrow, sometimes nonexistent. We passed giant hardwood trees, a type of mahogany, 100 feet high, and the branches were hung with woody vines, with great masses of moss. Everywhere, in all the trees, there were red parasitic flowers the size of basketballs. Looking up induced a kind of vertigo: all the smaller trees bent and twisted their way toward the sun, toward a patch of open sky, so nothing grew straight up and down. There was a sense, in this dizzying forest, that every living thing longed for the death of its nearest neighbor. The mosquitoes were fierce.

Our campsite was a limestone overhang, fringed with woody vines dropped from the trees growing on the ledge above. Octivilo shared my tent that night, and he told me that there were some nonpoisonous snakes in the forest, a number of small deer, a few ocelot, and a lot of foul-smelling bad-tempered peccaries. The monkeys were gone, hunted out, but there were plans to reintroduce them.

Not everyone, Octivilo said, agreed about how the new national parks of Honduras should be administered. There was some dissension in the capital city of Tegucigalpa. One group, noting the economic benefits Costa Rica was enjoying from ecotourism, wanted to open up everything, everywhere, to unrestricted travel. Another group was more cautious and felt some areas should be preserved to protect the wildlife and the watershed. Octivilo wasn't sure which was really the right approach, but he seemed proud that Santa Barbara wasn't all that accessible to the outside world.

There were times, he said, when it felt as if he were the only person in the forest. He especially liked the winter months, when it sometimes snowed in the higher elevations. There was a very distinct line at about eighteen hundred meters. Everything below was green; everything above, white. The snow bowed down the branches of the trees, covered the red flowers, and was knee-deep on the ground.

In the morning we puttered around camp, then walked back through a forest that was shrouded in clouds. Peggy said that while we were gone, there had been a gathering of townsfolk and we had been one topic of conversation. Her friend Pedro related the story of how badly we'd been stuck, how we had to unload the van and push it up the hill. He told the story in such a way that people were doubled over in laughter. Peggy—she said she was sorry about this, she couldn't help it—then told people that the big red bags we unloaded, the heavy ones, the ones we carried, sweating and cursing two miles up the mountain: those bags contained...boats.

Oceangoing boats. People had laughed until there were tears in their eyes.

Tim Cahill is the author of seven books, including Jaguars Ripped My Flesh, Pecked to Death by Ducks, Dolphins, *and* Pass the Butterworms, *from which this story was excerpted. He describes what he does for a living as "remote journeys, oddly rendered." He is also the editor of* Not So Funny When It Happened: The Best of Travel Humor and Misadventure, *and the co-author of the Academy Award nominated IMAX film,* The Living Sea, *as well as the films* Everest *and* Dolphins. *He lives in Montana and shares his life with Linnea Larson, two dogs, and two cats.*

EMILY HIESTAND

At the Station

Bargains can be subtle, and you need to hold up your side.

SKIFFS LEAVE BELIZE CITY FOR THE OFFSHORE CAYES AT UNPREDICTABLE times from moorings next to a Shell marine fuel station on Haulover Creek, whose water at this point is black as the asphalt and shimmers with the same rainbow of oil as the pools spilled near the station pumps. The city's open sewage canal runs alongside the shed at one end of the station and empties into the river at just this point. A foul odor emanates from the canal, but drizzling rain brings most passengers under the roof of the shed and under the canal's noxious thrall. None of us dares leave the station for even a moment; such folly would only prompt the skiff to arrive in our absence, so we steadily endure the afflictions of tropical weather and each other. Waiting for skiffs this morning are a platoon of off-duty Canadian sailors who are beginning to crack beers, and two women in paramilitary camouflage pants, hunting knives on their belts, t-shirts announcing the days of males are numbered. On the other side of the station, outside and near the river, under the marina's tiny roof overhang, is most of a Maya family: the mother and five shiny children arrayed around her full cotton skirts like a set of nesting dolls. Over the many hours that we all wait for skiffs, the children never once cry out or run around the station; even the toddlers are patient as old animals, brown eyes, luminous under straight, dark bangs, closing at times in sleep. There is also an assemblage of bare-chested young Creole men in oil-stained pants who want to jive someone, anyone, especially the two gay women. There is a character out of a Graham Greene novel, a seedy man with a faintly Canadian accent, whose story, one feels instinctively, has something to do with a racetrack and bourbon. There are two young mestizo boys, about twelve, in short-sleeve dress shirts, carrying knapsacks from which protrude books and fishing gear.

The atmosphere in the marina station is moody, oily, and raw. For solidarity, Katherine and I gravitate toward the other two traveling women, and are well into a conversation about their adventures in the Guatemalan jungle (matriarchal socialism among the ruins is the general idea) when the two leap up, responding to the Creole men's taunts by unsheathing knives and a venomous rhetoric. The men reply by swaggering closer in a lewd line dance. As the two camps bare their teeth and advance, Katherine pales and sinks to the ground, an unpremeditated act which—surprisingly—diffuses the situation. Everyone puts their knives and egos back in their cases, and though they clearly need no physical protection, we persuade our fierce sisters to "take some fresh air" and resettle with us on the sea wall, not far from the twelve-year-old boys who have mastered the trick of being left alone.

An hour passes with neither skiffs, nor torrential rain, nor gender wars. The sun comes out; the Maya children stare silently at the river. We turn to books to pass the time. Katherine reaches for her volume on Rome—brought as a stay against the tropics—adjusts her eyeglasses at the same time, and promptly knocks the latter into the open sewer of the river.

"Well," she says, "I am blind."

"Blind?" I ask.

"For all intents and purposes," she says formally, with the calm of the suddenly, catastrophically resigned, "blind. For example, I cannot make out where the river is. Can you see the glasses? Are they floating?"

They are not floating. We stare sadly, me into the murky soup,

Katherine into something murkier yet. Everyone, save the tactful, insular Maya, gathers to laugh, commiserate, or just see what will happen. From the gang of bobbing Creole men emerges one scrawny, barefoot fellow, maybe twenty years old. All morning he has been the butt of jokes by the other men, who consider him a pest not worthy of inclusion in their circle. His name is Cecil, and his face has the waxy, innocent look of some very brilliant, aging scientist, or of people who have been ill for a long time. He prances up to us, announcing that he will dive into the river of sewage and search for the glasses.

"Is it safe?" we ask.

He puffs up his chest. "I will do it."

Even the bullies are quieted by Cecil's proposal. He strips off his shirt and slips into the filthy gruel, here about four feet deep. Someone throws him a pair of underwater goggles. After ten minutes of diving, feeling with his feet, diving again, Cecil comes up with Katherine's glasses in one hand, his body dripping with dank sediment. Everyone cheers and laughs; even the Maya are smiling and Katherine seems about to swoon again—with happiness. Cecil struts up to her and proudly presents the dripping glasses as the wharf rats give their grudging approval. We thank Cecil profusely, glad to help his elevation. He has not asked for money, but we expect to offer him some, and he now hovers as artfully as a hotel porter. On the way to the station washroom where we insist that he rinse with hot water and soap, he names his price and we pay it. We praise him again in front of the still-watching gang and make him promise to go to a doctor for an antibiotic. He points out that medicine will cost more money; we give it without hesitation. Katherine washes her glasses in the washroom for about an hour, and when she comes out the skiff to Caye Caulker arrives.

Some days later, back in Belize City, Cecil comes to our guesthouse and shows us an envelope of small red pills that the doctor has given him so that he will not get sick from the water. The pills are very expensive, Cecil says, looking theatrically mournful. The choice is between seeming to be mildly duped or abandoning someone who did us a great favor because he was lowest on the pecking order and who would never have considered such a thing if he had anything resembling a promising hope in life. It is not much of a choice. We give Cecil twice what he asks for and tell him to get more pills if he needs them.

Traveling in places like Belize offers one a steady stream of ethical conundrums. Perhaps we have encouraged Cecil to consider future Americans as dimwitted customers? But surely we forfeited the right to resist his pleas and to another kind of relationship the instant we allowed him to dive into the open sewer? Yet stopping him would have been tantamount to patronizing him? And so on. We see Cecil one more time just before we leave Belize; he comes for a visit on the veranda and we can tell at once that he has come only to bask one more time in rare praise, to hear us use the word "hero" again. To have stumbled into this drama while waiting for the boat to Caye Caulker is especially instructive because the people of Caulker have organized a fishing cooperative that brings them economic well-being and independence from unwanted influence.

Emily Hiestand is a visual artist and the author of Green the Witch-Hazel Wood, Angela the Upside-Down Girl, *and* The Very Rich Hours, *from which this story was excerpted. Her writing has appeared in* The Nation, The New Yorker, *and* The Atlantic Monthly, *among other publications. She has received the National Poetry Series award, "Discovery"/The Nation poetry award, and the Whiting Writers' Award. She lives in Cambridge, Massachusetts with her husband, musician and journalist Peter Niels Dunn.*

PAUL THEROUX

Am I Glad to See You!

There is no escaping your fellow travelers.

THERE ARE TWO RAILWAYS IN COSTA RICA, EACH WITH ITS OWN station in San José. Their routes dramatize Costa Rica's indifference to her neighbors: they go to the coasts, not to any frontier. The Pacific Railway travels down to Puntarenas on the Gulf of Nicoya; the Atlantic Railway to Limón. The Atlantic station is the older of the two, and part of its line has been in operation for almost a hundred years. Outside that station there is a steam locomotive mounted on blocks for travelers to admire. In El Salvador such an engine would be puffing and blowing up the track to Santa Ana; in Guatemala it would have been melted down and made into antipersonnel bombs for the White Hand.

A Limón train leaves the Atlantic station every day at noon. It is not a great train, but by Central American standards it is. *The Brighton Belle*. There are five passenger coaches, two classes, no freight cars. I had been eager to take this train, for the route has the reputation of being one of the most beautiful in the world, from the temperate capital in the mountains, through the deep valleys on the northeast, to the tropical coast to which, because of its richly lush jungle, Columbus gave the name Costa Rica when he touched there on his fourth voyage in 1502. On his third voyage he thought he had reached the Garden of Eden, on the fourth he believed he had arrived at the green splendor of Asia. (Columbus tacked up and down the coast and was ill for four months in Panama; cruelly, no one told him that there was another vast ocean on the other side of the mountains—the local Indians were deaf to his appeal for this information.)

Costa Rica's railways no longer function after suffering severe damage in a 1991 earthquake, but the author's observations and descriptions are timeless.

—LH & NP

The most scenic of Central American routes; but I had another good reason for wanting to take this train out of San José. Since arriving in Costa Rica I had spent much of my time in the company of hard-drinking American refugees—Andy Ruggles and the diabolical Dibbs were but two. I was glad of their company; El Salvador hadn't been much fun. But now I was ready to set off alone. Travel is at its best a solitary enterprise: to see, to examine, to assess, you have to be alone and unencumbered. Other people can mislead you; they crowd your meandering impressions with their own; if they are companionable they obstruct your view. And if they are boring they corrupt the silence with nonsequiturs, shattering your concentration with *Oh, look, it's raining,* and *You see a lot of trees here.* Traveling on your own can be terribly lonely (and it is not understood by Japanese who, coming across you smiling wistfully at an acre of Mexican buttercups, tend to say things like *Where is the rest of your team?*). I think of evening in the hotel room in the strange city. My diary has been brought up to date; I hanker for company: What to do? I don't know anyone here, so I go out and walk and discover the three streets of the town and rather envy the strolling couples and the people with children. The museums and churches are closed, and toward midnight the streets are empty. *Don't carry anything valuable,* I was warned; *it'll just get stolen.* If I am mugged I will have to apologize in my politest Spanish: *I am sorry, sir, but I have nothing valuable on my person.* Is there a surer way of enraging a thief and driving him to violence? Walking these dark streets is dangerous, but the bars are open. Ruggles and Dibbs await. They take the curse off my boredom, but I have a nagging suspicion that if I had stayed home and lingered in downtown Boston until midnight I would have met Ruggles and Dibbs in the Two O'Clock Lounge (TWENTY COMPLETELY NUDE COLLEGE GIRLS!!!). I did not have to take the train to Costa Rica for that.

> It was a rare moment in traveling when I took a companion. Ray was a world class traveler of a different ilk, in territory I was familiar with, yet Ray allowed me to see more things in Central America, things inexplicable about myself, than I would have going it alone. This symbiosis worked, and Ray was a grand facilitator and diffuser, helping me spiral out of my angst and seriousness. Ray snatched me away from my save-the-world-from-injustice little world, and I was able to accept the larger view of what places like Guatemala and Belize had to offer from so many more perspectives.
>
> —Paul Haeder, "Paul and Ray's Exceptional Adventure"

It is hard to see clearly or to think straight in the company of other people. Not only do I feel self-conscious, but the perceptions that are necessary to writing are difficult to manage when someone close by is thinking out loud. I am diverted, but it is discovery not diversion that I seek. What is required is the lucidity of loneliness to capture that vision which, however banal, seems in my private mood to be special and worthy of interest. There is something in feeling abject that quickens my mind and makes it intensely receptive to fugitive impressions. Later, these impressions might be refuted or deleted, but they might also be verified and refined: and in any case I had the satisfaction of finishing the business alone. Travel is not a vacation, and it is often the opposite of a rest. *Have a nice time*, people say to me at my send-off at South Station. It was not precisely what I had hoped for. I craved a little risk, some danger, an untoward event, a vivid discomfort, an experience of my own company, and, in a modest way, the romance of solitude. This I thought might be mine on the train to Limón.

I found a corner seat by a window and watched the houses get smaller as we approached the outskirts of San José. They got smaller, but unlike the houses in the rest of the suburbs in Central America, they did not get dingier and more tumbledown on the periphery of the city. The campaign flags were still flying, and election slogans and posters were stuck to the walls of some of them. They were ranch houses, bungalows, square tin-roofed houses; houses of clapboard and concrete. They were pink and green and lemon yellow in the small settlements, and in the smart outer suburbs they were red brick and white and had rolling lawns. And then, without passing a dump or slum, or the dirty river with its gray froth of soapsuds that was the boundary of every other town I had seen so far, we sped into the countryside, past banana groves and fields of coffee. These were shady plantations, with wooded green hills surrounding them. It was sunny and cool on this day in late February, and there by the tracks was a Costa Rican beekeeper, like Sherlock Holmes in retirement, just as hawk-nosed and skinny. He looked up from his swarming hives and grinned at the train.

Even the poorest, the smallest house was neatly painted, the stairs swept, and starched curtains flapped through windows. In the yards were the piles of firewood, the vegetable garden, the borders of flowers. They were proud little houses, and the pride gave them dignity. There was a completeness to this, a certain formality, and it was reflected in the way the train passengers were dressed—the girls in sunhats, the ladies in shawls, the men in fedoras.

More than half the passengers on the train were black. I found this odd: I could not remember having seen any blacks in San José. Their baskets and shopping bags marked them out as Costa Ricans, not tourists, and for the early part of the trip they chatted with the whites on the train. They spoke Spanish, getting acquainted, laughing and joking. *I hope I've got enough food*, said a black lady in a sunbonnet. *My children are always eating.*

Then I heard, "Take you haid out de winda!"

It was the same woman, now yelling in English. One of her small sons, in a blue jersey, was hanging out of the window. But his head was so far out, he could not hear her.

"Tree gonna lop it off!"

Now he heard. He turned his head to her but did not withdraw it.

"You kyant do dat!" She punched his shoulder. The boy sat back in his seat and giggled at his sister.

"I have to watch them all the time," said the black woman in Spanish. Her English was singsong, her Spanish a stutter.

We passed through blobs of sunlight in a pretty, shady wood. It was unusual to travel in the shade, through woods that overhung the track. Normally there was heat on either side of the track and sun beating through the windows. But here the sunlight speckled the glass and flashed in the train, and the trees were so dense it was impossible to see beyond the pickets of slender trunks and the cracks of light. We were among mountains. A space between the trees opened like a gate and, far off, pine groves grew darkly on the hills, and below them in a ditch of shade there was a dairy and a sawmill and a village of timber houses and a wood lot. A river ran through it, sparkling just before it tumbled into the shady valley, and the place looked to me like a town in Vermont I had seen as a child, perhaps Bellows Falls or White River Junction. The illusion of Vermontness persisted even though in this village I saw a row of royal palms.

> Rural Central America smells unlike anyplace I have ever been and I wanted the windows down. For nearly all that there is to see can be found in the air as well; wood smoke from cooking fires, cattle pastures and fruit stands, diesel fumes of public buses, the saturated earth smells of jungle rivers. Here, the land still makes itself known.
>
> —Randy Wayne White, *The Sharks of Lake Nicaragua*

We came to Cartago. This was a market town. Here, in 1886, the railway line was begun by an American speculator, Minor Keith. The silver commemorative shovel, with an appropriate inscription, is on display in the National Museum in San José, along with pre-Columbian pottery and masks and gold jewelry and portraits of mustached Costa Rican patriots and presidents (their walking sticks, each one as individual as their mustaches, are also on display). In that museum is a painting of Cartago depicting the result of the great earthquake of 1910. It is an interesting picture, for right through the middle of town, in the foreground of the painting, are the railroad tracks, a whole section of them covered by masonry that had fallen from a convent wall. The earthquake had flattened Cartago, but the line was repaired; nothing else of old Cartago remains.

The seat next to me had been empty. Just as we left Cartago a young man took it and asked me how far I was going. He said he was going to Siquirres. Limón, he said, was interesting, but I might find it crowded. It would be hours before we'd reach Siquirres; he hoped I would teach him some English. He had tried to learn it but found it difficult. His name was Luis Alvarado, he said. I asked him if we could skip the English lesson.

"It is just that you look like a teacher. I think you could help me," he said in Spanish. "How do you like Costa Rica?"

I told him that I thought it was a beautiful country.

"Why do you think so?"

The mountains, I said.

"They are not so beautiful as those of Oregon. Or so high."

The river, I said. That was a lovely river in the valley.

"The rivers in Oregon are much more beautiful."

I told him I thought the people in Costa Rica were extremely pleasant.

"The people in Oregon always smile. They are more friendly than Costa Ricans."

It was a green country, I said.

"Have you been to Oregon?"

"No," I said. "Have you?"

He had. It was his single visit outside Costa Rica—a summer in Oregon, trying to learn English. It was a wonderful visit, but the English lessons were a failure. He had not been to Nicaragua or

Panama: they were loathsome places. He said that instead of my going on to Panama I should return to the States and visit Oregon.

The river was beneath us; the landscape had opened and become simple and terrifying, two parallel mountain ranges and, between them—so deep it made me anxious—a gorge. There were fountains of mist in the gorge, the flung spray of the foaming river. This was the Río Reventazón. It is a swift river, and its strength had pulled down the sides of these mountains and made a canyon, filled with the rubble of its destruction, and this—the fallen walls of boulders, the river heaving over rocks, the turbulent suds of rapids—lay 400 feet below the train. The low coffee bushes could not obscure the view. I saw how the gorge had been leveled by the rushing whiteness on the valley floor. The valley of the Reventazón is forty miles long. The mountains are in places so precipitous the train has to descend through tunnels (screams, exalted yells in the car, and the odor of damp walls) to a cliffside that brings it so near the river the spray hits the windows. Then up again, along a cut, to switchbacks and bridges.

The bridges were always approached at an angle, so that they were seen whole, from the side; they appeared as a framework of slender girders, or sometimes wooden beams, tensed across two cliffs. It seemed as if this were the view of a bridge on another track, as if we were going to bypass it. But always the train turned sharply and became noisy as it started onto it; and the torrent beneath it looked peculiarly menacing—a staircase of cataracts frothing into the greater torrent yonder. I wondered how it was that Costa Rica could be so cool and piny, and it was not just that it was so different from its near neighbors, but that it was cool and piny like Vermont, and freshly watered—here a sawmill and there a dairy, the cows cropping grass on the hillsides; and horses, oblivious to the train, tethered to fences. Later, I was to meet an American horse dealer in Costa Rica. He said, "My horses would bolt and hang themselves if I tied them that near the tracks."

It is, for the first third of the trip, a mountain railway, the train traveling along a narrow shelf that had been notched into the mountainside. How narrow? Well, at one point a cow had strayed onto the line. To the left was the sheer mountain wall; to the right, the drop into the river. The cow was baffled, and she lollopped ahead of the engine, which had slowed so as not to kill her. At times she stopped, put her nose against the mountainside, sniffed at the precipice, then started away again, rocking back and forth, stiff legged, the way cows run. The track was too narrow to give her space to allow us to pass, so she ran ahead rocking, her tail swinging, for almost a mile on this high shelf.

Nearer the river the coffee bushes were thick, and there was cocoa, too, the wide leaves, the plump, bobbinlike pods. It was easier to make notes here, as the train moved slowly on the flat tracks by the riverbed. But my notes were not extensive. *Boulders*, I wrote, *Valley—River—Spray—Frail bridge—Trapped cow—Cocoa.*

"You Americans like to travel alone." It was Luis.

I said, "I hate to travel alone. It is depressing. I miss my wife and children. But if I am alone I see more clearly."

"You never talk to each other, you Americans."

"You mean in Oregon?"

"Here, when you travel."

"We talk all the time! Who says Americans don't talk to each other?"

"There is an American," said Luis. "You see him? Why don't you talk to him?"

The man wore a blue cap, a Barney Oldfield cap with a visor; his shirt was bright green, his trousers cut like a sailor's.

Although he was seated, the strap of his bag was over his shoulder and he clutched the bag tightly, as if it had something valuable in it. He was sunburned, and I guessed he was in his sixties—the hair on his arms was white. He was seated near the blacks, who were talking in Spanish and English; but he did not speak to anyone.

I said, "I did not know he was an American."

Luis found this funny.

"You did not know *he* was an American?"

I suppose it was his cap, which Luis took to be foolishly youthful. Costa Ricans wore felt hats and fedoras. This man's cap was tilted at a rakish angle, and it did not quite go with his craggy face.

"Talk to him," said Luis.

"No, thank you."

Talk to this old man, just because Luis wanted to hear us speak English? I had met enough Americans in San José. It was the reason I had left the city, to seek out and assess the reputedly uninhabited Atlantic coast, perhaps wind up swapping stories with a grizzled black in a Limón bar, tales of muleskinning and piracy on the Mosquito Coast.

"Go ahead."

"You talk to him," I said. "He might teach you some English."

It was, mainly, my other fear: the distortion of companionship. I did not want to see things with anyone else's eyes. I knew this experience. If they point out something you have seen already you realize that your own perception was rather obvious; if they indicate something you missed, you feel cheated, and it is a greater cheat to offer it later as your own. In both cases, it is annoying. *Oh, look, it's raining* is as bad as *Costa Ricans have their own unit of length—the vara.*

I wanted to concentrate my whole attention on what was out the window; I wanted to remember this valley, this river, these mountains, the breeze freshening the train, the fragrance of the wildflowers that grew next to the track. *Pretty flowers,* I wrote.

Smiling nervously, Luis got up. He went up the aisle and mumbled to the old man. The old man did not understand. Luis tried again. You bastard, I thought. Now the old man turned and smiled at me. He rose. Luis took the old man's seat. The old man came toward me and took Luis's seat. He said, "Boy, am I glad to see you!"

Paul Theroux is the author of many books, among them travel classics such as Riding the Iron Rooster, The Pillars of Hercules, The Great Railway Bazaar, The Happy Isles of Oceania, *and* The Old Patagonian Express: By Train Through the Americas, *from which this story was excerpted.*

DAVID ROBERTS

Exploring the Place of Fright

A local archaeologist reveals secrets of the Mayan underworld.

IT WAS EARLY MARCH, THE MIDDLE OF BELIZE'S DRY SEASON, YET our faces streamed with sweat in the 95 degrees Fahrenheit jungle humidity. After a two-mile hike, we arrived at the cave. We strapped on our helmets, cinched down our dry bags, flipped on our headlamps, and started across the pool just inside the cavern's hourglass-shaped mouth.

There was just one problem: I have never learned to swim—and the water here reached depths of fifteen feet. Bound inside a puffy life jacket, I tentatively worked my way into the water, then flailed across and seized the shore on the other side. Tiny fish nibbled my calves, and dark shapes flitted overhead: vampire bats.

Discarding the cumbersome life jacket, I stepped back into the now waist-deep stream, following close behind Jaime Awe (AH-way), who is Belize's foremost archaeologist and who knows these caves better than anyone alive. Just behind us were photographer Stephen Alvarez and his assistant, Alan Cressler—expert cavers both. We shuffled forward until we came to what cavers call "breakdown"—a talus pile of collapsed boulders, here half-submerged in the wall-to-wall stream. I made my way over this chaos gingerly: The grotto was filled with limestone fins and prongs so sharp that a slip or fall might gash you to the bone.

Half an hour in, ducking to sidle through an unlikely slot, then stumbling shoulder deep against the current, I realized that, alone, I would now have been completely lost. We came to a boulder that looked like any of several dozen we had already passed. I would have plunged on upstream, but Awe said, "No, up here." He climbed the back of the boulder, stepped high onto a jutting shelf, and scrambled up a steep slope into the darkness. As we followed, the sound of the river faded below. And gradually, the slope eased, and the passage opened around us. At last we reached a broad terrace where rim stone dams sectioned off dry pools. The chamber lay 700 yards from the entrance—not far, if you were walking along a sidewalk, but a considerable journey inside a cave.

As my headlight swept the space, I caught my breath. In fourteen years of exploring prehistoric Anasazi sites in the American Southwest, hundreds of days of poking through canyons and across plateaus, I have come upon exactly six intact or nearly intact ceramic vessels. Now, all around me, ranging in size from a drinking mug to a vase big enough to hold a small tree—everywhere I looked were pots, dozens of them.

As I stood gaping at the extraordinary assortment of ancient vessels, Alvarez wandered deeper into the cave. Soon it was his turn to let out an involuntary curse of astonishment.

My eyes followed the beam of his headlamp. In the middle of the chamber lay an upright human skull, the eye sockets empty, the jaw still grinning in its rictus of death. The top of the forehead had a flattened, almost simian look about it. Each of the four incisors in the upper jaw had been filed into a tripartite fang.

On our trek to Awe's field camp the previous day, I had discovered that it's not just Awe's path-breaking theories or his unusual realm of archaeology that sets him apart from his more conventional colleagues.

We were no more than a hundred yards from the trailhead, and already we were bathed in sweat. Cicadas drowned the forest with their metallic whine. Suddenly, as we approached our first ford of

Roaring Creek, Awe flung his pack to the ground. I glanced over just as he launched into a headlong sprint, which culminated in a yawp—"I was born for this!"—and a belly-flop into the river.

The plunge and the cry, I soon learned, were spontaneously concocted by Awe one hangover-stricken morning some five years ago. They have since become an initiation rite for all new visitors to the field camp of Awe's Belize Valley Archaeological Reconnaissance Project (BVAR)—the official title of his pioneering investigations deep into the Maya world, both above and below the ground. Warming to the oddball ways of our leader (and seeing no real alternative), Alvarez, Cressler, and I dutifully followed Awe's lead: sprint, yawp, plunge.

If I was born for this, that birth happened just a few years ago, when, in the inland jungle of Guatemala's Petén, I tagged along with a Vanderbilt University team that was excavating royal burials. As I hiked toward the site of Dos Pilas, I passed by the mouth of a cave yawning in the gloom. "Just last week," the archaeologist at my side told me, "we found a whole trove of pots in there."

In that instant, I was seized with the insatiable itch of the explorer. The cities of the prehistoric Maya—one of the greatest and yet most enigmatic civilizations ever to emerge in the Americas—have been probed and pondered for more than a century. But the underworld, so important to the ancients, was only now beginning to be rediscovered by modern investigators. Here, I realized—in the cave systems that riddle the Central American rain forest—lay the new frontier of Maya studies.

Scholars trace the origins of the Maya back to more than 2,000 years before the birth of Christ. By 1000 B.C., the Maya were raising corn, making pottery, and living in small villages. Their heyday came between A.D. 250 and 900, a span known to archaeologists as the Classic period. During those centuries, the Maya realm extended from Tabasco in present-day Mexico, throughout the Yucatán Peninsula, south across Guatemala and Belize, and into the western edges of Honduras and El Salvador. The peak population has been estimated at eight to ten million. During the Classic period, the Maya built the most magnificent cities in pre-Columbian

America, civic centers such as Tikal, Copán, and Palenque. In Belize, their greatest towns were Caracol, Lamanai, Altun Ha, and Xunantunich. Here, soaring temple-pyramids bordered spacious plazas complete with ball courts: The whole city, oriented to the four cardinal directions, imposed a rigorous quadrilateral order upon the chaos of the lowland jungle.

> Honduras's famous Mayan town, Copán Ruinas, hosted an international conference on Mayan archaeology in July 2001—the International Congress of Copán: Science, Art and Religion in the Mundo Maya. In the midst of talks ranging from warfare to artifacts to postmodernism, the conference's biggest news emerged: the possible discovery of the legendary lost city of the Maya—called "Q," as in "Question"—by David Stuart of Harvard University. E. Wyllus Andrews, director of Tulane University's Middle American Research Institute, explained the potential importance of the find: "It's as if, generations from now, archaeologists knew there had been a New York, a Philadelphia, and a Chicago, but they had only found New York and Philadelphia. If this is true, he has basically found Chicago."
>
> —LH & NP

By the Classic period, the Maya had invented an astonishingly sophisticated calendar. They made astronomical observations that rivaled those of their Arab and Asian contemporaries. And they perfected the most complex writing system ever developed in the Americas, an immensely nuanced script of hieroglyphs that are partly alphabetic, partly phonetic, and partly logographic. In front of their temples, they erected stone slabs as tall as twelve feet, carved with elaborate depictions of rulers and gods and hieroglyphic texts.

Unable to read the hieroglyphics, scholars had developed by the 1970s an idealized concept of Maya civilization: a peaceful culture of pyramid-building philosopher-priests who spent their days contemplating the mysteries of time and the cosmos.

During the past twenty years, though, the language of the Maya glyphs has been almost completely deciphered, and the picture those texts reveal utterly upends the conventional one. The carved stelae erected before the temple-pyramids boast of the invincibility of elite rulers, of the torture and sacrifice of enemy lords, of great battles waged against other cities. In the words of the distinguished Yale archaeologist Michael Coe, "The Maya were obsessed with war."

And the underworld played a crucial role in the Maya conception of the universe. Myths and epics that survived the Spanish conquest of the Maya paint a vivid picture of this perilous, nine-tiered place. Into the underworld the Hero Twins (deities in the age before human beings were created) descended to face a series of ordeals that ultimately made the world safe for humans—defeating such lords as Jaundice Master, Pus Master, and Skull Scepter, evading traps laid in Dark House, Razor House, Jaguar House, and Bat House, which was full of "monstrous beasts, their snouts like knives." Each night, the setting sun was transformed into a jaguar god, which had to traverse the underworld with all its dangers before being reborn at dawn as the sun god. The dead dwelled there and had to pass through the nine levels before their souls could escape to heaven. The underworld was called Xibalba—Place of Fright.

The Maya believed that caves were the portals to Xibalba. This was borne out by finds of spectacular artifacts in the Yucatán Peninsula at Loltun cave and Balankanche cave by early modern archaeologists. Yet on the whole, Maya cave research was neglected throughout the twentieth century.

Enter Jaime Awe. As a boy growing up in San Ignacio, a midsize village in western Belize, he was well acquainted with things Maya. The small, partly excavated site of Cahal Pech crowns the town's main hill, and only six miles to the southwest loom the austere, jungle-swathed ruins of Xunantunich. Often Awe's family picnicked at Río Frío, a huge two-mouthed cavern some 600 feet long, 100 feet wide, and 80 feet tall at its apex, through which the cold river of that name flows. On other forays up the streams south of San Ignacio, Awe discovered his own caves, noticing the potsherds scattered just inside their entrances.

"When I was nine," he says, "I used to go out looking for mounds behind my parents' house. I'd collect potsherds, take them home, and square them off with my knife. Then I'd glue them together and make forts, put plastic toy soldiers on them, and blow the whole thing up with fireworks. I was a demented child!"

In college, this childhood fascination (demented or not) was rekindled by the teachings of an anthropology professor, whose faith in Awe's instincts helped him land the post of assistant commissioner in the government's Department of Archaeology. Ultimately, he went to Trent University in Ontario to get his B.A. and M.A., then to the University of London for his doctorate, becoming the first native Belizean to get a Ph.D. in archaeology.

In the late 1970s, just before Awe left Belize for school, a small cadre of die-hard cavers, mostly British and Canadian, led by an obsessed geomorphologist named Tom Miller, began to discover the country's caving potential. For these devotees, pushing new underground passages was an end in itself; the Maya artifacts they stumbled upon were of secondary interest. Word of their finds, however, got back to archaeologists. When Awe returned to Belize in the early 1990s, he decided to fully explore the caves. What he found there overwhelmed him.

A shallow pool of calcite had cemented the skull to the floor of the cave. Nearby lay a disembodied leg bone. "Flooding over the centuries separated the bones," said Awe. "But this is not a burial; there are no grave goods associated with it."

As I knelt to get a better look, Awe explained the flattened forehead. "It's called 'tabular oblique,'" he said. "His head would have been bound with boards for the first year of his life."

"Why?" I asked.

"Beautification. Same as the sharpened teeth."

During the past five field seasons, Awe's teams have spent a total of fifteen months working, often for twelve-hour days, in this cave system, which is called Actun Tunichil Muknal—Cave of the Stone Sepulcher. He has examined virtually every artifact and bone here. He knew exactly what we were looking at. "This is a human sacrifice," he said.

"How would he have been killed?" Cressler asked.

"We can't tell from the skull alone. Usually they sacrificed someone by holding him down, spread-eagled, and cutting out the heart. Or by decapitation. But he might also have been disemboweled while still alive."

In the ninth century, some terrible catastrophe struck the Maya world. The people built no new major temples after A.D. 830; the last date inscribed on a Maya stela corresponded to A.D. 889. By the first decade of the tenth century, Tikal, Caracol, and other great cities were essentially abandoned. Mayanist Robert Sharer, of the University of Pennsylvania, has called the collapse "one of the most profound cultural failures in human history." Most scholars believe that some sort of environmental crisis—most likely drought and deforestation—intersected with overpopulation and internecine warfare to lay waste a mighty civilization.

Now, as we pondered the grisly scene before us, Awe suggested a connection to the collapse of the Maya. "I'm almost certain," he said, "that the man was sacrificed to Chac, the god of rain. When this cave was being used for rituals, a severe drought gripped the countryside. Years may have gone by without a drop of rain. People were starving. This sacrifice would have represented the people's ultimate petition to Chac, to relent and restore them to the glory their forefathers had known."

At most Maya field schools, the local workers eat in separate messes from the gringo researchers. This is not Jaime Awe's style. That night, ten of us sat together around the campfire and shared a single meal, a gargantuan chile with tortillas, cooked by Awe himself.

The camp is set in a spacious clearing under the forest canopy, where workers have built four large wooden champas with thatched roofs and open sides. One serves as the commissary, complete with earthen stove. Low benches have been cobbled around the campfire hollow. Despite the heat and the bugs, we lingered around the campfire, drinking rum punch. At Awe's side sat his field director and girlfriend, Carolyn Audet, a twenty-three-year-old anthropology student set to start grad school at Vanderbilt in the fall. Athletic and assured, she had a smile that (to paraphrase Marlowe) could burn the topless towers of Xunantunich. Awe himself is forty-six, trim, clearly in good shape. His round face, crowned with black, curly hair, never showed a wrinkle of skepticism or doubt.

The couple met at Awe's summer field school in 1998—"and my life hasn't been the same since," he told me on the hike in. She was a volunteer on the project, an ambitious Princeton student seeking field experience between her sophomore and junior years. Now, while Awe dives through Tunichil Muknal and other caves, Audet works on above-ground excavations at Lamanai and Cahal Pech. Beside the campfire, the two held hands like teenagers.

The night was even buggier than the day. Audet spotted a sizable scorpion that had crawled over to investigate the fire; Pete Zubrzycki, a British Army veteran turned volunteer archaeologist, promptly extinguished it with a boot heel. Cressler picked up a roach the size of a mouse, which he turned over curiously in his hands, then released. On an errand to my tent, I caught a steely point of

The forest is so thick that you enter the city without knowing it is there. Then shadows deepen, and looking up through the leaves you see a stone tower blazing in the sun. The buildings might be cliffs or hills, except that here is a stairway smothered in roots, a mossy statue, a dark doorway to a dripping vault, an inscription. You walk all day yet never leave forest or city. The one seems to grow from the other—as if they have always stood together, as if the stones were cut and raised by the jaguars who make their dens in empty rooms. People of our time have come and dug beneath the streets and floors, asking What happened here? Where did the builders go? What silenced the writers? Why were the astronomers, who could see so far into past and future—projecting movements of planets over millions of years—blind to their own catastrophe? And if not blind, why powerless?

—Ronald Wright,
"A Pyramid Scheme"

light in my headlamp beam. It turned out to be the eye of a hairy black tarantula loitering near the tent door.

There are good reasons why caves in the Maya world have until now been so little studied. Most archaeologists lack the athleticism and the nerve to venture into even easy caves, let alone carry out intensive fieldwork within them. The dangers of caving are manifold: falling on the jagged karst, getting lost in labyrinthine passages, drowning in flooded caverns. And insidious diseases lurk in the stygian depths. While working in a cave two years ago, Audet contracted histoplasmosis, a kind of fungal pneumonia caused by spores from bat feces. "You get a terrible fever," she told me. "It feels like somebody's squeezing your lungs." Histoplasmosis is treatable, though the cure is almost as bad as the malady. Chagas' disease is not. Awe laconically described its course to me. "You get it from the assassin beetle, which lives in dry caves. When it pricks you, it secretes an anesthetic fluid; you don't know you're being bitten. It's a slow, debilitating illness that attacks the heart. It's fatal. Some people think Charles Darwin died of it."

Awe calls himself a speleoarchaeologist, one of only four cave specialists in the world of Maya studies. As such, he is a man on a mission. As he told me, "Even the people who studied caves like Balankanche in the 1960s spent only two or three days in them. If I worked a surface site only two or three days, my colleagues would laugh at me. What I'm fighting for is a cave archaeology as intensive as surface archaeology. We can't wrap up Tunichil Muknal in a week."

Yet Awe's mission faces twin dilemmas. Belize's economy is fragile at best; the average Belizean household takes in only $218 a month. Though the country exports sugar, timber, fruit, fish—and drugs—tourism looms as its potential make-or-break industry. So far the action centers on the cayes, where divers and sunbathers hang out. But the government, mindful of the drawing power of archaeological sites such as Chichén Itzá in Mexico and Tikal in Guatemala, has launched a campaign to promote its own Maya sites—with Jaime Awe in charge of the archaeological niceties. At the same time as our visit to the caves, Awe was supervising full-blown restorations (explicitly to make the sites tourist-friendly) at Cahal Pech, Caracol, Xunantunich, Lamanai, Altun Ha, and El Pilar. Yet in a cave such as Tunichil Muknal, can archaeology and tourism coexist? Even more troublesome is the threat posed by professional looters—who, thanks to the work of pioneers such as Awe, are getting wind of a whole new host of sites from which to pilfer pre-Columbian treasures.

"I'd become convinced that whatever rituals took place within the cave involved sensory deprivation. As an earlier experiment, a friend and I had spent forty-eight hours in complete darkness deep inside one of the caves.... For the first four or five hours we chatted away. But after that we suddenly ran out of things to say. It was as if the cave was demanding we listen. So we sat in silence. After a period of uncertainty and disorientation, we felt a presence that asserted itself first as a deep chill and then as a wave of energy. I began to feel as if I were everywhere in the cave at once; as if I were separated from it but part of it. Whatever it was, was older than the Maya. It was as old as the cave itself. It offered me a choice of time travel or apprenticeship.... I chose apprenticeship, which is a choice I've maintained. My career as a Mayanist is a result of it."

—Barbara MacLeod, quoted in *The Heart of the Sky: Travels Among the Maya* by Peter Canby

If cave research is the new frontier of Maya studies, the great question is just what these gateways to Xibalba meant to the ancients. Twenty years ago, most archaeologists had a pat, simplistic explanation: The pots had been carried underground to collect *zuhuy ha*, "virgin water"—water dripping from stalactites, pure because it had never touched the ground—for use in ceremonies. Because of the work of Awe and a handful of others, we know now that caves served a far more complex and profound role in the culture of the Classic period Maya.

One of Awe's key hypotheses has to do with what he calls "sacred geography." On

Roaring Creek a couple of days after our arrival, he demonstrated this notion with vivid specificity.

Less than a half mile upstream from Tunichil Muknal, on the same side of the valley, lies Actun Uayazba Kab—Handprint Cave. As we scrambled up a slope toward it, we caught occasional distant glimpses of its opening—twin apertures gaping darkly above a protruding horizontal shelf.

Despite the proximity of Handprint and the Cave of the Stone Sepulcher, they seem to have served utterly different functions. At the mouth of Handprint, Awe's teams excavated a series of human burials: not sacrifices, but orderly inhumations, complete with grave goods. Within the grotto, artifacts dating from the time of Christ all the way through a.d. 900 were found, including a number of pots.

Two of these—massive white ollas the size of small trash barrels—rest on a ledge fifty feet above the cave mouth, atop an unrelentingly overhanging wall. Invisible from the ground, they were discovered by a climber on Awe's team who rappelled from the cliff above the cave. Now Alvarez, Cressler, and I took turns performing the same rappel. Twenty feet below the lip of the overhang, as we twirled in space a good thirty feet out from the ledge, we won our hard-earned view of these hidden vessels. To place them in their precarious niche, the Maya must have used native trees to build a fifty-foot ladder arching from the ground over the void.

The most extraordinary discoveries in Handprint Cave, however, were not artifacts but art. At the mouth, the ancients carved foot-and-toe trails in the bedrock, as well as petroglyphs of footprints, all five toes carefully delineated. They also worked the corners of the protruding stone to etch three-dimensional masks or faces, visages that look like grinning skulls. Awe thinks these might be further representations of Chac, the rain god. The *pièce de résistance* of the cave lies in complete darkness, inside a small chamber reached only by a tight crawl. There on the wall stand four negative handprints, formed by placing a palm against the stone, then spitting a macerated paint forcefully against the surface, leaving a spattered outline of a spread-fingered hand. These were the first cave handprints found in Belize.

As Awe's headlamp beam played over these mute reminders of human presence, he mused, "Is this the testimony of a visit to a sacred place? Or the mark of having completed a rite of passage?"

With a little oversimplification, the importance of cave research to understanding the Classic Maya can be summed up in a psychological metaphor. The great cities, such as Tikal and Copán, with their monumental art, their stelae boasting of might and conquest, express the conscious, external Maya world. The caves represent everything that is murky, haunted, internal, unconscious. In these strange galleries, an air of secrecy, of the forbidden, prevails. Jaime Awe and his few colleagues in the world of speleoarchaeology have become the psychoanalysts of Maya thought.

Everywhere we walked in Tunichil Muknal, we came across pots. (The count of vessels inside the cave exceeds 200.) It took Awe's team three field seasons to map every artifact exactly where it lay, yet even now, in his fifth year in the cave, Awe kept peering into crannies for objects he might have overlooked.

As we worked our way deeper into the cave system at Tunichil Muknal, Awe's overarching theory—that what we saw in the cavern's main chamber represents a desperate effort by late Classic Maya to appeal to Chac and other agricultural gods—was steadily corroborated by artifacts we encountered in those deep corridors, which are off-limits to tourists: a stone bench, or "altar," bearing some eight or nine pots left exactly where they must have been broken at the end of some ceremony; a fragile filament of burnt pine torch lying among potsherds. In Awe's view, the Maya plumbed deeper and deeper into caves because their petitions to Chac in cave entrances had failed to work any change.

Yet it wasn't the logic of the place—its ritual clarity—but rather its sheer strangeness that struck me over and over the longer we stayed underground. The most beautiful pots often lay in the most hidden places. One sat upside down at the bottom of a shaft only a small child could have slithered into, yet from a different angle, it appeared at the end of another, horizontal shaft, as if in a display window. Another vessel could be reached only by a twisting crawl, yet there it perched, as bright orange as the day it had been painted, girdled by an exquisite band of some 80 to 100 thumbnail impressions. Three granite ax heads rested in obscure niches, their blades so highly polished that it seems doubtful they were ever used to chop trees. A huge metate—a grinding basin, also made of granite—sat in another niche, one corner smashed, apparently to retire it from worldly use.

Awe showed us an inverted pot with three of its four tiny feet intact. Within each foot was a handful of beads that would have rattled when the pot was moved. Awe had found the fourth foot a considerable distance from the others, surrounded by no other cultural remains. "They did that just to mess with the archaeologists," he said. Taken as a whole, this unrivaled ceremonial chamber deep beneath the surface of the Earth seemed to brim with some dark, somber purpose. But what exactly had been going on here, not even Awe could confidently say.

We climbed a slope and turned a corner. Awe pointed toward the ground ahead. I momentarily stopped breathing; there, in a hollow as neatly formed as a small coffin, lay the collapsed skeleton of an infant. "We can't tell the sex," said Awe. "The child was between nine months and a year old. The skull may have been smashed, or it could have simply imploded, since infants' skulls are so soft."

Approaching the spot, Alvarez groaned almost inaudibly and abruptly turned away. Awe went on, "As late as 1680, the Spanish chronicles record the sacrifice of infants in caves during times of extreme tribulation. Children are by definition *zuhuy*—virginal, pure. I can imagine them laying the child here alive to die. Its cries would have been heard rising up to implore Chac."

At the extreme upper end of the main chamber, we climbed a ladder that solved fifteen feet of vertical wall. (On the first modern ascent, Awe had made a brave climb to reach the ledge above.) Then we walked thirty yards down a passage that seemed to go nowhere. All of a sudden Awe's headlamp shined on the tableau he had brought us here to see.

I had seen skeletons in the American Southwest, in Egypt, in caves full of the disordered dead in Mali. I had seen skeletons and mummies in museums and archives around the world. In a refrigerated chamber in Austria, I had seen the exquisitely preserved corpse of the Copper Age mummy called the Iceman, found high in the Italian Alps in 1991. But no prehistoric human remains that I had ever seen struck me with the force of this single intact skeleton.

Known in the dry taxonomy of Awe's team's report as Skeleton Thirteen (out of fourteen sacrificial victims found in Tunichil Muknal), this was a woman of about twenty. She lay spread-eagled on her back, her left leg bent out at an awkward angle, her right arm thrown above her head, as if in salutation or protest. Half-imbedded in the floor of the ledge, detached by millimeters from the palms and soles, lay the individual digits of her fingers and toes. Her pelvis protruded upward like the twin horns on a saddle.

No flood had disarticulated these bones, but slow seepage over the centuries had crusted the entire skeleton but for the very top of the forehead with a fuzzy layer of brown calcite, which added a jolt of the grotesque to the scene. Its full horror, however, seemed focused in the skull, propped like a head on a pillow. The eye sockets were empty holes staring at eternity. The jaw gaped open, as if in a scream. The teeth were furred with calcite.

For the moment, none of us could speak a word. Perhaps the woman had died in this very posture, as men held her down and a priest cut out her heart. Perhaps that open mouth had indeed frozen her dying cry, but just as likely the skull preserved forever the transport of her sacrificial rapture.

Whatever the reason for her death, it was in vain. The gods ignored the people's petitions. Something—most likely drought and famine—drove the Maya from their homeland, and the countryside reverted to jungle. Tunichil Muknal became a forgotten place, not to be rediscovered for more than ten centuries, along with the collective nightmare that was Xibalba.

David Roberts is the author of thirteen books including A Newer World: Kit Carson, John C. Frémont, and the Claiming of the American West, True Summit: What Really Happened on the Legendary Ascent of Annapurna, *and* Once They Moved Like the Wind: Cochise, Geronimo, and the Apache Wars. *He was also responsible for the rediscovery of the lost Arctic classic* In the Land of White Death, *by Valerian Albanov, published in English for the first time in 2000.*

DOUG FINE

On Guatemala's Gringo Circuit

A culture of fertile indolence entices wanderers to abandon all plans and just stay.

ANTONIO WAS GIVING A LECTURE ON VIGILANTE DAY. HE IS THE wide-eyed American-by-birth who runs the solar-heated thermal waters and decidedly North American indigenous sweat lodge next door to where I am living in electricity-free luxury in the new, peacetime Guatemala. His student was Stephan, a tall German who endlessly lists and re-lists the cities he has visited in the United States and in India.

"So the whole village gets together, and if they agree Juan is a thief, they gouge his eyes out, then they string him up. Once a year."

It occurred to me that there is a whole Hallmark niche in this (congratulations for the acquitted, condolences for the mothers of the blindly hung), but I kept this thought and my greeting card poems to myself. Stephan thought that he might have had a traveler's check and a few hundred Guatemalan quetzals (about $40) ripped off from a money belt inside the house where we had both been sleeping since its American gringa renter had invited us as we walked off the boat from Panajachel.

A small-time volcano-climbing guide and ganja dealer named Chich was Stephan's chief suspect. Chich had come to hustle and hit on Claire, our twenty-two-year-old hostess at a beautiful two-story, green-trim house (with two decks). She had moved in a week earlier when its septuagenarian Mayan owner took a liking to her because her name was the same as his departed wife's. Chich had had five minutes alone in the house while Claire went to collect some water through the 200 yards of coffee groves that abut the place. The groves, along with ten acres of corn and black bean fields, lead down to spectacular Lake Atitlán and the surrounding lush velvet volcanoes, the whole a tourist haven in shaky Guatemala since the 1950s.

The village of San Pedro is a prime spot on the Gringo Circuit—the predictable nebula of young, guidebook-toting Western travelers settling into the nicer grooves of the developing world to study, screw, live, escape, learn, and read John Irving, Tom Robbins, and Carlos Castenada. They are here in numbers generally relative to the strength of their currencies: Germans, Dutch, and an inexplicably disproportionate number of Danes, Israelis, Canadians, people who call themselves Canadians, and the original gringos: *norteamericanos.*

> At two o'clock we came out upon the lofty table of land bordering the Lake of Atitlán. In general I have forborne attempting to give any idea of the magnificent scenery amid which we were traveling, but here forbearance would be a sin.
>
> —John Lloyd Stephens, *Incidents of Travel in Central America, Chiapas, and Yucatán* (1841)

Western tourism around the lake started in formerly mellow Panajachel, the lakeside town that has been dubbed "Gringotenango" for decades. "Pana," as its hundreds of expat neo-hippies call it, bears about as much resemblance to its 1960s incarnation as the Haight-Ashbury does to its. Each year, satellite Mayan villages around the lake grow, specializing in various sectors of the tourist economy: backpacker stoners gravitate to San Pedro; package tourists flock to see the semi-pagan *maximón* ritual at Santiago (wherein a mannequin is given cigarettes and prayed to out loud); slightly richer backpacker stoners and honeymooners make their way to Santa

Cruz, particularly the nearly communal Iguana Perdida guesthouse. All are easy motorized-ferryboat rides from Pana.

A sort of scraping, ringing sound was reaching me at my thatched, queen-sized hammock on Claire's second-story deck. The scary, nationalistic, six-foot-eight Stephan, an infected mosquito bite on his gigantic head like the mark of Cain, was sharpening a machete in preparation for a Vigilante Day of his own. I think he was misinterpreting Antonio's story.

Antonio, fortyish and rarely be-shirted, made a decision three years ago after a few decades of living on American communes (he calls them "ego factories") and working on Mexican ranches: he was going to pay $7,000 for a heap of rocks with a killer view of the powerful Guatemalan lake, live in a teepee made from morning glory and ivy and run the aforementioned hot springs and sweat lodge resort. He attends church weekly, and in his free time crafts cypress canoes. Antonio is widely regarded as a genius by the gringos who find him outside of the San Pedro village center.

More will find him now. He is listed, albeit as "eccentric," in the Lonely Planet guidebook. Among dreadlocked and multiple-pierced backpackers with a copy of Pirsig and a pocketful of parental cash, that is like a four-star Michelin rating.

The one sentence devoted to him will be read by about 20 million eyes in eighteen Indo-European languages over the next five years. As nostalgia is one of the great badges worn by those who consider themselves veterans of the circuit, I proudly and self-righteously look forward to lamenting how much "this place has changed from ten years ago." I've always wanted to do that.

Antonio knew about Stephan's possible theft because he lives adjacent to Claire and is surrounded only by man-sized banana trees for privacy, so Stephan and I had stumbled over to sweat and soak at his place right after Stephan had made his possible discovery. Antonio told Stephan—whom I had overheard earlier explaining to a Danish girl, "I have been to Los Angeles twice, then Miami, which I did not like as much as Bombay"—that this Chich was trouble and had ripped off a number of gringos.

It had turned into an interesting evening at Antonio's. After exhausting the fifteen minutes that a sweat lodge is enjoyable, I found myself naked and depleted, standing knee-deep in a hot tub, talking within fluid exchange range to an equally *au naturel* gringa from Michigan whom I knew from a previous Gringo Circuit pit stop—the Spanish schools of Xela in the mountains of western Guatemala. She was waiting for her bar exam results and trying to cheat on her boyfriend. Rachel, aware of the power of her chest, stood and talked while almost ultraviolet lightning flashed silently just beyond the closest volcanoes. This, for me, was a symbol of the tumult of Guatemala as watched from the haven of the lake.

This gringa had an incredible memory for names. There are no goodbyes on the Gringo Circuit. You meet people for two days, then run into them two weeks later on another guidebook-dictated stop (the Mayan ruins at Tikal in northern Guatemala, for example). If the memory of the previous meeting is positive, you are suddenly old and strong friends with dinner plans—for another day or two. It is far less common to remember names than not to. I often only remember the initial introduction after the addresses that no one follows up on are exchanged. These fill my notebooks.

Rachel remembered not just my name, but my schedule (on which even I wasn't clear), which I guess I had mentioned to her casually during those five days we had both studied at the same extremely progressive, intensive, and expensive school. She—whom I noticed was flirting with everyone in the hot tub vicinity, male and female—had just finished a book called *Using Your Perfect Memory,* or something like that.

Unfortunately, like most visitors to the lakeside villages, Rachel didn't know much about the bloody fifty-year history of modern Guatemala. But this ignorance is not surprising: Put on your conspiracy cap and try to do a library search on U.S. coverage of the region's CIA-supported reign of terror from, say, 1975–1995. It's about as bare as Stephan's money belt.

Above Nick's Restaurant in central San Pedro, American movies are shown every night (often, I'm told, suspiciously before they are out on video, but I've thus far seen only dated offerings like *Contact, Face-Off, Trainspotting,* and *Il Postino*). Rolling papers are stacked in the cash drawer and sold for $2.

The same people you see at Phish shows, wearing the same garb and body hair, spend parental cash, and smoke huge spliffs right at the tables at Nick's. It's not uncommon for spectators to collapse mid-film. This phenomenon has provoked an eerie feeling of déjà vu for me, because even in the States the same demographic dresses up in Guatemalan clothing. I expected to be asked for some spare change to get a friend out of jail.

Watching *The Truth About Cats and Dogs* over beers with Claire a couple of days before Stephan became homicidal, I asked Nick, who is a local bigwig and very amiable, if he ever worries about foreign law enforcement coming down here and poking around. He laughed and said, "This is a different country. They can't come here." Then his face clouded over for a moment. "At least, they haven't yet."

There is an "I am Mr. Rourke, your host; welcome, dear guests, to Fantasy Island" feel to the lake villages. Story after story is repeated, to the point of overplayed refrain, about the foreigners who came to the lake intending to stay two days (as Claire had) and wound up moving in. Almost everyone stays a little longer than expected. There are some haggard, shipwrecked faces here in San Pedro, like people who have spent too much time in the Orgasmatron.

Claire is in touch with the spiritual world to the point of clairvoyance and telekinesis. She says she knew this place was "it" because of a dream she had recently that pinpointed San Pedro right down to the hot tubs and the green-trimmed house. Next to falling in love, Lake Atitlán is the great schedule killer on the Gringo Circuit. Claire woke up the other day and, joining me on the second-floor deck and looking at her view, said, "5:15 in the morning is amazing. 5:00 P.M. is just...lavender and incredible. And all that time in between is unbelievable."

You start to wander around town and through narrow paths in fields, and the feeling of home sets in. An old man stuck his head out a window my first afternoon in San Pedro, invited me to share some bread, and told me about his leg injury.

Switching on my Allman Brothers tape later that day and thinking of the incident, I said, "This is paradise."

"This group?" Stephan barked, working on a halved coconut with a spoon.

"No, this place, my life."

But the breath of McWorld is already upon "this place": All around the lake, gringo dream houses with "No Trespassing" signs are springing up. The people from here—with my normal apologies when an opinion sounds liberal—have a traditional respect for the lake. The docks are few, and nobody but the resort owners build right on the water. Villages are high above the lake, for what I am told are security and aesthetic reasons.

There is a truly intense energy here, which one stereotype-defying Brit I've befriended calls "volcanic chaos." The unfathomably deep lake, with its shades from burnt sapphire to wavy turquoise, still has an ecosystem, but is plagued by nasty runoff from pesticides banned even in the U.S., by a predatory bass population introduced for gringo anglers, and by the fact that disposable Cheetos wrappers have arrived in Guatemala before weekly trash pick-up service. In the black bean field outside

For every traveler there is a place in his or her memory that is a Shangri-La, mysterious, beautiful, full of alluring secrets. A place where one can return to by closing one's eyes. A place that will never change in memory. Lake Atitlán is mine. I fell in love with it the minute I saw it. Quiche legend calls it one of the four lakes that mark the corners of the world. It is a crater lake surrounded by three volcanoes. The color constantly changes, from emerald to azure to steely gray. In the early morning or on calm evenings the water is smooth and still and reflects the huge volcanic cones. In the late morning or early afternoon "the wind that carries away sin," known as the *xochomil,* gusts defiantly across the lake and the surface turns dark and choppy.

—Judith Nolan, "Snapshots"

Claire's, each day on my way to kayak, I watch a farmer wearing a canister filled with God-knows-what spray every plant thoroughly.

If the lake is a Central American paradise, the real Guatemala is rarely seen by even the well-meaning Lake Atitlán gringo tromping around in Tevas. As soon as a village is too far away from the lake to be part of the tourist economy—say, a two-day walk—the issues that started Guatemala's civil war in 1960 are very much still in play: horribly lopsided land ownership, inflation, no educational system to speak of. People are hungry and desperate, even by "developing" world standards. One in three children dies before age two.

It's impossible to quantify the effect of all these foreigners on local culture. I hear progressive travelers hypocritically complain about "modernization" and "cultural poisoning," and yeah, the former real estate agent from Carmel who retires here and dresses her kids as Mayans—that's annoying, to me and to locals. But how far back do we go? Four-hundred years? Fifty? Were the Mexican Toltecs—who, before Cortés, pushed

> Outside Guatemala City, my colleagues and I drove up a dirt road to visit a community of women weavers whose festive clothes and beautiful smiles belied their impoverished state. They took us into their shacks for hot chocolate and cake. Then, they took turns displaying their hand-woven garments and accessories created on back-strap looms.
>
> Traditional Guatemalan textiles are well known for their intensity of color and design, and many Guatemalan Indians spin and dye their cotton then weave their own clothes. Hand weaving on back-strap looms produces narrow strips that are sewn together to make blouses and pants.
>
> I wondered how these women survived on the few dollars these textiles brought them. Nonetheless, our orders would feed many families from this cooperative.
>
> —Kathy Borrus, *The Fearless Shopper: How to Get the Best Deals on the Planet*

the various Mayan groups south from Chiapas and the Yucatán—"foreigners"?

I think of a contractor from Merced, California, who, smoking a fat one in Nick's, explained his trip to San Pedro this way: "One day I found out that not all the workers picking grapes near my house were Mexicans," he began, signaling the waitress for another liter of beer. "Guatemala? Belize? No one had taught me about these places. I wanted to see what was going on."

That's good. But an enlightened field trip for a country boy isn't going to transform Guatemala's future. And not all lake visitors have the bodhisattva mind-set.

An angry Stephan was apparently about to leave for Chich's house, machete in hand, when I offered a more diplomatic, perhaps face-saving suggestion: "Why don't you tell Chich you heard he had found some money, and you'd like to settle it without bringing the village authorities in?"

I wonder if I am going to see Stephan at the next Vigilante Day. I myself have now been trapped—perhaps not the best choice of words—on the lake four days longer than I had intended.

I think.

No one can tell me what day it is. After a week of volcanic chaos, one feels that one has changed…back into something. Who was that nice Brit who coined the volcanic chaos moniker? He had a guitar with him, and I argued that although he was right, the Doors and Huxley are indeed clichés, they are good clichés. I'm making a mental note to check at Nick's book exchange after *Shine* tonight for a volume called *Using Your Perfect Memory* some naked girl told me about. Ah, here comes Claire, asking me if I want to grab some homegrown hot chocolate at a restaurant called, as far as I can remember, Good Restaurant.

Doug Fine, while making a film in Alaska, is somehow also at work on a book about backpacking travelers in developing-world danger zones. He is an Alaskan daydreamer who travels the world seeking connections. A collection of his work from five continents is at www.well.com/user/fine.

NATANYA PEARLMAN

A Garífuna Awakening

A Caribbean interlude casts a spell.

YOU NEVER KNOW AT WHAT POINT IN A JOURNEY SOMETHING WILL make an impression on you. This particular afternoon in Honduras, the afternoon that things started to look a little different to me, we were in a van bumping along a dirt road, following the edge of the Caribbean out to a tiny Garífuna village named Miami. A few nights earlier, I'd had my first exposure to the Garífuna culture. Sitting on the hard cement ground of the Copán Ruinas town square, I had watched as a Garífuna dance troupe performed their traditional song and dance, called *punta*, providing an incongruent yet dynamic finale to a Mayan archaeology conference. After I'd spent three days learning about the Mayan Indians, a somewhat shy people, out roared the Garífuna—the women big-hipped and large-bosomed, the men taut and muscular, all moving together in a breathtaking display of sensuous rhythmic prowess, beating drums, pounding feet, swiveling hips, loud and passionate and vibrant.

The Garífuna culture is a hybrid one—Caribbean in its fishing practices, and African in its oral traditions, dance, and music, with a language that combines Arawak, French, Yoruba, Bantu, Swahili, English, and Spanish. The Garífuna's origins date back to 1635 when an English slave ship wrecked off the coast of St. Vincent, and, resisting slavery, the Africans on board began a new life with the local Arawak Indians. Generations later, the entrenched English shipped the Garífuna to the island of Roatán, off the coast of Honduras. But Roatán, the Garífuna discovered, was no paradise—it had no potable water or arable land—and soon most migrated to the Central American mainland, establishing fishing villages along the coasts of Belize, Guatemala, Nicaragua, and Honduras.

Miami was one of those fishing villages—one that now exists along the shores of the Jeanette Kawas National Park. We were heading out there following a morning of visiting botanical gardens, and a long, lazy lunch on the beach of another Garífuna community, Triunfo de la Cruz. After three days at an academic conference, and battles with a weak stomach that had left me in a food-deprived haze, I was finally starting to feel like myself again—up for anything, ready to take in the new sights and sounds around me. I was also slowly becoming cognizant of the tension within many of the Garífuna villages—between sustaining their authentic way of life and the eroding influence of tourism and the modern world.

Today approximately sixty Garífuna fishing villages lie scattered along the Central American coast. Although population numbers are hard to determine, estimates range from 450,000 to fewer than 100,000. In 2001, the Garífuna were named a World Heritage culture, a new United Nations designation that recognizes and urges protection for endangered ways of life.

—LH & NP

Rap music blared from a small hut as we pulled over to see a sea turtle on our way out of Triunfo. The turtle was upside down on a wooden table, its legs jerking spasmodically as a man hacked it with a machete. "It's dead," he told us, as we stepped out of the van to gape. Sea turtles are an endangered species, but catching them for food has long been part of the Garífuna culture, which is itself at risk. I took a picture of the man and the turtle, which I immediately half-regretted, and when I got back into the vehicle, my shirt and shorts were spattered red with turtle gore.

Back on the road, it became clear that the drive out to Miami was going to take a while—much longer than everyone had thought it would. Although we had all fit into the van, it was a tight squeeze, and two people had to sit in the very back, where, with no shock absorber, the bumping from the uneven dirt road was the worst. So, people were uncomfortable, but cheerful, and it was in this way that the ride progressed—passively, but with everyone happy to see whatever there was to see.

And it was during this period, when the ride out to Miami was getting longer and longer, and the people in the back were getting more and more uncomfortable, that the coconut trees appeared. Or, that I started to notice the coconut trees. For suddenly, it seemed, we were surrounded by them. During lunch a few had dotted the beach, but now they were everywhere—as far up the coast as the eye could see, and flanking every side of the van. But these were not normal coconut trees, with long, buoyant fronds and clustered, round brown coconuts. These coconut trees began as elegant, sleek stalks that rose up into the sky, but then they abruptly ended, their tops dramatically severed. It was as if someone had taken an axe and lopped off the heads of every single tree. At first we talked about it—hey, look at the strange coconut trees, the diseased coconut trees, the dead coconut trees. But then, eventually, we all became quiet. It was as if the sight of the topless trees, beautiful in an eerie, tragic way, was just too much. Eli, our guide, said that they didn't know what had caused the disease that had struck the trees five years earlier, but that it was a problem because these coastal villages didn't have much, but they did have coconut trees. Coconut oil for cooking, and coconut meat for eating, and the long green and brown fronds for building. But now all the coconut trees were dying, and all we could do was bump along in our van, looking out the windows, quiet and somber and contemplative.

It was at this point that something else started to enter my vision. In addition to the dead coconut trees, I realized that we were following the bluest, most beautiful water, and the whitest, purest sand,

and that for miles and miles now it had been just us in the van, the long stalks of the coconut trees, and this coastline. And even though I knew that we were in a national park, and that I shouldn't be surprised by the pristine and rugged beauty around us, I was. In this world of Everything Developed Everywhere, here we were, on the Caribbean, and there wasn't a resort or hotel or bar or even surfboard in sight. With the exception of the coconut trees, the view outside the van's windows mirrored every postcard of tropical paradise—every dreamy beach cliché that, once witnessed firsthand, disappoints. Only this didn't. And as I was starting to feel this, this awe, we arrived in Miami. And Miami was…

"It's like Africa," someone said. It's like the Blue Lagoon meets Bolinas, I thought. Here on a spit of sand, slipped between the Caribbean Sea, and the Los Micos Lagoon, existed a village of 350 Garífuna, who were still living and fishing as they must have two hundred years earlier. The spit was lined with simple huts, canoes peeking from every crevice. Brown pelicans glided over the lagoon, and hundreds of black cormorants and white egrets clustered above dense mangroves. Riding by on a horse, two young boys flashed giant smiles.

And it was here, in this moment, as I stood barefoot in the sand, taking in Miami, that I fully opened—that my pores and senses and brain and heart and soul cracked as wide as possible, and that finally I was fully in Honduras, every single part of me. If this place existed, I thought, and these people lived here, then the world was full of so much more wonder and pure, astonishing beauty than usually seemed possible. And looking around, I realized—I don't know how or why this is so, but I swear it is absolutely true—in Miami the coconut trees were still alive.

Natanya Pearlman is a freelance editor for Travelers' Tales and co-editor of this book.

PAUL BERMAN

In Search of Ben Linder's Killers

One person can make a difference.

DURING THE 1980S, THERE WAS A NEIGHBORHOOD IN MANAGUA, Nicaragua, known as Gringolandia—a district of hotels, flophouses, private homes, and open-air restaurants filled with visitors from Berkeley, Cambridge, Manhattan, Madison, and other American places. At one corner of Gringolandia stood the grotesque white modern pyramid of the Hotel Intercontinental Managua, and along the streets running west from the hotel were elegant Miami-style houses, some of them cracked and half ruined from a long-ago earthquake and from the revolution and the economic collapse. Still farther to the west were blocks of grim working-class houses built in the style of the Spanish Middle Ages, except with roofs of corrugated zinc, and on some of the weedy lots were tumble-down shanties made of wood scraps and pieces of cardboard. And in just that way the Americans, too, came in several varieties.

The largest number of them had come to see the Sandinista People's Revolution out of curiosity and sympathy, and wished by the mere fact of visiting to make a personal protest against the Reagan Administration and its anti-Sandinista policies. As many as a hundred thousand Americans tramped around Nicaragua in that spirit, and sooner or later all those people spent the night at a

Gringolandia hotel or gathered around a communal table at one of the restaurants.

A second group, much smaller, consisted of journalists in their twenties and thirties—not so much the salaried reporters from the big-time media (those people stayed away from Managua's American community) but the scrappy stringers and freelancers, the writers for alternative weeklies (I was one of those), together with a crowd of would-be reporters and photographers on the prowl for their first good story. The journalists rented rooms, and sometimes entire houses, from middle-class Managua families whose members had gone into exile, and they lived in a fairly comfortable style, by Nicaraguan standards—even if the running water was cut off two days a week and the electric power failed three times a day and the phones were always on the blink.

The people who gave Gringolandia its glamour and its spirit were neither touring protesters nor journalists. They were the "internationalists," which is to say the volunteer workers—people from around the world but especially from the American universities and the liberal churches who had come down to Nicaragua to lend their

The barrio outside Managua was lit as if for an evening soccer match as Daniel Ortega and four others sat listening to residents at the weekly "*Cara a Cara*" (Face to Face) town meeting.

"There's no working pay phone here, no way to call an ambulance if we need help," said one.

Ortega and his staff conferred briefly. "Be in the office of the Minister of Public Works at nine on Monday morning," they responded, "and we'll take care of it."

"*Cara a Cara*" continued for an hour and a half until everyone who wished to speak had had a chance. The air was charged with a sense of possibility and hope, a sense that things really were *different*, that *this* government put human needs before corporate profits.

—Mija Riedel, "*Cara a Cara*, September 2, 1983"

energy to the revolution. Most of the internationalists put in a few weeks or months of hard labor on the coffee harvest or building a health clinic, and then went home. But there were quite a few others—probably several hundred at any given time—who held regular jobs with the Sandinista organizations and worked on projects that lasted for years, sometimes in Managua, sometimes in the countryside. These people were poor. Mom and Dad back home might send a few dollars, but otherwise they had to survive on the salaries offered by the Sandinistas, paid in cordobas, the value of which depreciated by the hour. Unless someone lent them a decent house, the internationalists ended up living pretty much as ordinary Nicaraguans did—boarding in places where five or ten people might crowd into two or three rooms under a zinc roof, with a single fluorescent tube for light, a primitive stove, and an evil-smelling, seatless toilet that flushed only sometimes.

Life in Managua was exhausting. The buses were overcrowded and halfway broken-down, the sun was a blast furnace every afternoon, and nothing worked the way it was supposed to work. Still, the city was reasonably safe, and most of the provincial towns and the rich farmlands along the Pacific Coast were safe enough as well. But the Reagan Administration was backing the contra guerrillas in their effort to overthrow the Sandinista People's Revolution, and in several of the remoter regions the fighting was intense. The most frightening areas were in the frontier zone, where the hamlets and farms merged into the jungle: in the northern mountain provinces of Jinotega and Nueva Segovia and in a few other places, and along the Atlantic Coast, where the Miskito Indians lived.

The internationalists usually stayed out of those areas. Yet there were a handful whose work kept them there for months, or even years. The internationalists all entertained the idea that Sandinista Nicaragua was going to pioneer a new and better kind of society for poor countries around the world, if only the contras and the Reagan Administration could be beaten off; and the handful in the war zones staked their lives on that belief. And of those few, no one was graver in his commitment or clearer about the dangers than Benjamin Linder, of Portland, Oregon.

Linder moved to Nicaragua in 1983, freshly graduated from the University of Washington in Seattle with a degree in mechanical engineering—a short and skinny young man with eyeglasses and a plastic pocket protector to carry his pens. He spent a year and a half working for the electric utility in Managua, and in his time off he amused himself by teetering around on a unicycle, got up in a clown suit and a bulbous rubber nose. Everywhere he went, little children ran after him, astonished at the sight and nearly rioting with excitement. Then he moved north and went to work on a slightly harebrained but entirely commendable project to build a couple of tiny hydroelectric plants in the villages of Jinotega, where such a thing as hydroelectric power had never existed.

Jinotega lies on the border with Honduras. The contras maintained their headquarters on the Honduran side and slipped easily into the Jinotegan mountains to stage attacks. Linder's first village was El Cuá, which turned out to be a favorite target. The contras would come charging down the road, shouting, "We are the sons of Reagan!" The United States supplied land mines, and the contras laid them in the unpaved highway. Commercial truck drivers from Managua refused to drive anywhere near El Cuá. One day, Linder tuned his radio to the contra broadcasts and heard a voice describing his own project, El Cuá's proposed new mini-hydroelectric plant, as something that ought to be destroyed. He had written to his parents, "I'd be lying if I said that there isn't anything to worry about. There is." Yet he was not discouraged, and he made his way back and forth from Managua to El Cuá, arranging supplies and organizing the tasks and entertaining the village with his rubber nose and his clown act.

Linder's fellow workers were a couple of Americans—a machinist and a solidarity activist—and a team of local people. Under his guidance, the group put together a crude electric turbine and housed it in a brick shed beside a stream. They strung up a few power lines, and El Cuá entered the modern world. The Sandinistas maintained a health clinic in the village, and for the first time the clinic was able to refrigerate its medicines. Teachers offered night classes. Even the clothing styles changed. The villagers bought electric irons, and suddenly everyone's clothes were handsomely pressed—like city folk! No longer like hicks and peasants! Having performed his first miracle, Linder decided, with the permission of the Sandinista authorities, to build the second hydroelectric plant in the next village up the road, if you could call it a road. This place was Bocay (more formally, San José de Bocay), twenty miles north of El Cuá and more wretched yet. Bocay was a frontier settlement. It was in the mountains, where the river fords and the jungle prevented the Sandinista People's Army from providing even as much security as existed in El Cuá. In the hills above Bocay, the contras were everywhere.

> November 25, 11:32—The lights went on in El Cuá. I was excited, joyous, and amazed. We were back in the operator's house drinking beer while Oscar played the guitar in a yellow slicker. Days of staying up late had had an effect on all of us. I sat there looking at the table. Beer bottles, a pot of coffee, tools, guns. The whole image had a beauty of a team putting its all into an effort—and doing it. El Cuá is working...
>
> —from Ben Linder's journal, quoted in *The Death of Ben Linder* by Joan Kruckewitt

Linder was, of course, a puritan, not in his prescriptions for everyone else but in his own behavior—a Goody Two-Shoes, as one of his fellow-workers put it. He liked to dance, but there were no drugs for him, and no rum extravaganzas on a tropical afternoon except when socially unavoidable. Not much in the way of women, either, though after he broke up with his college girlfriend, back in the States, he did try, with notable ineptness, to find someone new—a Latin woman, ideally. But on the twin themes of the Sandinista revolution and practical technology his passions were uninhibited, and he got along best with people whose enthusiasms were the same. In Managua, he sometimes hung out with a freelance news photographer named Larry Boyd and with Larry's companion, Joan Kruckewitt, who worked as a stringer for

ABC Radio. Larry and Joan rented a pleasant middle-class house and paid a Managua woman named Hortencia Obando to do the housekeeping. Hortencia's children romped around the kitchen, and Linder would come over to bask in the luxury.

Joan was a Berkeley girl who had arrived in Managua the same year he had, and she would peer down at his scrawny figure—she was five-feet-seven—and reflect that he and she were schoolmates, in a fashion: the Managua class of '83, suffering together in the tropical revolution. Yet she never knew what to say when he was around. Linder was too much the nerd for her taste, and the circus clowning put her off. Larry, on the other hand, genuinely enjoyed Linder's visits. Larry was always out in front of the house, toiling on his beat-up Subaru. His idea of a good time was a lively discussion of car engines or camera lenses or the relative merits of Soviet and American weaponry, and he and Linder got along famously.

Now and then, Linder met real engineers, and those people were, in his eyes, more congenial yet. There was the case of Rebecca Leaf, who might have seemed an unlikely friend. Rebecca came out of M.I.T., though it had taken her a while to graduate, as a result of a long hippie interlude of pottery-making in a Massachusetts barn and socialist virtue on a kibbutz. She arrived in Managua, ready to put her skills to use, and Linder took her for a walk through the streets. They came across a giant puppet, double human size—with a normal-sized man inside—clowning around with a couple of drummers and a guy improvising poetry. The performers recognized Linder as the famous unicyclist, and the poet launched into a mischievous verse about a gray streak in Rebecca Leaf's hair. She thinks she is pretty but looks like a peeled coconut, the poet declaimed. Linder loved that kind of thing. A city of color and theater—that was his Managua. But Rebecca was restrained. Linder invited her to sit with him at one of the innumerable bars and restaurants, where people with a pocketful of cordobas listened to high-volume scratchy music tapes. She preferred to stay at home.

Linder and Rebecca did have a few points in common; both were the children of Jewish doctors, for instance. But engineering was the main connection. They conferred about the work habits of their Nicaraguan colleagues, which were, from their American engineers' point of view, unbelievably sloppy; and about the lack of supplies. "How many Nicaraguans does it take to screw in a light bulb?" Linder liked to say. "None—there are no light bulbs!" Rebecca worked at the Managua electric utility and served as the Managua coordinator for Linder's project up in Jinotega. They boarded in the same house in Managua for a while and they thought about pooling resources to buy a place of their own somewhere in the capital—just to make life less of a struggle. It was not because of anything romantic between them. Dealing with practical problems was their shared pleasure.

It must have been his engineer's passion for problem solving that brought Linder to Bocay. The hydroelectric plant at El Cuá was a success, but he could easily imagine something better and stronger. And so, on April 28, 1987, he and his crew of Nicaraguans took their shovels and tools and climbed a hill about a mile above Bocay to work on a small, temporary dam called a weir. The Nicaraguans brought assault rifles, and Linder, too, came armed: in the matter of guns, he drew no distinction between his workmates and himself. Construction, not combat, was the idea, though. The weir would allow Linder to measure the flow of a mountain stream and help him identify the ideal site for a permanent concrete dam, whose waterfall would power the proposed new hydroelectric plant. Only, by climbing the hill he and his crew stumbled into one of the largest engagements of the contra war.

Congress had voted a hundred million dollars for the contras the year before, and by April of 1987 the contra *comandante*, Enrique Bermúdez—known as 3-80, his number in military school—was using the money to move his headquarters to the border of Jinotega and launch a big push southward. The contras began staging pinprick ambushes up and down the Bocay River. A little unit showed up on the hill where Linder and the crew were building the weir. Whatever happened next was over within minutes, and Benjamin Linder was dead and his body was stripped of his wallet, watch, camera, and cartridge belt. Two of his workers were dead at his side, and the four other members of his crew had fled down the hill to Bocay.

Linder's body was carried into the village but the Sandinista officials there were nervous about having a dead American on their hands, and no one wanted to take charge. An American religious activist named Gary Hicks happened to be traveling through the region, and the Sandinistas put Hicks and a couple of other people on a helicopter with the corpse and sent them southward, out of the zone. Word of what had taken place arrived in Managua via the very shaky telephone connection to the electric utility. It was Rebecca Leaf who answered the phone…

> Why? Why do we do it? Because [the Nicaraguans] deserve it. They sacrifice and continue sacrificing. They deserve a better life. I have the honor of helping them. Risk is accepted or rejected and I've chosen to accept it. I know it's meaningless to say "don't worry." I want you to know what I'm doing and why I do it. Rest assured that I don't take "undue" risks but "undue" is very relative.
>
> —from a letter Ben Linder wrote to his parents, quoted in *The Death of Ben Linder* by Joan Kruckewitt

Eight years later I traveled into the northern zones where Linder had been killed, and, on my way, a number of people told me that, to their knowledge, Linder's widow, a gringa, was still living in the area. I was surprised to hear it. I had never heard that Linder was married. But, at the Five Star restaurant in Bocay that I met the widow Linder—a gringa for real, with a long face and delicate hands and a broad strand of white running through her hair that did in fact make her look like a peeled coconut. She was Rebecca Leaf…. No, she was not really the widow Linder, she explained to me. Yet her friendship with Linder had certainly turned out to be the fateful element in her life. The phone call announcing his death still rang in her memory. It had been her obligation after receiving that call to go across the street from the utility office to the telephone office, where you could make international calls, and to try to reach Linder's parents in Oregon. She wasn't able to get through. She called her own mother, in Massachusetts, and asked her to telephone the Linders. Sitting with me at the Five Star Restaurant, Rebecca trembled, ever so slightly, as she remembered those moments.

She was one of the people who had organized the protest march from El Cuá to Bocay after Linder's funeral. When the march reached Bocay, she and a couple of Linder's fellow-workers would have liked to go up the hill to see what was left of the temporary dam that he had been building, but the contras were around, and going up the hill was out of the question. Still, even without inspecting the weir, Rebecca could see that if Linder's work in Bocay was not to have been in vain someone would have to take up where he had left off, and that person would have to be a trained engineer. Someone who knew how to build a hydroelectric plant. Herself, namely. At first, she lived in the agrarian-reform building in the Bocay plaza, which must have been somewhat like her hippie experiences in the Massachusetts barn, except a million times as extreme. When it seemed safe to climb the hill, she discovered that the weir was intact, though unfinished. Eventually, the commandos blew it up, but by then Rebecca had been able to calculate where to build the permanent dam.

A number of Linder's American friends—Don Macleay and Mira Brown, from the El Cuá project; a machinist named John Lewontin—came and worked on the project for periods of up to a year. The Linder family's tours around the United States raised a good deal of money for Rebecca's project. A solidarity campaign of American machinists and engineers sent lathes and machine parts. But that was before the 1990 election [when the Sandinistas were voted out of power].

Afterward, what was left for Rebecca Leaf? Suddenly it was obvious that a worldwide socialist revolution of the poor countries was not going to occur, and Sandinista Nicaragua was not going to be a light unto the Third World, and the political excitement that had led people like Rebecca and Linder to think of building hydroelectric plants in jungle villages was gone forever. The engineers' and machinists' solidarity campaign pretty much disintegrated.

Life in Bocay was monotonous and filthy, and was not getting any less so.

There were matters like malaria and cholera to worry about. It was always possible that one of the old contras might someday resume the attack on the hydroelectric project—especially after the re-contra rebellion got going. Rebecca had organized a machine shop in El Cuá, and the re-contras kidnapped one of the workers. She watched in horror as the Talavera brothers' 3-80 Front went around blowing up electric lines.

Yet the issue of whether to stay on in Bocay seemed simple enough. The revolution was finished, but the revolution's purpose, in its original, uncorrupted version, had always been to improve the life of the very poor, and that was still possible. There was not going to be a socialist society; but there could be a hydroelectric plant. In the United States, the Linder family and some of Linder's friends were willing to go on raising funds, if Rebecca wished them to do so. People in Berkeley sent contributions. There was aid from the government of Sweden. The

---

The re-contra rebellion occurred after Violeta Chamorro beat Daniel Ortega in the 1990 presidential election and the contras, at her request, turned in their guns and returned to civilian life. The expected reforms didn't happen, however (for instance, the army remained under Sandinista control), many former contras were killed either by assassination or in murky circumstances, and disgruntled peasants and former contras took up arms again. They wanted government benefits rather than an overthrow of the regime.

The Talavera brothers' Comandante 3-80 Northern Front was a re-contra force formed by members of a prominent landholding family from the north who had fled into Honduran exile when the Sandinistas, in an effort to nationalize agriculture, embarked on a wholesale confiscation of rural property.

—LH & NP

Nicaraguans who had gone to work for Linder and had been trained by him and his American fellow-workers—and, later, by Rebecca—were willing to keep on laboring. They organized themselves into a committee called the Benjamin Linder Rural Development Workers' Association. It consisted of thirteen Nicaraguans and one gringa graduate of M.I.T. Rebecca never doubted what was the right thing to do. She was exactly like Linder in that regard.

She was known as Doña Rebecca now, a respected lady in her mid-forties. I walked with her along Bocay's street, and she received the greetings of people we passed. She had long since made peace with the old contras. The original laborers on her dam had been Sandinistas, but she was clever enough to recognize that her hydroelectric project could never get anywhere as the partisan enterprise of an unpopular party, and she swallowed hard and hired veterans of the contra army to aid in the construction. The contras were glad to have the work, and were surprised to get it, and afterward were grateful, too. Rebecca was a little nervous about telling the Linder family that she had hired the contras to work on Ben's project. But the Linders trusted her judgment.

A new handful of Americans came down to work with her. One of them was Benjamin Linder's older brother, John, who toiled over the billing system and a few other tasks connected with the project. John Linder marveled at the austerity of Rebecca's life—her barren room with her clothes stuffed in a coffee sack, the outhouse down the hill, her insomniac nights of counting out bolts and washers by flashlight. But this life of hers was visibly productive. The permanent dam was built. It was eighteen meters across, a wall of concrete.

Water from the runoff tumbled 200 meters down the hill to a square concrete house, where she put the turbines and the generator. In May, 1994, the Linder family flew from the United States to Managua, then to Bocay by military helicopter, and observed as the Benjamin Linder Hydroelectric Mini-Power Plant was inaugurated, with balloons, clowns, a unicycle, and cockfights. Electricity flowed through suspended wires down the hill to Bocay. The village's dental offices went electric. The public school added night classes. The stores began to sell cold drinks. A corn mill and several carpentry shops were electrified. A video theater opened. That was Rebecca Leaf's achievement—that and the perpetuation of Benjamin Linder's memory. Near the Benjamin Linder Mini-Power Plant dam was the Benjamin Linder School. In another school, the assigned topic for commencement addresses was "Benjamin Linder." A new settlement was constructed a few miles away, and Rebecca ran a cable out to the new houses, and the householders responded by naming their neighborhood the Benjamin Linder Barrio.

Rebecca ushered me into the power plant to show off the machine-tooling. The place was the size of a one-car garage. The turbines gave out a tremendous roar. She took me up to the dam. A wooden boom in the stream had got out of place, and I went into the woods and found a long stick so she could poke at the boom. When everything was back in order, she stood at the edge of the dam and surveyed her little empire and the rushing water, and the women washing clothes downstream, and the concrete house that gave out a roar from the whirring turbines, and the green jungle all around.

Her two sisters in the United States hoped, Rebecca confessed to me, that one day she would awaken from the terrible insanity that had obviously overtaken her, and would return to America and lead a normal life. She didn't rule out such a possibility. Meanwhile, the European Union had opened an office in Bocay and come up with money for a potable-water project, and Doña Rebecca was running around with her shirttails hanging out, supervising the water technology. There was a rice-hulling project. She was a busy woman. Yet, for all her plans and activity, the weight of the past seemed not to have grown very much lighter. I mentioned that I was interested in finding anyone who might have participated in the events of April 28, 1987—that I would like to find one of the contras from the task force that had killed Linder. Doña Rebecca looked as if she were going to tremble again and asked in a whisper if I happened to know someone named Joan Kruckewitt. I told her that Joan was soon coming up to Bocay, and that she and I were going to make the search together.

⁂

I met Joan back in Managua, and we hired a driver and a jeep and set a day to drive up to Bocay on our own. But just then El Charrito's group, from somewhere deep within the north, issued a proclamation—handwritten on 3-80 Northern Front stationery, and sealed with a contra stamp from the mid-1980s—forbidding road traffic anywhere in Nicaragua for one week. The re-contras had no chance of enforcing such a ban in most of the country, but Bocay was their terrain. The staff of the European Union office there thought it wise to pull out of the region for the moment, and Joan had a few errands to do in Managua, anyway. She had brought a sewing machine down from California and wanted to present it to her old housekeeper, Hortencia: a brilliant new idea for setting up Hortencia in business. A few days later, we read in the Managua papers that, sure enough, El Charrito and his men did go out on the northern roads, and burned five or six vehicles and beat up one of the drivers.

So we arrived in Bocay later than planned, and ended up booking stalls—you couldn't call them rooms—in Bocay's single lodging house, where the posted rules forbade anyone to drink liquor or to introduce explosives into the building. Bocay was not a restful place. At three in the morning, the East German truck pulled up in front to collect the farmworkers, and the noise and the fumes drove me out to the front porch, where I sat in the dark and listened to a grizzled peddler in a Philadelphia Flyers hat whisper about Sandinista massacres.

The Sandinistas had just slaughtered some of their own followers in the north, he said. The Sandinistas were going to blame the Resistance—the re-contras, that is. The Sandinistas were Communists, the people were Christians. Another man on the porch nodded vigorous assent. And at sunup Joan and I went off to pay courtesy calls on Bocay's contra veterans and to see if, by any chance, some of the former commandos of the Francisco Rodríguez Task Force might be found.

We were particularly curious about the man known as Williams—his real name was Santiago Girón Meza—who, according to what Bull's Eye, the regional commander, had told Joan, might be living nearby. Williams was one of the commandos who had described Linder's killing to the American official back in 1987 and had signed his statement with a real signature, not just a thumbprint. We sat in the home of a former contra officer named Seven Seas, and Joan cracked jokes and brought up Williams's name. Seven Seas said that Williams might be living in the mountains, two or three hours distant. We met someone else who knew the way and agreed to guide us. And we set out, up the steep hill in our jeep, past the Benjamin Linder Mini-Power Plant, then higher still, to the concrete dam, where the jungle swallowed up the path and we had to leave the jeep behind.

The terrain we walked through had the strange quality of being wilderness and farmland at the same time. Leaves the size of elephants protruded from plantain trees, and the bigger the leaves the tinier seemed the farms—stick-pile hovels surrounded by pathetic patches that could hardly have supported a human being. The ground was muddy, making it hard to walk, and when we found ourselves in purer forest the walking became harder still, until we were hopping from stone to stone across rivulets and pulling our ankles out of sinkholes. Yet just when the going seemed impossible we arrived at a farm more impressive than any we had seen—a field with three horses, a couple of dozen ducks and chickens, a few head of cattle, and patches of land growing coffee, corn, and beans, with a shack at the center. This was the farm of Williams's father, Don Rosa Girón, and his family. They came to sit with Joan and me and our guide on the porch: Don Rosa's wife in a brocaded, handwoven cotton dress; a young woman chic in red polyester; another young woman and a young man; and infants and small children. We expressed an interest in speaking with Don Rosa's son, the war veteran, and Don Rosa sent one of the little boys galloping off on horseback to find him.

Don Rosa was not a man of wide experience. Sometimes he traveled to Bocay to sell his beans and corn, though not often, because the trip took five hours there and back, not counting the time in town. Otherwise, he hadn't seen a lot of places. Even El Cuá lay beyond the periphery of his travels. But Don Rosa had accomplished something large in his life, which was to carve out his farm from pure wilderness. He had bought the land thirty years ago, and he and three sons had spent a year clearing out the growth with axes, machetes, and handsaws. They had lived in a straw hut, and eventually his oldest son had chopped down the tropical laurel trees and hewed the planks and built the shack that was now their home. Unfortunately, no sooner did the house go up than war came to the farm. Two battles between the Sandinista People's Army and the contras were fought on Don Rosa's land.

The little boy trotted up on his horse and told us that Williams was waiting for us at another farm, and we said goodbye and praised the beauty of Don Rosa's land and plunged back onto the path. The second farmhouse was a dismal shed with cocks and a pig and a couple of little children peeking at us from inside. The mountain vista was grand, though. The farm was on a slope, and the ground fell away into the valley of a hamlet called Agua Zarca, with mountains beyond. Because of the rainy season, the mountain peaks and the valley seemed to radiate every color of the spectrum, if you can imagine every color as green. Williams was leaning over a railing on the porch. He was a man of twenty-five, three or four inches shorter than Joan, with black hair, a round bronze face, and an amiable smile, glinty with gold fillings.

Williams had grown up on the farm with his parents and his brothers and sisters. But in 1982—the year before Linder's arrival in Nicaragua, and Joan's—the two older Girón boys decided to run away to join the Resistance, and, because brothers follow brothers, Williams insisted on going along, though he was only thirteen. The oldest of the boys, the one who had built the house, was captured a year later by the Sandinistas and, Williams told us, was murdered. But Williams and the second brother made it through the war in one piece.

Williams spent part of the time in a Resistance camp in Honduras. The camp was full of preachers, he said, and one commando after another began to hear a personal message from God. The commandos learned that Catholics were not really Christians, as they had always been taught. True Christians belonged to the Assembly of God. And God spoke to Williams in Honduras of 1987. Somebody lent Williams a Bible that came from the United States. His narrative of conversion leaned on that fact—for my benefit and Joan's, or perhaps because the American provenance lent the Bible authority. Williams promised God that if he survived the war he would live the upright life of a good Christian. Then it was 1990, and he and the other commandos from his unit returned from the war, and he set out to fulfill his promise.

God's word had spread by then to the hamlet of Agua Zarca, and though the Girón family as a whole remained Catholic, many other people became true Christians. They met for services at the chapel of the Assembly of God in Agua Zarca. Williams was one of the new preachers. He preached to his neighbors about the coming of Jesus Christ—soon, soon, before the next millennium. He did not drink or dance or use bad words or engage in dishonesty in business. Whenever he had the chance, he made his way through the jungle into Bocay and attended Bible class. The teacher was a man who had studied in Managua. Williams was now newly married. The stylish young woman in red back at his father's farm was his wife.

Williams and I had been talking together up to this point, but now Joan asked about the war. Wasn't it around here that a North American had died?

Williams had a poker face.

"What was his name?" he asked.

"Benjamin Linder," she said. "I think your group was involved."

Williams had been enjoying our visit until that moment—had seemed to be, anyway.

"I think it was," he said.

But he was cautious. His unit, yes, had killed the North American. But he himself had been elsewhere—on another mission. Or lagging behind. Either way, he wasn't there, wasn't responsible for killing a North American—even if it was true, as Joan reminded him, that his name, and even his signature, appeared in the State Department reports. But he could definitely tell us about the event, down to its tiniest particulars. He could tell us why the unit had attacked the group at the dam. It was because the people in the area had said that Cubans were working on the dam. Killing Cubans was a basic task. And so the commandos in his unit had walked two hours through the jungle to the dam, and they had lain in wait two hours more for the Sandinistas and the Cubans. The commandos opened fire and then threw hand grenades.

Just at this point in Williams's story, a bare-chested young man carrying a machete in each hand came wandering down the path to the shack and peered at us with wide-eyed wonder. The man was an apparition out of Joan's worst fantasies, and mine. I jumped up and left Joan to go on with the questioning, and I tried to strike up a cheerful, diversionary conversation with the new arrival, and at the same time, to block his view.

Behind us, the conversation between Joan and Williams was lumbering on, and with a phrase here and there the gist of Williams's descriptions was audible. That was exactly what I didn't want the newcomer to overhear. So I asked, "Are you from around here?"

The man with the two machetes tilted his head.

I rephrased the question.

His chin pointed up the hill.

"And how are the crops?"

"Good."

"How is your own farm?"

Silence. "We are poor," he said. "We have always been poor. We do not have a farm."

The situation was awkward beyond all awkwardness. "It is a beautiful view from here," I said.

Two Machetes looked at me with wonder.

"Yes, what a view!" I went on. "Very beautiful. Very, but very. What is your own opinion?"

But it was of no use. Behind us, Joan, in the bell tones of her radio announcer's voice, was probing for details. "I thought that during the attack Ben Linder was wounded."

"No, he died at once," I could hear Williams answer. There was no torture or execution, in short. "He died. Because—as I told you—the information was that he was a Cuban."

The ambush, he said, was from fifteen meters away. Anything closer would have allowed the Sandinista group to begin firing. "The Resistance shot first," Williams said. This was a new admission—not at all the version that had appeared in the official documents. Raccoon, the unit leader, had searched Linder's body without ever discovering that it was the corpse of a foreigner.

"He had a camera. He was next to a gun that...I don't know if he was carrying it or not." That, too, was new. In the official reports, the contras had claimed that Linder had fired his weapon.

Our guide had been standing at a discreet distance from Two Machetes and me but now came over to join the conversation. We talked about regional accents, and, as we rambled on, Williams described to Joan how, on the day after the ambush, the unit received an extraordinary order to leave Jinotega at once and return to Resistance headquarters, in Honduras, on foot. The trek took eight days, and only when they had reached the camp did they learn that in the fighting outside Bocay they had killed a North American.

Comandante 3-80 spoke to them in person, in a harsh tone. He called their attack on the hill above Bocay "the failure." All kinds of people came to speak to the little unit—journalists, Americans. Williams had the impression that Linder's own family were among the people who came to the commandos demanding an explanation. It was a terrifying time. The secret cemeteries that surrounded the contra military camps in Honduras were not really a secret, after all. Everyone knew what happened to people who incurred the displeasure of the contra *comandantes*, and, as for what might happen to people who incurred the displeasure of the United States, that was beyond knowing. At that very moment, with his eyes trained on Joan, Williams must have been sick with worry about the consequences of incurring the displeasure of the United States.

And what about the soldiers in Williams's unit, the Francisco Rodríguez Task Force, and their fate? Williams paused to recall. About half of those men were killed in combat. The survivors came back to Bocay and the jungle hamlets at the end of the war, and most of them settled down into civilian life—all except Raccoon, the man who had searched Linder's body. Raccoon had joined the

Resistance back in 1981, when the Sandinistas confiscated his father's farm, and now, Williams told Joan, he was still at war. He was with the re-contras north of Bocay.

A violent squall broke out, and we huddled under the tiny porch roof. When Joan and I and the guide headed out in the direction of Bocay, the mud was squishier and deeper than before. It was late afternoon before we reached the concrete dam. We rode in the jeep down the steep hill into Bocay, and Joan and I went to the Five Star Restaurant and exchanged impressions. Granted that Williams had very sensibly insisted on his own absence from the attack at the dam, he had given us a thorough account, full of visual memories. His story countered the State Department and the official contra versions of the attack, and the more extreme Sandinista accusations, too. Linder and his fellow-workers had not started the fighting. There had been no order to execute an American. He had not been tortured. What about the theory of a gunshot at close range—a *coup de grâce*? Williams's version denied any such thing. The ambush at the dam had been an incident of war based on a rumor about Cubans—nothing more. Mostly, though, Joan and I had learned about the people who had done the killing.

We had learned that Linder was killed by a group of poor peasant boys who came from the neighborhood of Bocay itself—by the very people who were supposed to benefit from the new hydroelectric plant. We had learned that Williams was an earnest and religious man, concerned with his duties to God and with living a moral existence, as he conceived it; he was someone who, through his preaching, enjoyed making his own contribution to the community life of his hamlet.

We had learned, we had seen with our own eyes, that Williams was strikingly like Benjamin Linder, a Goody Two-Shoes, let us say. Where Linder's Two-Shoes spirit of militant virtue had come from a puritanism of the left, though, Williams's came from a Protestant fundamentalism, or from capital "P" Puritanism itself. The one man had been fervently idealistic and perhaps a little blinded by his fervor, though likable even so, and, in his way, admirable; and the other man was the same.

It was just that one was living and the other was dead. And the one who lived, on those occasions when he trekked into Bocay to sell coffee and corn and to attend the classes that were held by the Assembly of God, was the beneficiary of the one who was dead. For when Williams left home as a thirteen-year-old to go to war, Bocay had had no electricity, and now, when the young husband and war veteran wished to study the Word of God, Bocay was a town with lights, refrigerators, videos, and night classes—a place where you could study and improve yourself, using the Bible or any other book (though other books were not exactly prominent among the items for sale), according to your preference. And so Linder, together with Doña Rebecca, had won a triumph, and men like Williams were better off for it.

> I'm writing from my favorite godforsaken corner of Nicaragua. Here I am where I was last year at this time, fighting to get this 100KW mini-hydro in. Everything goes wrong. Every piece of metal has a story of how it would fit one day but not the next. I've never seen such bad luck. Yesterday I came back to my room in town, took a slug of rum and lay back in the hammock and thought about my karma. I just lay there and wondered about my role on this earth. I finally decided that this really is what I'm here for, like it or not, and that I just have to keep fighting.
>
> —from a letter Ben Linder wrote to his friend Peter, quoted in *The Death of Ben Linder* by Joan Kruckewitt

The next afternoon, Joan and I joined up with a new O.A.S convoy to return to Managua. On the way out of Bocay, we ran across a group of refugees. We were told that a number of re-contras high on marijuana had attacked a hamlet called Santa Teresa de Kilambé and burned a house, and forty people had fled to Bocay. The O.A.S. gave these people some emergency rations, which turned out to be packaged meals from the United States Army—the meals that are famously loathed by all American soldiers. Joan and I were called on to explain how to tear open the packets and convert the contents into food. Gravely, the crowd of refugees watched our demonstration.

Down the road, on the way south to El Cuá, we ran into two more refugees. They were a woman, riding a dappled horse, and an infant, swathed in cloth, on the pommel of her saddle. We stopped the jeep and asked what happened, and the woman told us that her name was María Navarrete Chavarría. She was twenty-four years old and the mother of five children. Three re-contras had come to her house and had taken her husband away and murdered him. She and the children had fled into the mountains, and she was now on her way to Bocay, and as she told us these things her voice wavered and her lungs heaved and she stroked her infant's hair. These were not scenes of triumph after all. The story of Benjamin Linder and his death is the story of how the war in northern Nicaragua was more bitter than anyone in the outside world has appreciated. And it is the story of how, in some very remote places, the war has never come to an end—there in a couple of jungle villages, where the people now enjoy the blessings of electricity but not those of peace and safety, and where, because of an American woman's spirit of defiance and undying comradely love, the honored name of Benjamin Linder has virtually been engraved in the backcountry geography.

Paul Berman is a journalist and literary critic who writes for a number of magazines. His reports on Latin America have appeared in The New Yorker, The New Republic, *the* New York Review of Books, Village Voice, Mother Jones, *and* Dissent. *He is the author of* A Tale of Two Utopias: The Political Journey of the Generation of 1968, *and is a fellow at the Center for Scholars and Writers at the New York Public Library. He lives in New York.*

PART TWO

Some Things to Do

JASON WILSON

Corn Island and the Festival of Crabs

On a small Nicaraguan island, two strangers and the author find paradise.

THERE WAS ONLY ONE VACANT ROOM AT THE HOTEL PANORAMA.

Marco and Elisa, the Dutch couple with whom I'd shared a taxi ride to this point, glanced at each other in horror over the predicament. Hanging palm fronds brushed softly against the bright yellow and white paint of the pleasant, tiny, eight-unit hotel. A young girl with a straw broom lingered under the cool shade of the porch and awaited our decision while straightening a hammock. Marco and Elisa composed themselves and Elisa said to me, "If you really, really want to stay here, I *guess* we can find *somewhere* else." Her eyes, however, begged me to go away.

I humbly insisted that Marco and Elisa take the room, then continued by taxi along bumpy roads with deep puddles that had been gouged by tremendous downpours and dried quickly in the hot sun. We drove from hotel to hotel, but there were no rooms at any of the other seven inns. "Too many people in town for the fiesta," said the innkeeper of the twenty-six-unit Bayside Inn, the island's grandest accommodations. At most destinations, "no vacancy" wouldn't necessarily mean a crisis. But here on Corn Island, forty-five miles off Nicaragua's eastern coast in the middle of the Caribbean, it presented a special dilemma.

When I had exhausted every possible lodging option, my driver dropped me in front of the small government office that housed the only public telephones on the island. I could see the orange sun beginning to set over a blue lagoon, casting shadows off several scattered fishing boats. There wasn't a soul on the beach. I almost began to panic, but standing inside the office with a telephone receiver in my hand, I realized worry was senseless. I was here, and there really wasn't anyone to call anyway. So I went back to the Hotel Panorama and drank beers with Marco and Elisa on their porch.

The first thing you need to know about Corn Island is that the airstrip doubles as the main thoroughfare. It is the only paved section of the island. When the planes arrive from Managua, 100 people line the runway to watch. Smiling men grab luggage straight out of the cargo hatch and throw it into taxis. First-time visitors like us just follow along, mouths agape. Gorgeous giant palm trees line the strip.

The second thing you need to know is that Corn Island has fallen under the auspices of the Nicaraguan government for many years. Before that, the island was a British colony. You can see the effects of both governments in small but significant ways. Corn Island's "taxis," for instance, are

I remembered how, a few weeks after Somoza's downfall, a well-known Latin-American Trotskyite had burst into the lobby of the Hotel Intercontinental here, just off a plane from Mexico, his face alight with discovery. "I understand!" he bubbled. "It seemed impossible that a guerrilla group could force the collapse of a state so quickly, but I've just driven here from the airport, and, let me tell you, Nicaragua was not a state. It was a hacienda—Somoza's private hacienda! And the National Guard were not an army, they were his private watchmen!" He was right: Nicaragua was not a state until the Sandinistas made it one.

—Alma Guillermoprieto, *The Heart That Bleeds: Latin America Now* dilapidated Russian surplus jeeps. They were brought here during the Sandinista rule in the 1980s, a subtle hint to the islanders that comrades in Managua were watching. The local language, unlike the Spanish of Nicaragua's interior, is a West Indian dialect of English, which dates back to earlier days of British rule. What Spanish Nicaragua calls "Corn Island" refers to two islands: Great Corn Island is about three-and-a-half miles long with a population of about 2,500; Little Corn Island, relatively uninhabited, is reachable only by boat from Great Corn Island.

Before I flew to Corn Island, I'd been told by my Nicaraguan friends that it was "virgin" and completely removed from the rest of the country. I was hopeful it would be uncrowded, since there were still no paved roads that connected the Pacific and Caribbean coasts of Nicaragua. But I was also skeptical, since these same friends had also told me their nation's government was finally stable and after several weeks in Managua, I'd realized that stable is a relative term. By "virgin," I only hoped my friends meant Corn Island would be a break from the desperate poverty and the danger that lurked in the capital.

Myths swirl around Corn Island. It is reputed to be a stopover, a safe haven, for the Medellín drug cartel's shipments on the way to Miami, and, according to locals, kilos of cocaine often wash up on the beach. But this rumor is only the contemporary version of Corn Island's tradition of being a frontier, outlaw place—a reputation that dates back to British and Dutch pirates in the seventeenth and eighteenth centuries. It's a place many have touched and claimed, but none have truly conquered.

I'd met Marco and Elisa on the scary propeller airplane to Corn Island, and they told me the trip was a vacation from their real purpose in Nicaragua—to provide health care outreach to street kids in León. The plane stopped once in the coastal outpost of Bluefields to drop off passengers and for the pilot to catch a smoke, and we continued on.

When we landed, we were joined in the taxi by a Peace Corps volunteer from Los Angeles named Tim, who told us he'd been trying for months to establish an efficient lobster fishing cooperative on Corn Island. As we disembarked, we saw several boxes marked "Spanish Bibles" unloaded by a group of sincere-looking, English-speaking men.

"¿A donde va?" asked the black islander driving our rusty old jeep. His casual assumption was not unfounded: We'd all just arrived from Managua, were white and, therefore, must certainly speak Spanish. At Tim's suggestion, we headed for the Hotel Panorama.

Tim explained that the island would be crowded on this particular weekend because it was the annual La Fiesta de Cangrejo—the Festival of Crabs. "Everybody here says the fiesta celebrates the emancipation of the slaves by the British in 1841," he said. "Legend has it that their ancestors cooked a huge pot of crab soup in celebration. That's where the name came from."

As Tim continued, he spoke about the island's lobster fishermen—the ones whom the Peace Corps volunteers were trying to assist. "It's hard to get these people together for a meeting," he said. "I scheduled one last Sunday and it rained and nobody showed. Like they never got wet before." This was the first time in twenty years that the Peace Corps had been invited into Nicaragua.

Tim slightly bemoaned the fact that the Festival of Crabs was happening that weekend because another Sunday meeting with the fishermen would fall by the wayside. "These people have no concept of how to market their product."

Marco asked, "Do you have experience in lobster fishing?"

"No, I have a business degree," Tim said.

"Oh," Marco said, smiling broadly and winking at me.

Our driver honked and yelled to his friends, who were yanking a giant sea turtle out onto the white beach, and making short work of the animal with a machete. "Turtle soup, mon!" our driver shouted. The sun sparkled off puddles in the road as we approached the hotel, which was tucked away in overgrown brush.

Night on Corn Island means a darkness so clear and thick it feels tangible. Although I still didn't have a place to sleep, Marco, Elisa, and I decided to get something to eat. The girl at the Hotel

Panorama pointed us toward a light atop a hill, which overlooked a cove. "That's the closest restaurant," she said. We had to carry flashlights to find our way up the path, and we could see the flickering blue glow of televisions in the little ramshackle homes as we passed.

When we reached the top of the hill, we realized the restaurant was basically someone's home—about six tables set up in the living room. Two island women rushed back and forth down a hall toward the kitchen while a middle-aged American man ate at the front table. The man told us that the restaurant/home was his and that he'd come to Corn Island to catch lobsters. "Been here four years," he grunted, adding that one of the women in the kitchen was his wife.

Merle Haggard's *Greatest Hits* played on a small boombox and we ate a tremendous dinner of shellfish. Later, when I tried to use the restroom, the door was locked and I heard the shower running. Soon enough, the American lobsterman walked out wrapped in a bath towel.

We drank more beers on the porch. Haggard changed to reggae and mixed with the soft lapping of the bay. Suddenly, from out of the darkness, a man wearing rubber surgical gloves and no shirt appeared at the porch. He carried a bag of shrimp and asked if we wanted to buy some. We said no, then he patted my stomach and disappeared once again into the darkness. We walked back down the hill by flashlight, and searched for the man with the rubber gloves.

Then we decided to take a taxi back to the main drag. People with AK-47s occasionally appeared from the darkness in the taxi's headlights. As we approached the airstrip, the street teemed with islanders gripping beer bottles and falling in and out of bars with swinging saloon doors. Roulette wheels lit by lanterns spun as the crowds screamed. Motorcycles and taxis flew through the darkness with or without lights.

When we tried to pay our taxi driver in Nicaraguan cordobas, he first refused, then claimed he didn't have any change. The making of change became a community event: He shouted at drunken friends in the street, asking for cordobas. Finally, we produced a $5 bill and he gladly made change out of a wad in his wallet.

Three of us stumbled through the doors of Bar Morgan, which

felt like a sauna inside. Dance-hall reggae pumped and we screamed at one another and laughed. The skull and crossbones of a huge Jolly Roger hung over the dance floor. According to the waitress, the bar's owner was a descendant of the legendary pirate Captain Morgan. We paid for our beers with cordobas and she brought us two packs of Chiclets as change and we laughed again. I danced with Elisa and a giant woman wearing pink curlers. We saw Tim was sipping a beer by the door and yelled at him to join us. "Don't Peace Corps volunteers dance?" Elisa asked.

"I'm not really in the mood, man."

"What?" we shouted.

I spilled onto the street for air and a man who smelled like a rum distillery wrapped his large arm around my shoulders and yelled, "Whoever doesn't enjoy themselves on Corn Island is a fool!"

At the end of the night, Marco and Elisa insisted I stay in their room at the Hotel Panorama. "I like you," Marco said. "It's funny, usually I don't like Americans." He smiled. "I'm sort of a Marxist, you see. Back at the university in Amsterdam you might have even called me a communist."

I followed them back, sweaty and happy, and fell into the extra bed. In the middle of the night, I heard a crash and awoke to find the electricity off. I didn't bother to grab for the flashlight in my backpack. There, away from the excitement near the airstrip, the night was silent and stars gave off the only light. The fan never came back on, and as I waited to fall back asleep, I could hear Marco and Elisa panting and whispering amorously in the darkness across the steaming room.

In the morning, the Festival of Crabs began early with a parade that wound through the muddy streets to the beat of a makeshift drum corps. I scrambled down the beach and was nearly run over by a boy on horseback. Army surplus trucks carried costumed children, and the young festival queen in an orange gown was carried through the streets on a pony.

During the parade, it started to rain—a warm, peaceful island rain—and I dashed back to the Hotel Panorama, following two little girls with long, braided hair along a shortcut through the trees and past a house. Men standing on the porch yelled, "Hey, dreadlock girls! Hey, dreadlock girls!" as the two covered their heads.

Later, I treated Marco and Elisa to breakfast at the Restaurant Rotunda, across from the airstrip. After our forty-five-minute morning hike from the hotel toward the southern beach to find the only public phone on the island, we decided we wanted "Tomasa's Pancakes." We settled into a table on La Rotunda's porch and ordered.

Tomasa herself took our order and whistled for a little dreadlocked boy who bounced over. She whispered in his ear and the boy tore off across the street. About fifteen minutes later, he ran back, shrugging his shoulders. Tomasa returned to our table. "We can't make pancakes," she said.

"O.K.," Marco said. "Can we have eggs?"

"No. No eggs. That's why I can't make the pancakes." She added: "The boat was supposed to come in yesterday with my supplies, but it didn't."

"What do you have?"

"I have chicken and toast. You can have chicken sandwiches." So chicken sandwiches it was. And toast smothered in maple syrup. Perfect. And beers. A breakfast of champions.

As we ate, a bare-chested American man covered in tattoos and his female companion sat next to us. He told us they'd come over by boat from nearby Little Corn Island for the festival. "Little Corn Island is even more primitive than this," he said. "There aren't any taxis or electricity and the only lodging is a small pension with an outhouse." The tattooed man said he'd sold his house, car, and business and moved there on a whim. "It was just a little piss-ant business anyway." The couple was starving for news of the Atlanta Braves.

Apparently, the two of them owned the only small pension on Little Corn. "We have to grow everything we need," the woman said. They'd planted melon, bananas, peanuts, and, of course, corn. "The people have really helped us with our crops. We thought our peanuts looked great, but somebody told us we had to stomp them down, so we did."

As we ate breakfast, dozens of islanders strolled by in their Sunday best. Little girls and women dressed in pink and white twirled parasols and tried to keep their dresses and shoes from getting muddy. The tattooed man waved to one of his neighbors. "Everybody's so excited about the festival," the man said. "It's funny. I've been here for over a year and nobody can tell me the significance of it. They all say, 'It's when they freed the slaves.' They say, 'The slaves made crab soup.' But nobody can tell you any more than that. It's all been forgotten."

When it came time for the bill, Tomasa eyed our cordobas and demanded exact change.

Under the midmorning sun, hundreds of islanders stood on a crumbling basketball court and watched their festival queen crowned on a makeshift stage. People cheered as the emcee introduced her in English. Following her coronation, the politicians took over the stage. The Managua-appointed governor began his speech in Spanish and people wandered into the shade. He told everyone they must unite in order to solve Corn Island's problems: unstable electricity, unclean drinking water, unemployment. He said Managua understood that the islanders were still hurting from a terrible hurricane in 1998. He assured them the government pledged 10,000 cordobas (about $1,300) and fifteen new basketballs to the island. Near the end of his speech, someone blared reggae music, drowning him out, and the islanders danced in their bright Sunday clothes. Bottles of beer were already opened. The only politician who spoke English yelled over the music, "We must make it a point to preserve the beauty of our island!" Everyone cheered again.

Later, bongos and steel drums banged while two local baseball teams played an exhibition. Women in curlers served an enormous pot of crab soup. A sweating man stared at us with bloodshot eyes. "You all had some?" he asked, handing us three bowls. Hot sun beat down and we were the only ones outside the tent.

Soon, we decided to go swimming and found a small path that led to the beach. Lizards and huge crabs crossed back and forth in front of us. We passed a pig and trailed through a tiny farm. Under a mango tree lay a half-naked man, passed out, snoring, his bottle of rum and a machete on the ground. Eventually, the path opened up to blues, whites, and greens that previously had existed only in my imagination.

"This is like a cliché," Elisa said. "Like a beach a child would draw." And so we entered the cliché as we were supposed to: We left our sweaty clothes on the beach and swam naked, the water so clean and salty it burned our eyes. I strolled along the white sand alone for over an hour and didn't pass a soul, and suddenly the idea of a crowded island seemed laughable.

When I returned, Marco and Elisa were drinking milk out of a coconut and the three of us grinned at one another. We'd been on Corn Island for less than two days, but we already knew we'd stumbled into one of those truly special places in this world: just close enough to the real world to know what it lacked, but thankfully, far enough away not to care. As we cracked open another coconut, none of us wanted to return to the Nicaraguan mainland, or even to our own countries, ever.

Elisa was right. The beach, the whole island excursion, was certainly rife with clichés—the carefree islanders, the posturing foreign volunteers, the backwater politics, the tourists' wacky encounters with Third World amenities. Even the beauty and the epiphany could be summed up as cliché. But what does it matter? It's certainly not the kind of story you'd trade in a hostel, late at night, when all the backpackers hold forth, trying to top one another's most sordid tales. But is that all we travel to find?

On that beach on Corn Island, we were simply three people greedily sharing a brief, odd, fleeting moment. It was a quiet moment of happiness. Can that be enough?

Eventually, as the sun went down, we put our clothes back on in silence. Together, we walked back along the path, careful not to disturb the man sleeping under the mango tree.

Jason Wilson is the series editor of The Best American Travel Writing *anthology. He has written for the* Washington Post Magazine, Condé Nast Traveler, National Geographic Traveler, Travel & Leisure, *Salon.com, the* North American Review, *among many other magazines and newspapers. He is currently at work on a novel.*

TOM JOSEPH

Bones and Heads with Hussein

Fishing is more than sport—in Belize it can mean becoming one with the tides.

"TIM. THEY RIGHT IN FRONT OF YOU. SEE 'EM? BIG SCHOOL, TIM." Hussein stood at my right shoulder, pointing. He didn't even have his polarized glasses on.

I pulled my hat down and peered into the turquoise water of the Belizean lagoon, trying to distinguish between the brown swirling clumps. Shouldn't be that difficult—the one that was the school of bonefish should be moving. I cast at one.

"No, Tim. That grass. They over there now."

It was hopeless. Either the fish moved before I could get off a cast, or the wind blew my fly far from its target. I couldn't get my leader to lay straight out, so most of the notoriously skittish bones saw the curled line and spooked. My retrieve was too fast or too slow, too regular or too jerky. And when, by the greatest of coincidence, I got a strike, I set the hook too soon or too late.

Not that it mattered, but my name isn't Tim, either.

I took a minute to reflect. I knew Hussein had done this hundreds of times, stood in waist-deep water trying to put some dumb American on fish. Yet the excitement in his voice was unmistakable, its measured quality that of a deep well of patience, not frustration. His wiry body gave off the same signal, coiled and ready, but for the moment securely fastened.

I cast at a clump. "Good shot. Strip, strip, wait. Now!" I set the hook. Fish on! My eight-weight fly line went zinging out as if attached to an arrow. I'd learned from fishing salmon—the hard way, of course—to keep clear of the reel handle, which can machine gun your hand at about 80 hammer-strokes per second. This fish was running at more like 800. My first bone.

The fish was three-quarters of the way across the lagoon when his run slowed. I began reeling, stole a glance at Hussein, who stood beside me, arms bent at the elbow, palms in, thumbs up, as if cupping a fly reel.

"Reel, Tim. Reel, reel, reel." Suddenly, my line was running a million miles an hour straight at me. I must have had the fish well hooked, though, for despite the slack, he stayed on. I played several more runs until, eventually, I brought the fish close.

Kaboom. My line went smoking back out. What the—?

"Barra."

I looked across the lagoon. Sure enough, instead of a twenty-inch bonefish at the end of my line, I was now attached to a four-foot barracuda.

"Dogfish," said Hussein, resignation heavy in his voice.

"What do I do?"

He shrugged. I found out why in about twenty seconds when my line went limp. "Barra bit you off, scared all the bones. We try later." He waded toward shore.

I reeled in my hookless line, followed him in. "Hey, Hussein. Thanks. That was fun."

He adjusted the baseball cap over his jet-black hair. "Fun for me, too, Tim." And though his taut and tawny Middle Eastern face was unsmiling, I knew he was telling the truth. Hussein was a true fisherman; fishermen tell stories, but they don't lie.

Before coming to Belize, Hussein had never held a rod in his hand. A refugee from war-torn Beirut, Hussein somehow scraped the funds together to leave Lebanon in 1980. Out of money by the time he reached Belize City, Hussein shared a cab with a man who had a similar Semitic look. Mike Feinstein turned out to be a

Belizean Jew. The unlikely duo became friends and eventually built Manta Resort together, carving the eleven-cabana retreat a machete slash at a time out of the four-acre mangrove island.

This Belizean atoll halfway around the world may have been an unlikely roosting spot, but here, on Glover's Reef atoll, Hussein had found not only a home but a calling. This year, his fifteenth, he'd resigned as manager so he could guide full-time. Taken a pay cut in order to put dumb Americans on fish they'd probably blow, and done it with a satisfied non-smile.

An eighty-square-mile atoll that rises from the depths of the Caribbean, Glover's Reef is the furthest offshore of the three Belizean atolls, about thirty miles out. My wife Jeanne and I had cruised out on the *Pelagic*, the resort's fifty-footer. An administrative snafu had us booked the week the resort was supposed to be shut down, so we shared the island with a skeleton crew. Talk about your desert islands.

The entire atoll was nearly as uninhabited. There was one kayak camp on the next island up, and, on the one after that, a government station to remind commercial fishermen that the twenty-by-four mile atoll and surrounding waters are all marine reserve. Hussein told us that there are 700 shallow reef patches on the inside, and only four cuts where a boat can pass through the surrounding barrier reef. Whereas the inside waters are no more than twenty-five feet deep, outside the reef the bottom drops quickly to a hundred feet, and after that in a sheer wall to half a mile. The contrast of the dark navy of the blue water, the blotchy blue-and-turquoise of the deep reef, and the aqua-and-sand of the inside made for a kaleidoscopic tidal wave of color. A guy could stare at that all day, if he weren't busy bonefishing in the lagoon, trolling the outside for grouper, kings, tuna, and wahoo, or casting jigs for snapper on the inside.

Fishing first for subsistence, then as a guide, Hussein probably knows more about angling these waters than any other human. Considering his late introduction to the sport, his grasp of both equipment and technique was amazing. But his fish sense was even more so. Maybe he smelled them with his long Lebanese nose, maybe picked up their vibes with the twin radar dishes protruding from his ever-present baseball cap. Maybe it was something less tangible. It seemed Hussein, the wanderer, understood the ebb and flow of waters which twice a day are pulled from one end of the world to the other. Hussein had the tides in his soul.

Jeanne and I spent nearly all our waking hours that week with him, falling into an easy routine. Up at dawn for a morning troll, where we'd catch bonito, Spanish mackerel, barra, and, hopefully, something big. I learned the importance of heavy-duty tackle when a wahoo snapped a treble hook clean off a brand new Smitty, and another straightened a hook on my biggest Grandma. After that we used Hussein's personal stash. His seven- and nine-inch Rapalas looked like they'd been chewed up in a meat grinder, but they held up. Jeanne got a thirty-five pound king and a forty pound grouper.

We'd come in before noon, so I'd have time to fish bones before lunch. Hussein usually accompanied me with his own fly rod, which he'd cast patiently, measuredly, successfully. He taught me to sneak up on fish in the shallows, their forked tails seductively wiggling in the air, staying upwind so I could cast better to them. I began seeing fish better, even catching some. What beauties bonefish are, shimmering

Schools of yellowtail snapper, barracuda, and several species of reef jack are cruising here—I know because I snorkeled this spot this morning. I pinch on a split shot and cast beyond the blue water line marking the drop-off. Giving the big fly a moment to sink, I strip in as fast as I can. Again and again. Nothing.

My stomach growls again. Getting these suckers to bite a fly is harder than I thought it would be when snorkeling among them....

My hopes sink with the sun. Then miraculously, I get a hit on the next retrieve by a small but strong fish. Carefully I play the fish around the fan coral and walk it up to the beach. A foot-long yellowtail snapper. Dinner.

—Doug Peacock, "Easy in the Cayes," *Islands*

silver, built like bullets. Each release left me full of pride and slime.

After a snooze in the hammock, it was more bones, or more trolling. When there was a lag in action, we talked of the state of the atoll, and of the world. I told Hussein that I was Jewish.

"My friend," he said, "why do our people have to fight? What is the difference, my God or your God? Don't we all have to live on the same Earth?" He shook his head sadly, and I recognized the weight that holds his face short of a smile. "I left all of my family in Lebanon. All. But here I have found something better. I have found peace."

I think that's what all fishermen are looking for.

Sometimes we had silences, too, where we ran a zigzag line between the deep blue Caribbean and the upreaching coral, or where we stopped to rock on the swells and watch the thin white line of the waves breaking on the barrier reef. Hussein sometimes seemed far away, but always, if there was a strike, he was on it instantly, goosing the throttle if he sensed a big fish, pulling in a line if it was in the way.

Late in the afternoon we'd return, switching to a tarpon-sized MirrOlure as we crossed into the shallows. We hooked one once and saw it jump high into the air and spit the hook before either of us could grab the rod. Then Hussein cleaned our supper on the pier which led to the thatched-roof bar and dining room built over the lagoon. We'd stay at the fish-cleaning station until sunset. There was blood in the water, fish-scent in the air, salt-spray on our faces, rum on our breath. And maybe a bit of the tides in our soul, too.

Hussein filleted, skinned, or scaled deliberately, threw the entrails to the nurse sharks that cruised in for supper, two reds and a light-colored one called Blondie. Sometimes a huge stingray would try to hide the carcasses by smothering them. Gigantic bonefish up to eight pounds swam inches from the sharks. I tried to catch them and failed. The sharks didn't bother. Fortunately, neither did they bother with humans. Late one afternoon when I was bonefishing, one practically swam between my legs.

After catch-of-the-day dinner, we'd walk with Hussein to the entrance of the lagoon and shine flashlights on the eagle rays that swooped in for an evening foray. Hussein knew the "every when for every fish" at Glover's Reef Atoll.

Of all the fish we caught that week, the most memorable were the headfish. Never did a half-day go by without bringing in one of that species. I learned to tell when one was on—I'd be playing a fish, and suddenly my line would go dead. Not limp, as if I'd been cut off, though. I'd reel in my still-heavy line, and on the end would be a head. Hussein could tell, by how cleanly the fish had been severed, whether it had been cut off by a shark or by a big wahoo, king mackerel or barracuda. The lone black fin tuna we caught was a half-tuna—the other half was a shark snack. We salvaged enough meat for a sushi appetizer. Our frequent catch of headfish proved there were countless monsters down there, just waiting for prey giving off distress signals. A sobering thought.

"And you let us swim and wade in those same waters?" I asked Hussein.

"Is different," he answered, and of course it was.

That's what we learned from Hussein. Every situation in his ocean was different, every moment fresh. Hussein knew the tide was always moving in his Belizean waters. We treasured the chance to hop on.

Tom Joseph writes essays, humor, and fiction from northern Wisconsin. There are few things in life that he enjoys more than travel, yet he returned from a trip to Southeast Asia to be home in time for the opening of Wisconsin's fishing season.

SUE HUBBELL

In Search of Blue Butterflies

The jungles are full of fantastic creatures both abundant and elusive.

I AM CAUGHT IN A TANGLE OF THE ARMS AND LEGS OF FOUR OTHER Americans, huddled on the bottom of a rubber raft, pinned among the boulders in rapids of the Pacuare River, on the Caribbean slope of Costa Rica.

Our guide, Miguel T. Cabrera, a student of biology, had warned us that we might get in trouble on these rapids. And trouble we are in. I can tell because Miguel mutters, "Oh, damn," and tells us to get down. This section of the Pacuare River falls at a rate of forty-six feet a mile, and it has wedged our raft, and us, between just two of the many exposed rocks. Any moment now, I am sure that the river's force is going to flip us, and we frail creatures will be hopelessly squished against them. But after only the merest of eternities, Miguel pries us free, asks us to resume our perches on the raft's edges, and begins paddling again. Fast. We hurtle down the river to a protected cove to assess the damage (one paddle lost) and to stand by in case rescue is needed for the other two rafts and supply boats.

My raftmates leap out in glee. They have come for the experience of white-water rafting. I follow with weak knees. I am here for the butterflies.

For years, lepidopterists have described to me the beauty of blue morpho butterflies, found from Mexico to South America. I've stared at their representations in books: the males or individual species in brilliant blues, azures, and purples, in contrast to the duller browns of the females. They are big, some three inches and more in wingspread. Their color is structural; the effect of light passing through the prismatic scales on their wings makes their perceived hues shimmer and change. I knew that pictures could never do them justice. The males typically patrol the edges of forests, such as those along riverbanks, and I longed to see them, free and flying, glinting in the sunshine.

Crumpled into a ball, I was certain I would be dead within minutes. I was whitewater rafting in Costa Rica when thunder boomed despite the cloudless sky. A palm tree shaking atop a sixty-foot riverbank shot out of the ground. The cliff upon which it rested tore open and began to fall toward us. "Back paddle!" the guide screamed. Terrified, all I could do was quiver on the floor of the raft until we reached an island. Standing on land but not yet safe, we were jerked in every direction by short, violent spasms. All around, the riverbanks exploded. Trees and rocks flew through the air. Suddenly it all stopped except for the brown, opaque water oozing by. Hello! No guidebooks listed earthquakes as an attraction.

—Isabelle Selby, "Earthquake"

So, when I had a chance, recently, to visit Costa Rica, I asked a travel company that creates custom-tailored nature tours, to advise me where I would be most likely to see blue morphos. The Pacuare River, I was told. The company was already arranging for a small group to go down it. I could join them. Would I like to take a river trip? A river trip. That sounded like floating on the calm, beautiful river that runs past my farm in Missouri, so I said, yes, please. I was busy with other matters and paid little heed to the description of the Pacuare River in the material the company sent me, noting only that it was a "Class IV" river. A few days before leaving, I stopped by the library and took out *The Rivers of Costa Rica*, by Michael W. Mayfield and Rafael E. Gallo. My heart sank when I read the definition of a Class IV river: "Long, difficult rapids with constricted passages that often require precise maneuvering in very turbulent waters...conditions make rescue difficult." There followed a detailed description of the river and, worse yet, pictures. One showed a kayaker coming through a set of rapids, invisible in the churning white water except for two hands holding up a paddle. I nearly canceled the trip.

My raftmates and Miguel are waving their arms and cheering as the supply boat finally pulls through. They are busy and miss what I see. It appears to be a shimmering ball floating high in the air, a tiny flying saucer, blue, but successively cobalt, lilac, violet, purple. It plays tricks with my eyes, gleams, and slow dances above the water's edge. It is a male *Morpho cypris*, a midsize butterfly, one of the three common morphos to be seen along the river. All morphos flutter their wings in a slow, floppy, almost indolent flight; the cypris's distinctive wingbeat, along with its pattern of coloration, creates an optical illusion that makes it appear ball-shaped. The cypris in flight is a picture I will hold in my mind until the end of my days.

During the past two of them I had seen males of two other species of morphos. *Morpho peleides limpida* is the most common—I must have seen a dozen or more of the shimmering blue males, their wings rimmed with a dark brown band. Their lazy dip of wings made them easy to watch. We often saw these at stream edge when we stopped to hike back into the forest to clear jungle pools where we could swim.

When I walked into the rain forest for the first time, I had a shock of recognition—it was filled with house plants. This is what happens when your dieffenbachia, philodendron, ficus, and begonia have exactly what they want. Big trees are swathed with carpets of epiphytes and then epiphytes upon epiphytes until it is hard to figure which are the leaves of the original trees. They have become layered, intertwining masses of green with leaves in every shape and pattern. The rain forest is the "Goldberg Variations" of green.

Here, in the light gap, Miguel tenderly plucked from the air a butterfly with orange oblong wings, banded in black and yellow. He showed us its four walking legs and the two short front ones covered with chemical sensors that define the pretty dappled creature as one of the family *Nymphalidae*, the largest butterfly family in the world. It flew off as he released it.

There were no mosquitoes, black flies, or obnoxious insects in the forest or out on the river. But at one stop, named Fer-de-lance, we all carefully minded our footfalls lest we meet one of those dull-colored, well-camouflaged poisonous snakes. I saw bustling stingless bees—*Melipona*—everywhere, and out on the river, we paddled through clouds of pieridine butterflies, white and yellow, and commented on the birds: cattle egrets, herons, both great blue and little blue, kingfishers, yellow-tailed orioles, cormorants, swallows, and sun bitterns. At a rest stop, Miguel scooped up and handed us a tiny, cute, bright red frog, a poisonous-dart frog, whose skin contains a poison used in former times by Indians to tip their arrows. We passed it around. Once, while paddling, Miguel called out to me, "Susanna!" and pointed upward. There, floating above us, was one of the biggest of morphos, *Morpho amathonte*, his wings perfectly azure, unbanded but with a dark brown edge toward his body. I saw a couple more of them on my own later.

After we climbed back into our rafts, the river held no more terrors. We paddled through the Dos Montañas gorge, a deep set of cliffs, and then took the rafts out of the river. Dos Montañas is the proposed site of a hydroelectric dam to be operational in the coming century, unless conservationist and white-water enthusiast groups stop its construction. It will create a lake over some fifteen of the eighteen miles we had paddled, obliterating significant amounts of rain forest, home not only to the morphos and other animals we had seen but also to the scattered Cabecar Indians. We had camped in the front yard of one Cabecar family on the night we spent by the river and had shared our food with them. These Indians are representatives of the 25,000 indigenous people still living in Costa Rica. Coincidentally, their number is just about the same as that of resident Americans: 20,000 (the total population of Costa Rica is 3 million). "These Indian kids," Miguel told me, "are absolutely fearless in the river. They make themselves little rafts out of balsa wood—the tree grows wild around here—and start playing in them when they are small. The grown-ups ride on the same flimsy rafts with incredible skill." Miguel, handsome, short, with a broad face, told me he is mestizo—of part Indian, part European descent. "Indians," he said, "make the best river guides there are."

The land along the Pacuare is not protected and therefore may be lost to the dam, but more than a quarter of the land in Costa Rica, a country slightly smaller than West Virginia, is a treasure house of biodiversity, with only a fraction of the plants and animals yet described and named.

This richness is the product of a benign climate, varied terrain, and the country's position as the last geologic link in the land bridge formed between North and South America. It is a place where species from both continents mingle in at least twelve different life zones, habitats distinct enough to support different sorts of plants and animals. In 1950, 72 percent of Costa Rica was forested; today, only 30 percent is, nearly all of it in reserve land. Outside of the reserves, land was deforested, first for timber, then to develop crop land and pasture for beef cattle. The beef is largely exported, much of it to American fast-food restaurant chains.

In the early 1970s, Costa Rica began to create a national park system to help preserve its rich biodiversity and also to develop a tourist trade. In *The Quetzal and the Macaw: The Story of Costa Rica's National Parks,* David Rains Wallace quotes Mario Boza, one of the system's founders, speaking about a visit to the Great Smoky Mountains National Park in Tennessee: "The first time I saw the whole park working was in the Smokies. I saw the people going back and forth using the facilities. And Gatlinburg [a city with a sprawl of tourist-service businesses], and all the things that had grown up around the park because it was there. And I thought Costa Rica was ready for that."

The day I left the Pacuare River, a nor'easter smashed into North America with high winds and snow. The storm forced the trade winds across Costa Rica, bringing rain with them. It was raining in the rain forest. But I put on foul-weather gear, and, in the company of Arturo Jarquin, an American-trained botanist, a man who also knows his bugs and birds, I spent several days hiking through some of the parks and reserves in the central part of the country. Arturo increased my understanding of the complex plant communities we saw, but sensible butterflies and birds were tucked away in hidden spots. Arturo and I were the only large mammals to be seen.

The skies cleared the day we drove up to the highland cloud forest at Monteverde, a 27,000-acre biological reserve in northern Costa Rica, one of the most important in all of the tropics. I had made arrangements to visit the butterfly garden there. Biologists study in the reserve, but it is also a popular destination for Americans, who are drawn not only by the excellent birding but also by the knowledge that the reserve was first staked out by Americans. They were Quakers, pacifists, who were attracted to Costa Rica as a stable, democratic country that had abolished its army in 1948; in 1951, they began dairy farming there. The Quakers soon understood the biological importance of the area and, in the late 1960s, approached the Tropical Science Center, a nonprofit Costa

> A streak of vibrant red and green shot across the sky, followed like a comet by a long tail. The male quetzal landed on a small branch about sixty feet away, exposing his lustrous colors and flowing tail feathers. He flitted from branch to branch, his tail undulating like a wave. Before me was a bird I'd dreamed of viewing, never expecting I would. Until this moment, it had been mythical to me, a bird of stories and legends, of bank posters and currency. How could it be real? The brilliant scarlet breast, a back of outlandishly luminescent green and blue feathers, and—as if the Great Spirit were saying, "So you still don't believe I can do whatever I want?"—a finishing flourish of three absurdly long emerald tail feathers.
>
> —Michael Shapiro, "In Search of Guatemala's Resplendent Quetzal"

Rican research organization in San José, and suggested that the T.S.C. manage it as a preserve. In the early 1970s, the T.S.C. began acquiring land. It had finally taken action at the urging of George Powell, a researcher who had come to Costa Rica to study the quetzal, the symbol of Monteverde. One of the showiest birds in the world, the quetzal is rare throughout its range—wild highlands from southern Mexico to Panama. About the size of a pigeon, the male is emerald green with a red breast and green tail that measures two feet or more in length. Among birders the quetzal is considered the ultimate trogon, a widely distributed family of beautiful birds.

The butterfly garden is a well-developed, well-presented live display of many of Monteverde's share of the 1,500 Costa Rican butterfly species. Indoors, butterflies can be seen mounted in cases and also alive—egg, larva, pupa. I saw a fat, furry, hearty *Morpho peleides* caterpillar munching happily on leaves, soon to pupate and transform itself into a winged beauty. Shannon, an American biologist volunteer, showed a few of us through the garden. She took paper envelopes with her, placing in them those butterflies that—having emerged from pupation and dried their wings—were ready for release. The gardens are artfully arranged to re-create three of the local microenvironments into which the butterflies could be appropriately let loose. My walking companions were a young English couple, he a shaggy-haired physics don from Cambridge, she, a medical writer with a long blond braid.

In the proper garden, Shannon handed the don an envelope containing a big owl butterfly, one of the *Caligos*, somber brown with large eyespots on the hind wings, eerily recalling an owl's eyes. Which may both attract and startle a predator. Following directions, the physicist gave the envelope a sharp rap and the *Caligo* walked out onto his hand. A slow smile spread across his face and he stood rapt, transfixed, as the butterfly daintily stepped across his palm.

In the gardens, there were also clear-winged butterflies, another group I had always wished to see. Members of the genus *Ithomia*, they have transparent or translucent wings. Sitting on a leaf, the butterflies blend into the background, their visible wing veins resembling the very slimmest of twigs.

Arturo and I met at six the next morning, early enough to see birds during their early morning feeding. The sun shot golden shafts down among the tangle of vines and green leaves as we walked soundlessly along one of the trails. Arturo told me that a favorite food of quetzals is wild avocado and motioned me to stop near one such tree where we could hear seeds falling to the ground. A group of Americans mindlessly talking and laughing approached, and the sharp cries of the quetzals told us that, alarmed, they had taken flight. I raised my binoculars in time to see a female, her colors slightly more subdued and her tail shorter than that of her mate. The male had faded into the shimmering foliage and disappeared. But then I saw something even better—a female Elegant Trogon, a cousin of the quetzal. Metallic green, with a brownish-orange breast and white- and black-banded tail, this trogon can be seen as far north as southern Arizona, but I had never seen one. The bird had just captured breakfast: a walking stick of enormous length. Gulping the oddly shaped insect, a straw with legs, she swallowed hard and intently for several minutes until it had disappeared inside her. Then she tidily wiped her beak on a twig and hopped away.

Sue Hubbell is the author of many books, including Shrinking the Cat, A Country Year, A Book of Bees, *and* Waiting for Aphrodite: Journeys into the Time Before Bones. *She lives with her husband in Maine and Washington, D.C.*

SCOTT ANDERSON

The Last Penal Colony

Where wildlife and felons live side by side.

THE ISLAND OF COIBA RISES OUT OF THE PACIFIC OFF THE COAST of Panama, a tangled beauty of pristine jungle wilderness, home to countless species of the most exotic wildlife in the Americas and some of the best diving anywhere. It is kept pristine by its only other inhabitants: 250 murderers and thugs.

On the second-floor veranda of the command center at Central, the senior officer eyes me warily. "You're not one of those social reformers, are you?" he asks.

Since I'm wearing a filthy Tintin t-shirt and I haven't shaved in a week, his suspicion is understandable, but I assure the man that social reform is the farthest thing from my mind.

"Very good," he says, ushering me to a chair, "because we've had trouble with those people in the past."

From the veranda, Central—a cluster of dilapidated, tin-roofed buildings on a bluff over the Pacific Ocean—appears to be some backwater army garrison where discipline has succumbed to jungle torpor. In the noonday heat, a few men in camouflage pants shamble about the compound, but the more comfortable-looking ones have stripped down to shorts and plastic sandals and have sought out the shade of trees. Just about the only clue to Central's true function is the crude balsa-wood raft propped against a tree. HANDICRAFTS OF COIBA, its wooden sign reads.

"Always they are trying to escape," the officer mutters, gazing disdainfully at the raft, "but I don't think these guys were serious—very unprofessional."

"Multi-use" has become a popular catchphrase in the field of nature conservation, but the concept has taken an interesting turn on the Panamanian island of Coiba. While most of the 190-square-mile island, perched twenty miles out in the Pacific, has been set aside as a vast nature preserve, it also doubles as a sprawling penal colony (the inmates are the ones in the comfortable clothes). From its headquarters at Central, the colony extends to six smaller camps scattered along the coast, each under the tenuous control of a three-guard detail. Tenuous because the outnumbered guards lock themselves in their command posts at night and let the prisoners roam free.

For the visitor, this presents a clear-cut set of pros and cons. On one hand, Coiba is a naturalist's paradise, with great tracts of virgin jungle and miles of untrammeled beaches. Its forest canopy is home to colonies of capuchin and howler monkeys and the rare scarlet macaw, while its coral reefs and waters offer world-class scuba diving and deep-sea fishing. On the other hand, there's the whole restless natives thing: some 250 convicted felons, many of them members of gangs back on the mainland, who periodically take advantage of the lax supervision to take to the high seas or to lop off one another's heads with handcrafted machetes.

"We have all the gangs here," says a prison official. "Los Hijos de Dios [Sons of God], Los Tiny Toons, Los Chuckies. We try to keep order by giving each of them their own camp, but there are still problems at times."

Considering they took their name from the *Child's Play* horror films, I place my bet on Los Chuckies being the most obstreperous, but as it turns out, that honor actually goes to the Sons of God. A few years ago, the Sons ambushed five Perros (Dogs) of San Joaquin who were making a break for the mainland aboard a balsa-wood raft but who had the misfortune of drifting into shore near the Sons of

God camp at Playa Hermosa. One of the Dogs managed to escape into the mangrove swamps, but the Sons captured his four companions and decapitated them. And that—in the opinion of the various Panamanian conservation and prison-reform groups that are trying to close down the penal colony—is precisely the sort of incident that gives Coiba a bad name.

The non-felon seeking admission to an island penal colony has to clear a few bureaucratic hurdles. In the case of Coiba, I had been told, it is actually quite easy, simply a matter of showing up at the regional office of the national conservation ministry (ANAM) in the mainland town of Santiago with a halfway decent cover story. At that office, however, the approvals clerk studied me with a doubtful expression. "You're a bird enthusiast?"

Perhaps I had overreached in stating the purpose of my visit to Coiba—"to observe the scarlet macaw in its native habitat"—but I was stuck with it now.

"Not all birds," I conceded. "Just macaws."

"You understand that you are restricted to the ranger station," she said, stamping my permission papers. "The rest of the island is off-limits."

It seemed a good time to feign difficulty with the Spanish language.

Over the past few years, Panama has become an increasingly popular travel destination, especially among so-called ecotourists looking for something more woolly than the well-trodden, sign-post-and-handrail nature parks of neighboring Costa Rica. As Panamanians like to point out, their country has more of everything than Costa Rica—more wildlife and nature preserves, more indigenous Indian cultures, more history—as well as more bird species than all of the U.S. and Canada. The miniboom in tourism is now evident most everywhere, from the Bocas del Toro archipelago and the San Blas Islands on the Atlantic coast to the cloud-forest highlands of western Chiriquí province, even in the jungles of eastern Darien, the largest true wilderness left in the Western Hemisphere. In all this, however, the authorities have never quite figured out what to do with Coiba.

For now, most visits to the island tend to be of the offshore kind.

A cruise ship operated by an ecotour company out of Panama City moors off the coast for the scuba diving portion of its weeklong sail, while a few intrepid yachtsmen have discovered the sheltered cove of Coibita, or "Little Coiba," just off the island's north shore. Even this limited traffic has dropped off since 1995, when an American couple anchored by Coibita were attacked by a group of escapees from the penal colony and the man was murdered. As long as the prisoners remain, the waters around Coiba are restricted and regularly patrolled by police launches, while all potential visitors must first get clearance from the ANAM office in Santiago.

Traveling in Panama wasn't always easy, but the experience—despite, or maybe because of, the complexities—thrilled us. We decided the country is, in fact, a long way from being the next Costa Rica. Call it the next next Costa Rica. There are few luxury lodges on the outskirts of its rain forests, few English-speaking wildlife guides, no safari vans ferrying nature-lovers about. But we had encounters we will not soon forget, and we loved the feeling of being someplace most of the traveling world has yet to discover. There is still much talk about turning Panama into an ecotourist's dream come true, but from what we saw, it's going to take a while. And for that we were glad.

—Kimberly Brown Seely, "A Family, a Plan, a Canal," *Travel & Leisure Family*

Once I had those coveted permission papers in hand, I made for Puerto Mutis, a hamlet of perhaps fifty houses and nine bars at the mouth of the Gulf of Montijo, where, rumor had it, I could charter a fast boat that would cover the seventy nautical miles to Coiba in about two hours. With an ease that should have aroused my suspicions, I made arrangements with Teofilo, a laid-back Mutis fisherman, and we set out across the Montijo estuary on his coastal fisher, the *Itzel II*. After a few minutes of gauging our progress against the jungle shoreline—if we weren't stationary, we were pretty damned close—I diplomatically asked about the two-hours-to-Coiba reports.

"In a fast boat, that is definitely true," Teofilo nodded. "In the *Itzel*"—he patted the side of the boat—"maybe eight."

Finally reaching the open sea, we stayed within sight of the coastline, only the occasional tiny village or remote farmstead visible amid the vast expanse of forested hills. Schools of dolphins came out to race alongside the *Itzel II*—well, maybe not race as much as loll—and leap before its bow. It was well after dark on the night of a lunar eclipse before we puttered in to the ranger station, still called Club Pacifico from the days when it was the exclusive fishing camp of a wealthy American.

Built along the shore of a small cove and surrounded by jungle, the station consists of a few low concrete buildings and a half-dozen little bungalows reserved for guests—of which, in mid-January, I am the only one. At 11 P.M., the generator is turned off and Club Pacífico is plunged into darkness, but the only sign of menace I can find on that first night is the scorpion under my pillow, its tail raised and quivering.

"The scorpions aren't so poisonous here," Ivan Tunon, the Pacifico administrator, assures me the following morning. "Normally, just your tongue will go numb for a few hours and then you are very thirsty."

The laconic, thirty-five-year-old Ivan oversees an odd little community at the station, a collection of conservation workers and police officers, as well as two dogs, Volvo and Fula (Blondie), a tame deer, and a less tame crocodile, Tito, that comes in to be fed at high tide. Technically, Pacífico is a scientific field station, but most attention seems to focus on the two-base softball games played in the afternoons. Those, and the meals prepared by Castillo up at the open-air canteen.

Castillo Varga, forty-six, was brought to Coiba fifteen years ago for murdering a man in his hometown of Chiriqui, in western Panama. For the first few years of his captivity, he toiled in the fields of the Central prison farm, but eventually he found advancement through the food-services industry, first becoming the penal colony's chief butcher, then one of its cooks.

"For an *interno*, it is the best job," he says, patting his well-endowed belly with a grin. "And, of course, it is how I came to Pacifico."

Four years ago, when the last trustee-cook at Pacifico was paroled, Castillo was transferred over from Central. His skills in this capacity might be described as rustic; to prepare a large fish for one of the evening meals, he decides against the time-consuming fillet approach, choosing instead to hack the carcass into small pieces with a rusty hatchet.

During his tenure on Coiba, Castillo has seen the penal colony's population ebb and flow, from a high of nearly 1,000 inmates in the early nineties to its current low of 250 or so. He's also been witness to the periodic gang wars that, by his estimate, have led to more than forty murders. "Ninety-two, that was the worst." Castillo shakes his head. "Back and forth the killing went."

In that year's wars, gangs took to crossing through the jungle at night to attack rival camps, usually picking off the unlucky inmates who had drawn short straws and been made to stand sentry. Before the year was over, at least twenty *internos* were dead.

On a happier note, he recalls the days when Manuel Noriega used to chopper in, usually accompanied by some of his generals, several cases of champagne, and a bevy of beautiful women. "They would stay at the commandant's house up on the hill," Castillo recalls, "or in the bungalows over at Playa Hermosa, but Noriega would always come down to say hello to us. From what I could see, he was normal, just liked to drink and be with pretty girls."

Lazing about the Pacífico station, it's easy to imagine that, so long as they avoid the gang wars, prisoners on Coiba have a pretty easy go of it—left to wander unshackled about a tropical island. Such a view, though, overlooks the hard side of doing time on Coiba. With no telephones and no visitors allowed, the *internos* are almost completely cut off from the outside world, from their families, from their former lives. It's little wonder that so many of the convicts—up to 20 percent by some estimates—eventually try to escape to the mainland or *tierra firme,* as all those on Coiba refer to it.

"What they normally do," Ivan explains, "is hoard food for a time and then leave the camps for the jungle. There they build a raft and wait for good currents and a dark night."

Very few make it. If they get past the crocodiles and sharks and patrolling police launches, which have been known to dispatch fugitives by the "law of the sea" (a quick burst from a machine gun), their rafts usually break up in the waves or are swept out to sea. Making for the Coiba interior is an even worse option. The forest teems with a variety of poisonous snakes, including the deadly fer-de-lance, and is so dense that getting lost is almost a given. Hiking one of the better marked trails near Club Pacífico with a guide one day, we came to a stream that had turned into a mud bog; cutting a fifty-foot detour around the bog meant a half-hour of hacking through vines and brush, the trail completely invisible in the foliage until we stood back on it.

"They also forget about water," Ivan says, "that it is very hard to find drinking water in the jungle. Every few months, one of the *internos* who has gone into the forest will come into the station. They are hungry, thirsty, all cut up, and all they want to do is surrender. We feed them and then turn them over to the police."

Even though he gets along well with the police guards stationed at Pacífico—certainly, the softball games would be impossible without them—Ivan firmly believes that the penal colony should be closed. In his opinion, shared by conservationists both in Panama and abroad, Coiba represents an untouched biological laboratory, a place that should be both extensively studied by scientists and lightly developed for ecotourism. That cannot happen as long as the colony remains.

But this, I decide, is something I need to judge for myself, and at Pacífico, I'm just six or seven miles up the coast from the main prison compound at Central. Mindful of the restrictions placed on my visit by the ANAM office in Santiago, I scope out Pacífico's resident policemen and make for the one who seems the softest touch. By lucky coincidence, he's also the one holding the field radio connected to Central.

"But I thought you were interested in macaws," he says upon hearing my request.

"Well, sure," I reply, "macaws and island penal colonies." I launch into a complicated disquisition about some research project I'm doing on the cultural and philosophical underpinnings of various prison systems around the world and their effect on native flora and fauna—even I can't make sense of it—until the policeman implores me with a raised hand to be silent.

"Maybe we should just tell them you're curious to see it," he says.

"That's good," I nod. "Let's go with that."

He gets on the radio and, in less than thirty seconds, gives me a thumbs-up signal. Climbing back aboard the *Itzel II*, Teofilo and I trundle down the east coast of Coiba, passing miles of empty beaches and untouched jungle before putting in to the long pier at Central. There, a guard leads me up the hill, past small workshops and the prison cemetery, to an open-air gazebo that is also the compound's entertainment center. A few off-duty guards sit on the wood benches watching a B movie about life on a prison farm in Louisiana, while a half-dozen prisoners watch from outside, leaning on the gazebo rails. Posted below the VCR is the one stern sign I've seen since arriving: "It is absolutely forbidden to change channels without authorization." After a few minutes, I'm led up to the command center, to the senior officer waiting on the second-floor veranda.

As we talk, it gradually emerges that the official is close to agreement with those environmentalists who want to close the prison, although not for the same reasons. Coiba imposes deprivations on his charges, and those deprivations have grown worse in recent years. Until the early 1990s, guards' families lived on Coiba, and inmates were allowed visitors; there was even a little store where convicts hawked their wares to those coming ashore. All that was stopped by the Panamanian government, which also shut down the Central hospital as a first step toward closing the colony altogether, but then seemed to forget about the other steps.

"So maybe the prison should be closed," the official says, "because this is a hard existence for the men. Yes, they are allowed to walk around, but there is very little for them to do, no training for when they get out, and they are lonely for their families. I think that is why there is so much violence between them."

He steps into his office for a moment and returns with a cloth bundle. Spreading the cloth over the table, he produces eight crude daggers, all recently confiscated from the *internos*. The knives are dull-edged but very sharp at the tips, with handles fashioned out of rolls of gauze bandage; being killed by one of these would take a long time.

"On the other hand," the senior officer says, staring at his display, "one could say that by staying here we are actually preserving Coiba. If the colony is closed, then people from *tierra firme* will come over and settle here, destroy the land. That has happened on other nature preserves. As long as we are here, the settlers are afraid to come, so Coiba stays the same." He motions to the daggers. "Take one if you like. We have plenty more."

It is an interesting rationale, this idea of men like Castillo Varga as some odd kind of ecowarrior vanguard. At the same time, the murderer-cook from Chiriquí is a man both physically and psychologically marooned by his time on Coiba. Eight years ago, he was given a two-week furlough to visit his family on the mainland, and the experience left him disoriented.

"So much had changed," he says. "Not just my family, but all Panama—new buildings everywhere, all the cars and televisions, the way people acted. It was strange for me."

Later this year, Castillo finally comes up for parole, but he is considering staying on in Coiba.

"Maybe so," he says, squinting at the mainland coast, "maybe so. I've been away from *tierra firme* so long that maybe it is better I stay here."

On the *Itzel II*, during the long, slow voyage back to Puerto Mutis, Teofilo manages to find a sandbar in the middle of the Montijo estuary. After a few minutes of struggling to get the boat free, he gives up and kills the engine. "We'll have to wait for high tide," he says—"maybe four or five hours."

It is nearly midnight, and in the estuary the only sounds are those of calling birds and small waves tapping against the side of the boat, the only light that which is reflected from the stars and moon. Across the expanse of calm water, the jungle's edge rises up as a forbidding wall of black.

As we settle in for the wait, I think how this is a pleasant way to spend a few hours: surrounded by the sea, suspended in the darkness and silence. Not for fifteen years, perhaps, but for a few hours it is not such a bad thing to be lost on the earth.

Scott Anderson is a journalist and novelist who lives in New York. A contributing editor at Harper's Magazine*, he also writes frequently for the* New York Times Magazine *and* Esquire*, usually on foreign, war-related themes. His most recent books are* Triage*, a novel, and* The Man Who Tried To Save The World*, a nonfiction investigation into the mysterious disappearance of an American relief worker in Chechnya.*

KEVIN NAUGHTON

Surfing La Libertad

Three decades ago it had Central America's best waves, and it still does.

ALMOST THIRTY YEARS HAD ELAPSED SINCE CRAIG AND I WROTE our first surf travel articles on Central America. We were stationed in El Salvador at the time, and although we'd made a foray into Costa Rica in search of unexplored surf, Salvador was the place.

Our original intentions were innocent enough. Traveling for waves was all that was on our minds. If Craig could fire off a few good shots with the twenty or so rolls of film at his disposal, and if we could couple those photos with dispatches concocted over a card table littered with lousy hands and empty bottles of *cerveza*, then all the better. Whatever it was, the timing was right, and what was meant as a means to finance our explorations turned into an all-out enticement for the masses to start heading south. Way south.

Two years after those first articles came out, we blew through Salvador again on our way back from West Africa and the Caribbean. It was 1975, and my, how things had changed. I remember walking out to the cobblestone point on a six foot day at Punta Roca—made famous by our articles—and watching in dismay as forty or so Texans and Floridians dropped in on one another with reckless abandon. It was raining single fins on anyone unfortunate enough to be caught by a set paddling out. Having just come from six months of seeing nothing but empty waves in Africa, it was a real shock to our surf psyche. Any illusions we harbored about the special quality of the place were dispelled by the shouting and finger pointing in the water. We looked at each other in tacit acknowledgment that the responsibility for the debacle in the lineup that day fell squarely on our shoulders. It had to rate as one of the low points in all our surf travels.

"I don't know about you, but I didn't come here to surf in this," said Craig.

We both got up, boards under arms, and turned our backs on one of the finest waves we'd seen in any of our travels. Little did we know that twenty-five years would pass before either of us would walk out to the point at La Libertad again.

We'd heard lots of rumors about El Salvador since the twelve-year civil war ended in the early '90s. After the war broke out and the whole country really went to hell, surfers pretty much stopped coming. The gradual return to normalcy has been tenuous at best, and yet the flocks of surfers seen in the free-for-all '70s have yet to return.

By the early '80s, the mystique of El Salvador had run its course. What started out as a great adventure at the beginning of the '70s had deteriorated into a crowded and drugged-out way station for all manners of surfers, smugglers, and losers on the lam from reality.

The focus shifted to Costa Rica. The country was everything El Salvador was not: clean, safe, urbane, and stable—a political anomaly in Latin America. High-profile surfers staked their claims there and the media was quick to follow. Costa Rica, already famous for its beautiful women, embraced them all with open arms. On its pristine beaches—far from the upheavals in El Salvador, Nicaragua, and Panama—surfers could mingle with Europeans and Canadians fleeing the harsh winters of their homelands.

Meanwhile, the ragged cousin to the north, El Salvador, had come apart at the seams. In fact, the only safe space to be in the whole country was La Libertad. Expatriate Bob Rotherham had opened a restaurant there in the late '70s, and he was doing a booming trade. "The place was packed every weekend," Bob says. "Everyone who wanted to get away from the war came to Libertad. No surfers. Just all 'Salvos.' It was the best of times for business." Indeed. For surfers passing through and scoring waves without getting shot at, it was also the best of times. Because for all Costa Rica's charms, and there are many, she doesn't have a wave like La Libertad.

From our aerial view in the pre-dawn light, we could see tiny lines wrap off the headland into the bay. On the horizon line a scorching sun was creeping up on another day.

The old airport we used to fly into near the capital didn't fare so well during the war and has been replaced by an international airport located out in the country. A new road, one guarded by the country's ubiquitous soldiers, runs from the airport to La Libertad, less than a half-hour's drive away. Still, the guards couldn't prevent a couple of tourists from losing all their belongings to bandits two months earlier, when they were unfortunate enough to choose the wrong cab driver at the airport.

I had to smile as we drove through the countryside. If you had been gone from anywhere in Southern California and returned twenty-five years later, you'd hardly recognize the place. But here in Salvador, virtually nothing had changed. Only when we pulled up to the bay at Libertad were things discernibly different. Rotherham's success in the restaurant biz had not gone unnoticed, and now several other restaurants and hotels surrounded his place.

At the Hotel Rick, an affable surfer from North Carolina showed up. It was his fourth trip to Salvador that year. A "surgical strike" mission for surf. He told us that according to the most recent surf report, the waves should be double overhead by the middle of next week.

I was skeptical. Like everyone else, I'd put my dollar in the slot only to hear the frenzied hype of surf forecasters whose ultimate message is to deposit more dollars for further updates. "Indeed," said our North Carolina compatriot. "I believe that as we speak there's a southwest swell on its way."

Juan, a.k.a. John Sverko, one of my California buddies who accompanied us here, showed up with a couple of Salvadoran *compadres*. Although he hadn't been back in twenty years, he couldn't walk down the street without running into someone who remembered him. He quickly filled us in on the *pupuserias* where the locals ate, who sold what in the *centro mercado* (all of them old women who shouted "Don Juan!" at him), the place to buy fabric and the tailor who made shorts, who had the best deals on fish at the local pier, the time schedules and fares for all the buses, the locations of the cat houses, the best coconut vendor, where to get the cheapest beers, what was fresh at the town bakery, the good deals on hammocks, and the name of a guy who repaired surfboards and would drive us to all the local breaks. I asked him if he was thinking of running for local office.

Friday night pulled around and the human carnival from the capital hit town. Rotherham's biz, which on weekdays could get so slow it would have to pick up to be dead, was suddenly hopping. The weekend turned into a two-day party on the stretch of restaurant road where we were staying. Out in force came the mariachi musicians, the street vendors, the kids selling jewelry, the hustlers, and the migrant molls following the cash flow. The music never stopped and, as in all of Latin America, the *louder* the better. From our upstairs balcony at the Don Rodrigo hotel, we took it all in from the safety of our hammocks. Doc, my buddy who has a weakness for assuming the best in human nature, made a comment about all the fathers who were taking their daughters away for the weekend. "Those aren't daughters," Craig told him.

Soon, the street kids were delivering messages to Greg, our traveling filmmaker, from unknown female admirers. It got to the point where we couldn't walk to the restaurant without Greg, nicknamed "Boy Wonder," getting accosted by some young lovely. As for the rest of us, all we got were smiles of benign pity and comments like, "Isn't that nice of his uncles to take him on a vacation?"

We were three days into the trip and the surf was still small at Libertad Point. Juan's point man in El Salvador, Ruben, showed up and we all piled into his truck for a surf check up the coast. We ended up where everyone who is desperate for waves ends up: at Zunsal. The point at Zunsal sticks out enough to catch even a ripple of a swell. When we got there, it was small, and it was gutless. We stared at it so hard the gravitational pull of our eyeballs seemed to cause it to pick up by several inches, so we paddled out. Only Doc, who being from the East Coast knew a bit about gutless surf, seemed genuinely enthused.

Zunsal is where I lived on three trips to El Salvador in the '70s, so I've got a soft spot for the place. At Zunsal, the water's always warm, tensions run low, and there's always something to ride. Kind of like a rest home for aging surfers.

Zunsal had its share of detractors. Chief among them were Rotherham and the resident kingpin of Libertad for the past fifteen years, Lee. Both these guys dismissed Zunsal outright. Lee, whose nickname around Libertad was "Macho," a nom de plume only a professional wrestler could love, had nothing but contempt for the waves there. In truth, it's hard to defend the place beyond the scope of the aforementioned criteria. Although Lee didn't mind driving us to Zunsal almost every day, he only went out once and came in after one wave. Still, it was enough for us to give him a nickname he'll never live down: "Zunlee."

The Zunsal camp and the Libertad camp—that's the way it has always been in El Salvador. There are several other breaks in the area and some of them have their days. But the groups of surfers passing time in the country tend to gravitate toward these two spots. The Zunsal crowd generally prefers the cheap living, consistency of surf, and rural nature of their area to the noise and pollution found in Libertad. The Libertad surfers have only disdain for Zunsal because it's, well, Zunsal.

One thing we came across there that didn't exist in the '70s was an eclectic mix of surf nationalities. You begin to realize just how global wave riding is when you tour the planet. What hadn't changed was the basic philosophy behind it all: a bit of adventure away from the mainstream.

Greg was looking for a new generation surfer to interview who best personified the spirit of travel as we knew it. It was our job, Craig's and mine, to find that person. About a week into the trip I approached Greg and said, "I found her. The one you want to interview."

"Her?"

"Yeah. She's from Canada."

"A chick from Canada?"

"Yeah."

"A *girl*?!"

"Hey you said find someone. You didn't say what gender."

I had had a feeling that Greg's estimation of us was taking a slow descent, but now I sensed a real tailspin. I quickly added, "Juan and Doc talked to her too. She's the one."

Her name was Dawn. She was twenty-two. She had flown into Mexico City from Vancouver and traveled overland with a surfboard on local buses the rest of the way. She was renting a room near Zunsal and finding it so cheap that she decided to extend her stay there by a month. Her plan was to continue on down to Nicaragua and Costa Rica via bus with her surfboard. By herself. The point is she was out there doing it. Alone, no less.

She showed us where she was staying. It was exactly the sort of Spartan quarters that we lived in way back when. Cheap, too. I felt a pang of shame when I compared her

> So I *went*, spun my board toward shore and stroked for all I was worth until I felt myself sharply rising; and then suddenly I was on my feet—a quick and flawless transition to standing is absolutely vital on a wave like this—and for a split second contemplated the view of the twelve-foot drop I'd be presently making, like it or not, either standing up or somersaulting, board flying, into the impact zone.
>
> You're pretty much weightless for the first third of the way down on a wave at Salsa Brava, and unable to make adjustments. Pursued by some ridiculous volume of cascading seawater, you stoically just hope for the best until you reach the trough, whence you project yourself in the logical direction—away from the freight-training breaking part of the wave, which, thankfully, you can't see because it's behind you.
>
> —Allan C. Weisbecker, *In Search of Captain Zero: A Surfer's Road Trip Beyond the End of the Road*

place to our rooms at the Don Rodrigo. Craig said nothing but looked grim when I asked, "Are we getting soft?" At least my wife was not within answering distance.

After Greg interviewed her, he seemed well pleased. Our credibility was up again. For the time being.

Probably the biggest change on the surf scene since the '70s is the increase in local surfers. The first generation of surfers in El Salvador are the ones who started on the boards left behind by traveling surfers like us. A lot of them have natural abilities and are limber in the way all kids are who learn in tropical waters. That generation has come and gone.

The ones out in the lineup now are far more savvy to the ways of the surf world. They know what's happening. They've got the look. They've arrived. There's a surf shop in Libertad, The Mango Lounge, where locals can hang out and watch surf videos. There's also a board repair garage by the beach that could belong in any beach town in California. Our driver, Ruben, had his own shaping room and skateboard ramp in the back of his house. It costs Ruben and his pregnant wife about sixty to one hundred colons ($7–$12) a week to live. We gave him one hundred colons every day for driving us to Zunsal.

The current scene in the water includes a mix of body-boarders and local surfers. Most of these guys are friendly once you make the initial contact. On the weekends, when the *rico* kids from the capital descend on the beaches, it can get quite crowded. Mind you, it's nothing like in Brazil where the situation in the water is completely out of control. Still, there's something about Latino *machismo* the world over that compels them to paddle up to the line no matter what. The Hawaiian/California tradition of actually completing the ride is still a foreign idea to them. In vogue is the nouveau approach, which goes something like this: Try the latest radical moves you see in the mags, and eat it. The innate ability is there, and someday they'll make those moves, but that day is still a ways off.

We were ten days into the trip and it was still a no-show on the big swell. We were getting antsy. Sure, there had been waves at

Zunsal every day, but nothing over five feet. The North Carolinian had been conspicuously absent since the double overhead surf he predicted failed to appear.

Zunlee showed up at the Don Rodrigo before sunrise to tell us we were not like the usual raft of idiots that drifted in from the States. As such, he'd take us to a secret spot. After some grumbling over why it took so long to decide this, we piled into his late-model pickup truck and set out from Libertad.

Driving the coastline of a foreign country is one of the simple pleasures of travel. Especially in warm-weather countries. A set of wheels, a board on top, and a tropical wind blowing through it all—*la dolce vita.*

In fact, one of the safer places to be in El Salvador is in your vehicle. It's not like Mexico where *bandidos* at remote surf locales set up roadblocks where you have to wait in line to get robbed. In El Salvador, aside from the occasional *loco* driver, it's an open road.

Zunlee soon clued me in on his ulterior motive. La Libertad was the last stop for him in a lifetime of chasing waves. He bluntly told me that he doesn't want to see a shower of assholes every time he paddles out, compliments of us. He and Rotherham had had it good, real good, for a solid fifteen-year stretch. During those war years they pretty much had had it to themselves. And now, just when he thought it was safe to go in the water, Peterson and Naughton show up again. He was concerned.

The previous evening, Rotherham had bent my ear extolling the merits of Libertad now that the war was history. Bob sang a different tune twenty years ago, but times change—as they do for each of us—and now it was all business. I told Zunlee that, Bob's good intentions notwithstanding, tourism was a hard sell in a country with so many unresolved problems. Zunlee agreed that it was hard to promote a place like that. But he was concerned. And knowing our track record, I could see why.

After about an hour, we got to his secret spot. It was one of the most scenic places in the country and the waves were good to boot. Hard-breaking peaks slammed onto sandbars formed by a river-mouth. About a dozen local surfers and body-boarders were out.

After mushy Zunsal and small Libertad, it felt good to pull into a few waves that could punch back. One wave drilled me so hard, I think it left a permanent indentation of my considerable bulk on the bottom.

The swell finally started to pick up on the last couple of days. Not big enough to make it epic, but strong enough to show promise. We got a few good sessions in, and then suddenly it was time to leave. The day before we were scheduled to go, Zunlee took me aside and said the latest surf fax was calling for a swell to hit in the next couple of days. It was going to be an overhead at Libertad, he added. I phoned my wife with the news. She was less than enthusiastic. But she knows a bit about surfers, and said it was all right by her if I stayed longer. My boy and girl were not so easily convinced. "It's snowing in the mountains, Papa!" they chimed.

The photographer Craig kicked in, "If it's good, I'm staying."

It was Saturday. I calculated the amount of time I'd need to make good on my ski week promises. "OK," I said to Craig. "Three more days max, and only if tomorrow morning it's really showing." Craig agreed.

We were up before sunrise on Sunday morning, and the big swell Zunlee predicted wasn't there. Ruben showed up to take all of us to the airport. He gave each one of us a La Libertad surf t-shirt as a going-away gift. Zunlee appeared and changed his overhead surf prediction to midweek. Despite what he'd said about us blowing open his quiet niche, he'd have liked us to stay. "Midweek is too far off at this time in my life," I told him. We piled into Ruben's truck and headed for the airport as the sun turned the heat up on another day. In a couple more days, I'd be skiing with my kids. Times change, all right, for Bob and for everyone.

Between travels afield, Kevin Naughton spends time with his French wife and two children in Laguna Beach, California. Currently, he's working on a book about his adventures as a travel correspondent for Surfer Magazine, *and has a couple of screenplays in development in Hollywood.*

STEVE WILLSON

Pacaya!

Is the volcano crawling with bandits?

IT BEGAN WITH GERMAN FRANK BANGING HIS FIST ONTO THE TABLE in our hotel kitchen. He was drinking cheap orange wine as he did every night, seeking visions of our future.

"Pacaya!"

"What?"

"Pacaya! We climb Pacaya!"

"Okay, calm down. We'll climb it."

"Pacaya! Pacaya! Pacaya! Pacaya!"

This was not unusual. We had followed the sound of Frank's voice from town to town through Mexico and into Guatemala.

"We climb Pacaya!"

One of four active volcanoes in Guatemala, Volcán Pacaya has been continuously active since 1965, often erupting up to several thousand times a day. Located only eighteen miles from Guatemala City, Pacaya is the most accessible and most often-climbed volcano in the country.

Probably because of that, Pacaya also is reputedly crawling with *bandidos*. Mention Pacaya to your hotel owner, say, or your Spanish teacher, and receive an earful of warnings. I soon had an image of a mountain covered in short Lee Van Cleefs, all of them hiding in the dark and rattling with weapons. According to rumors, the hills around Pacaya hid more highwaymen than trees.

However, from what we saw around town, it seemed more likely that Pacaya would be covered with tourists. Every tour company in Antigua offers a volcano trip, and on every corner in Antigua stands a tour company. That's a lot of traffic on one volcano.

"Pacaya!"

"Shut up, Frank. We'll go tomorrow."

We would go on our own out of pride and poverty and a certain sympathy for the unemployed. If we were to be robbed, we decided, let it be by Guatemalans with guns, not gringos armed with cash registers and minivans.

In the morning we set out for the Offfice of Tourism for help in finding the right bus. Our assistant was called Señor Fernandez, a fat squat man behind a big desk, his face as round and emotionless as a dinner plate. He stood without speaking, crossed the room, and halted before a road map of Antigua. He pointed to a street corner.

"Go here," he said sternly. "There is a tour agency. They will take you to the *volcán* in a nice microbus, with an armed guard. If you go to Pacaya alone you will die." He paused dramatically and without expression. "I will not be held responsible for your deaths."

"We don't want to go with a tour group," I said. "Can't you tell us which bus goes there?"

"No. I would be sending you to your death."

"I promise that if we die we won't hold you responsible," said Dave.

Señor Fernandez gave him a look.

"Last week three people were robbed. People are killed. It is very dangerous. If you choose to take it lightly, do so, but I will not be part of it." He turned and retreated to his desk.

"Not very helpful," I commented.

"Maybe we should hire a guard," Alex said.

"That'll cost too much."

"We could buy our own rifle," said Dave.

"Who's going to shoot it?" I asked.

"I will," he said.

"You'd shoot a man because he tried to rob you of twenty dollars?"

Dave thought about this.

"Okay, forget the rifle."

"Let's go," said Frank. "We just go. We don't bring a lot of money. They either rob us or they don't."

"The *bandidos* will never rob us," said Dave. "We'll stick to the shadows and move silently, like wraiths in the night."

Raving in the night was more like it. From bus to bus we traveled, emerging into waning daylight at the Pacaya turnoff, a dirt road bordered by the endless confused tropical green. We waited.

A pickup turned off the paved road onto ours.

"Ah, our chariot."

"Pacaya?"

"Si."

The truck bed was full of women and children who stared or giggled as we clambered in. We sat with butts over the edge, shoulder to shoulder, and hip to hip. Next to me sat a wiry gent in his forties wearing spotless clothing, whose temples shone in the sun like polished stone. The shining-faced man watched Alex, who is clumsy, Frank, who is large. He gave the bedrolls consideration.

"You are climbing Volcán Pacaya?" He spoke softly and earnestly.

"*Ja*," said German Frank.

"There are many bad hombres."

"Bandidos?"

"*Sí*—you should have a guide."

"We have weapons," said Frank.

"They have *pistolas* too," the shining-faced man said, shrugging.

"We have more," Frank insisted. "Pistols, rifles, machetes…"

The shining-faced man nodded seriously. The shining parts of his head slid through the sunlight.

I asked, "How can you tell they're *bandidos*?"

"You will know when you see one."

"How do we avoid them?"

"Walk with guns in your hands."

"What if we stayed off the road and walked through the woods?"

He shook his head. "That is where they hide."

"You seem to know a lot about *bandidos*," Dave said.

The man shrugged.

Frank said, "We're here to make sure nobody hurts any of the tourists."

"You are mercenaries."

"*Ja*."

"Where is your tour group?"

"They will be coming soon."

"Oh."

"*Ja*, we're advance scouts, you see."

I looked away, up the road. Frank often lied for the sheer joy of it, but I assumed that these lies had a purpose. We had been told repeatedly that everybody on the mountain was a *bandido*, or a *bandido* scout, and evidently Frank had decided to believe it. And why not? I believed it, too. Perhaps the shining-faced man was one. The reflective surface of his skin was efficient enough to send messages. *Bandidos* could be appraised of potential customers through Morse code. Perhaps appraised of our arrival. Waiting. Guns and mustaches.

We bumped past milpas of maize tended by the moving forms of thin, bent farmers. Because of the cramped seating arrangement and uneven road, it became difficult to sit upright. To keep from falling backwards we linked arms with the person seated opposite.

Far below, Guatemala City glinted like dirty ice spilled over the valley floor. On opposite ends of the valley, miles apart, loomed the volcanoes Fuego and Agua. Agua we knew because it was the first thing we saw when looking out our hotel window. It was huge and solitary, a tall tight peak that seemed to be pushing itself away from the earth's center and taking the land with it. Fuego looked identical but Fuego was active and Agua dormant. Smoke often drifted away from Fuego's peak.

As we gained in elevation the road passed between fields of coffee, leaving the tropical lushness and entering a region of thin, malnourished pines. When the road branched downward, toward a small village, the truck stopped.

"Pacaya is that way," the shining-faced man said, pointing up.

We climbed out. He addressed us again, in a quiet and secretive tone.

"It is a strange place, Pacaya…it is high and it is cold, but it is hot. Very windy. You should not go alone."

This last suggestion seemed to linger as he fixed us with his radiant temples. The truck lurched off. The children waved good-bye.

"What a strange man."

"He was like a character out of a fairy tale."

"Do you think that was a bad omen?"

"You should not go alone."

Dave giggled. "Who's alone?"

We started walking. You should not go alone. Mysterious advice from a mysterious stranger. It would be quite fitting if there were dozens of these shining-faced men standing at strategic locations along the road. They could stop the tour busses, deliver their cryptic messages, and vanish before everybody had stopped saying, "What?" It would add a little atmosphere to the trip.

Night fell as we walked. Lit by stars and the lights of Guatemala City, our road was a wide sandy gash through the darkdark green. At crossroads

Toward evening we set out for Santa Maria, an Indian village situated on the side of the Volcano de Agua, with the intention of ascending the next day to the summit. At dark we reached Santa Maria, perched at a height of two thousand feet above Antigua, and seven thousand feet above the level of the Pacific.… Soon there was an irruption of Indians, who came to offer their services as guides up the mountain.… They represented the ascent as very steep, with dangerous precipices, and the path extremely difficult to find, and said it was necessary for each of us to have sixteen men with ropes to haul us up, and to pay twelve dollars for each man. They seemed a little astonished when I told them that we wanted two men each, and would give them half a dollar apiece, but fell immediately to eight men for each, and a dollar apiece; and after a noisy wrangling, we picked out six from forty, and they all retired.

—John Lloyd Stephens, *Incidents of Travel in Central America, Chiapas, and Yucatán* (1841)

we made guesses, flipped coins, and followed tire tracks. We were standing at one intersection, arguing over which way to go, when a Volkswagen bus drove by, honking. On the side of it was written, "Volcano Tours!"

"At least they're good for something," I said, as we strode after them.

The village of San Francisco, the last village on the road, consisted of twelve buildings, several disheveled dogs, and one electric light inside the one *tienda*. Leaning against the *tienda's* front wall were three swarthy men who stopped talking to observe us. Above them was a photo of the *Rubio* Man (the Marlboro Man's Latin cousin) having a smoke on a ridge next to the words, *"Esta Tierra Es Mi Tierra."*

"Subtle *bandido* humor," Dave said.

One of the three men approached us, a shy gentleman wearing a straw hat and an unshaven smile. He stopped before us, thumbs in pockets.

"You climb Pacaya?"

"Yes."

"You would like a guide?"

"Why?"

"It is dark, and easy to get lost, and there are *bandidos*. I can take you there safely."

"We were O.K. last time," said Frank.

"You have been before?"

"Dozens of times," said Frank, with a loose, dismissive wave of his right hand. "We're geologists. We climb every week to measure the lava output."

The guide shrugged and stood there listening to us for a while before slowly turning and walking back to the others.

"Do you think he was a *bandido* scout, too?"

"Probably everybody in this town is a *bandido*. I mean, if you had a choice between that or picking coffee beans, what would you do?"

Frank, who had climbed Pacaya six years earlier with a tour group (in the daylight), led us away from the *tienda*.

"We go this way," Frank said confidently.

We went down a broad track between widely spaced houses. After the houses it narrowed, then stopped. Frank asked an old man for directions.

He pointed to the forest to our right. Frank thanked him.

"You should have a guide," the old man said, shaking his head.

Not another one, I thought. This is getting silly.

We followed Frank into the woods on a narrow path past trees no thicker than my wrist. There was little foliage and we could see stars through the tangle of branches. Under the branches we could barely see each other. Of course, nobody had remembered to bring a flashlight. This was annoying until Alex stumbled and fell with a splendid thud.

"He moves like a wraith in the night," I said.

Dave and Frank were cackling with laughter.

"Hello, *bandidos*! Here we are!"

"Nice *bandidos*! We're walking through your forest!"

The trail reflected a slight silver shine, like the path of a slug, that vanished and appeared between the shadows of trees. We followed it, lost it, followed another. Lost in the woods. It's not so bad in a warm land, where there are no bears, and people live in the middle of nowhere and can rescue you. Better to be lost in Guatemala than in Alaska.

"Is this the way you went last time, Frank?"

"Oh, no, we stayed on the road."

"Maybe we should be on the road, you know, just for old times' sake."

"So where are they?" Alex asked.

"Who?"

"The *bandidos*."

"Probably lurking and pillaging."

"Do you think we'll meet any? I'm kind of surprised we haven't."

"Maybe they all take Sunday off?"

"They're probably closer to the volcano," Dave pointed out. "They would have more clients there. I mean, they're not going to be roaming around in the woods waiting for idiots like us."

"You're the expert."

In Peru, Shining Path rebels had captured Dave and two Israelis at gunpoint on a mountain path. They were blindfolded and led to a cabin, where they were questioned about their political beliefs, then lectured on the errors of Imperialism and the virtues of Marxism. After a couple of hours, realizing he was not going to be shot, Dave said aloud, "Nobody is ever going to believe this."

One of his hosts, hearing him, asked how they could help him convince people. His reply: How about a picture?

"This was not a very popular idea with everybody, and I was wondering if I'd said the wrong thing," Dave told me. "There was this big discussion and then they decided it was appropriate as long as their faces were masked. So we went outside and all the Shining Path put hats and sunglasses on, you know, or scarves across their faces, and the Israelis went and sat on the ground in front of them."

He had showed it to us, a group photo of these masked men and women standing close to each other with very serious expressions, each one with a gun raised beside his or her head. And kneeling before them were two curly-haired men grinning as if it was a photo of their college graduation. The whole thing looked like a farce—perhaps a photo of the attendees of a costume party.

Dave said, "It was interesting how much power that camera had. Even though they had all the guns, I was definitely part of the ruling class there, with a dominant social status. Nobody suggested that one of the Shining Path take the photo. It really changed the whole dynamic of the meeting. We became sort of honored guests, rather than prisoners. Although we still couldn't leave."

The next morning, after each made a voluntary donation, they were released.

"You shouldn't have stuck to the trail," Frank said. "You never would have been captured if you were lost."

Dave said, "Yeah, I think that getting lost in the woods is a pretty good strategy for avoiding *bandidos*. But you know, I had a thought about these *bandidos* and the *bandido* scouts. I think they work for the tour groups."

"What?"

"Yeah, all these guys warning us about the *bandidos*, they work for the tour groups. Maybe the *bandidos* even work for the tour groups. Their job is to scare the tourists into paying for the trip."

"That's very devious."

"Makes sense, though."

It did make sense. Maybe the *bandidos* didn't exist at all. The whole thing could be a construct of the tour companies and the wretched Señor Fernandez.

We followed the trail to a barbed wire fence that enclosed a small garden. Wide dark leaves covered the ground. A small white house lurked down the hillside. We stepped quietly and carefully through the garden, then back over the barbed wire and onto another trail, or the same interrupted trail.

Almost immediately we came across a clearing. Frank, who was the first to enter, stopped suddenly, pointing. We froze. I heard a stick break, then saw the bushes on the other side of the clearing move.

"Steve," he said loudly, *"dame la pistola."*

> When we began our hike, I noticed our two young tour guides were each carrying Little League baseball bats, the so-called "defensive weapons" that were supposed to protect us from the *bandidos* and guerrillas. I'm sure those hillside warriors were shaking in their munitions belts when they saw us coming—fourteen tourists being led by two five-foot-three teenagers who probably couldn't hit a softball if my grandma pitched one right over the plate.
>
> —Doug Lansky, "Playing with Fire"

"Here is the pistol," I shouted from ten feet away.

"Danke für die pistole," he yelled.

"De nada."

We watched the bushes. Nobody moved. My heart thumped. I was ready either to run or fall to my knees, begging for mercy.

Dave giggled nervously. There was the sound of something pushing past branches, then two horses clopped into the clearing, chewing on something green. A slight embarrassment passed between Frank and me.

"Perhaps the *bandidos* dress in horse costumes to lure their victims into a false sense of security," Dave commented.

We looked carefully at the horses. They continued to chew.

Very briefly I had the thought that a group of *bandidos* might be hiding nearby, watching our reactions to the horses, to see if we actually did have weapons. But this was just a fleeting fantasy. The bitter, disappointing truth was that we were unworthy of the *bandidos'* attentions.

We left the clearing and within five minutes were standing on the road. Before us was a hill, nearly bare of vegetation, topped by a television transmission tower.

"We go this way," said Frank.

We climbed to the top of the hill, where the strong wind blew our shirts against our left sides and flapped them away to the right. We could see the MacKenney crater, a dark, rocky depression in the top of the mountain created when an earlier cone had exploded. The new cone, about 300 feet high, grew out of the middle of the crater like an island in an ancient, dry lake bed. The cone was smaller than I had expected.

As we watched, it erupted. From the tip of the cone burst a bright red fountain of red-hot rocks (called bombs), lighting up the sky around the volcano. The bombs shot high into the dark sky, then plummeted in slowly curving arcs back to the earth while a huge cloud of evil-looking black smoke blew off to the west. The erupting lava was surprisingly red, like neon. Suddenly, climbing to the top of an active volcano seemed like a very stupid thing to do.

"We're all going to die," I said.

"But what a glorious death."

"You see what a great place I bring you to?"

"You're our hero, Frank."

No more than five minutes passed between eruptions. Pacaya, a Strombolian-type volcano, is mostly full of hydrogen gases, its lava very liquid. Pacaya mostly lacks the solid matter necessary to block a vent, which can create the buildup of pressure that leads to a top-blowing explosion.

Although Pacaya's major eruptions have been small in comparison with those of other volcanoes, such as Mt. St. Helens, it occasionally builds up to some large blasts. In March 2000 a powerful eruption caused two nearby villages to be evacuated. A few months earlier, Pacaya sent 800-meter-high fountains of lava into the air. Villages were again evacuated and the ash from the eruptions shut down the Guatemala City airport.

The large and small eruptions had turned the area surrounding Pacaya into a zone of lifelessness. Even at night we could see that the land was built of shades of gray and brown, rocks and dirt and ash. A few scrappy plants had pushed their way through the ash cover to the air, and didn't look too happy about it.

To our left a ridge curved around the crater, losing elevation until the two met. We followed a well-worn path along the ridge, through a bit of ragged forest, and down. Just before the ridge ended, on the barest, most windswept section, we were stopped by an odd sight. A dozen people in sleeping bags, enveloped by huge, clear, plastic tarps. The ground was so barren that they appeared to be camped on the moon. It was a tour group. I felt sorry for the paying customers—they must have been freezing. It was cold enough to see our breath. The tarps snapped and popped in the wind.

From one of the sleeping bags came a flashlight beam and an unclear query.

"Don't worry," said Frank, "we won't harm you. We only want your women."

"What?"

"Why don't you guys camp in the woods?" Dave asked.

"Bandits," the voice said. "Don't you guys know anything? This mountain is crawling with them."

The only thing this mountain is crawling with tonight are tourists, I thought. Maybe we were too eager. There must be certain rules the *bandidos* operate by, and one of them must be to rob only those people who do not wish to be robbed. If sought out, they hide.

At any rate, we were at the base of the volcano, and we had seen neither blade nor bullet. The *bandidos* would have another chance at us on our way down. But now Pacaya beckoned. It roared and rumbled. It burst forth like the end of the world. Frank and Dave were the first to move, walking then running toward it across the crater floor, through soft silty ash.

Pacaya's cone was covered with ash. Not just covered with it, but built of ash, layer upon layer of ash and rock. From a hole in the ground the cone had been spewed one piece at a time. The ash was both thick and chunky, like burned scraps of peanuts, and fine as the soot of a burnt paper bag. It gave way easily. Step up two feet, slide back down one. We stopped often to breathe and look at the view.

> I thought of what I knew about volcanic eruptions, about weak continental plates submitting beneath thicker ones, and heat from the friction melting the plates into molten rock, compressed gasses squeezing the magma until it bubbles like liquid fire through the earth's thin crust. But as I watched it happen before my eyes, I thought the ancient Mayans had understood it better. Volcanoes are alive; they have heartbeats. They are gods, furiously spewing their admonitions at mortals.
>
> —Lucy McCauley, "Up the Volcano," *Women in the Wild*

When Pacaya prepared to erupt I could feel the rumbling in my legs. We stopped to look up, then looked at each other nervously. As we approached the peak the eruptions felt stronger. The ground kept shaking and stopping and shaking again.

Then we were standing on the rim, looking into the cone. My heart was pounding from excitement and fear and thin air. The rim was about thirty yards across. The wind was very strong and I thought that if it gusted it would blow us in. We peered over the edge. The interior of the cone sloped down, toward its own center, like a funnel. At the lowest and narrowest point were two holes beside each other, both large enough to drop an elephant through. Bombs popped up and fell back through the holes. We could see smoke and a lambent red glow, as if from a hidden forge.

Below us we could see the lights of Guatemala City, and in the other direction, a few stars. Dave ventured to the other side of the cone, where the gases and rocks were thick and moving, and came back coughing to tell us not to.

We were giddy with excitement. Thoughts of *bandidos*, tour groups, horses, the shining-faced man, all were gone. The volcano was all we could fit within our skulls.

Pacaya erupted again, with the sound of an avalanche. The ground shook, smoke rushed and boiled into the air, and red-hot bombs lit the smoke as they plunged through. The smoke slipped over the edge with the wind, as smooth and fluid as breath. The bombs plummeted onto the far side of the cone, invisible and loud.

"Yahoooo!"

"It is high and it is cold!" Dave yelled.

"But it is hot!"

We all laughed and swore as Pacaya shook with another rush of noise and smoke and fire, so sudden it made me jump. The molten rocks rose in clumps, separating and curving away from each other like flaming cannonballs. Smoke filled the air above the cone and immediately was blown down the western slope of the cone and away. Nobody had words to express their excitement. We were reduced to jumping and shouting, which is sometimes the best way to express yourself.

"What do you think?" I yelled at Dave, over the noise of wind and eruption.

He shook his head.

"It's too much," he said, tapping his head, "it's too much!"

Steve Wilson writes regularly for Transitions Abroad *and contributed a story to* Travelers' Tales Hawaii. *He lives in Portland, Oregon.*

PART THREE

Going Your Own Way

JOHN KRICH

Viva Sandino Koufax!

During the Contra War in the mid-'80s, baseball was the common denominator for hope and peace.

AT SIX IN THE MORNING, THEY'RE POUNDING DOWN THE DOOR TO our Managua motel bungalow. Tim sits up in the nearest cot, throws off his flimsy sheets and greets the caller, buck naked. It's not the secret police. A grizzled farmer clutches his straw hat to his chest and his young son to his knees. The two of them have driven down to the capital just to see our first baseman. Our tour will get used to this peculiarly Nicaraguan habit of well-wishers turning up unannounced in one town or another, in spite of gas rationing and frequent transportation snafus, as though the country were one hacienda kitchen. All night long, says the farmer, his son stayed awake talking about the big *primera basista*. Now this frail boy in his best gingham shirt presents his idol with a letter. The boy doesn't seem to register that Tim's in the buff. Father and son encourage Tim to read the letter aloud. In formal Spanish, the first baseman is requested to give greetings from the children of Nicaragua to his children back home—they can't imagine that Tim has none. And to please ask his president, personally, to stop the war. The letter also inquired humbly whether Tim might think to send this boy a Wilson-brand first baseman's glove so that he might follow in the path of his hero. Half asleep, Tim reaches in his backpack for a spare ball. Father and son back out the door, bowing.

"There I was with my hand on my dick!" Tim mutters before trying to get some more shut-eye. "Then I'm handing out my autograph! Man, this has got to be baseball heaven!"

The former Cub farmhand and current red bear has found his nirvana: a place where his sweet swing can be hitched to his politics, or vice versa—and where each cursed Yankee dollar buys a wad of continually devalued cordobas. Tim will remain here after our tour to serve as a batting instructor for the first-division team in Matagalpa. In the meantime, "Baseball Heaven" becomes the title of our group's epic poem, our stanza of Nicaraguan free verse. In what other firmament could we find sworn revolutionaries who interrupt their dialectics to remind us that their favorite player is Ernie Banks? Where else would our chief guide, a mischievous mustachioed union leader and nerveless street-fighting veteran named Emigdio Siqueiros, spend most of his time glued to game broadcasts on his transistor? Or could we, simply by showing up, get the finest players in the land to stay up in darkened hotel dining rooms patiently offering their trade secrets on which seams to grip for the slider, the scroogie, the forkball? And where else could our ragtag squad get ogled like superstars, asked to scrawl our worthless autographs on dozens of souvenir balls? I sign mine "Sandino Koufax."

It's all too *perfecto*—the word used all the time in a country where a simple yes is never good enough. In Nicaragua, where everyone's presumed to be a poet, we're presumed to be ballplayers until proven otherwise. Hitting the back roads like a bunch of old-time barnstormers, we experience the grinding bus rides that are the staple of life in the minors. In this instructional league, we work out the kinks by spreading mirth and equipment to hitherto neglected locals. Each stop begins with the announcement of our names and positions from speakers propped against cattle posts, and ends with brew, barbecue, and kind words at the nearest tavern or hacienda. When everybody's drunk enough, the Nicaraguans rip off their hand-sewn, sweat-stained uniforms and give us the shirts off their backs. In return, we leave 'em with a rousing, off-key rendition of "Take Me Out to the Ball Game." This is the leftist equivalent of a baseball fantasy camp—the sort of place where oral surgeons pay thousands to play an inning or two with their boyhood idols. The Natural meets Walter Mitty meets Fidel.

In Matagalpa, as close to the war as we ever get, we're told that "whenever the troops have a moment away from the front, the first thing they do is pick up a ball and a glove." At a welcoming breakfast, a Paris-educated lawyer named Marco Gonzales speaks on behalf of the region's coffee growers. "We would no longer be Nicaraguans if we stopped playing baseball. What was once the opiate of the masses has become the balm for our wounds." Gonzales claims that Nicaraguans remain "mentally very healthy people," despite losing thirty-five thousand lives in five years. And baseball, this legacy of prior wars, is "our way of coming away from war, of making certain that our people never yield to the war mentality."

It's just beyond the next hill that one never crosses: *la guerra*, invisible yet omnipresent.

Somewhere nearby, a game adds up its score in casualties inflicted and families uprooted. For us, the threat takes a slapstick form. A softball designed for the blind, emitting a steady beep, sends the Nicaraguans scattering in fear of a time-bomb. On the way back from an exhibition in the hinterlands, our van often gets mired in puddles that have stretched to small ponds across the single, unmaintained lane of brown dirt. In the mountains, three hours from nowhere with darkness closing fast on the jungle, none of us dare speak our fears. If our Unión Nacional de Agricultores y Ganaderos [UNAG] driver Silvio doesn't get us through these washouts, we'll be easy picking for the contras. The whole team has to evacuate the Toyota and watch the moves of our most valuable player. Mission accomplished, he winks and flashes his gold-filled front teeth. In designer jeans and polo shirt, Silvio always looks dapper. Each morning, he rises an hour before the group to hose all the mud off his treasured vehicle. Near the end of the trip, I hear he first learned to handle a set of wheels as an ambulance driver. Life in Nicaragua is one controlled skid and Silvio, a wizard in a Red Sox cap, knows just when to spin his wheels.

Riding beside him is *compañera* Lisa Rosenthal. Like so many

Below Acoyapa, we were educated in the way of Nicaraguan roads. The road was wide, but only because of decades that drivers had spent trying to skirt this hellish bed of wild rock and crevices. There was little commerce here, so the few houses were built of bamboo or scrap planking, the roofs of palm thatch sloped like pyramids. In the yards, naked children tottered among goats and dozing horses. And every few miles or so, I noted the worn footpaths of makeshift baseball diamonds. One such field was in a trash dump—one of the few flat places available—where more than two dozen boys played using bare hands and an old ball mended with black electrical tape. I stopped and watched their game for a few minutes before lobbing a new white ball to the pitcher. This was an unprecedented event—I could read it in their faces; a look of wonderment and pure joy that I carried with me down that bastard road.

—Randy Wayne White, *The Sharks of Lake Nicaragua*

North Americans settled here, even those who have gained positions of trust, her presence in Nicaragua is almost entirely accidental. An aspiring modern dancer from Los Angeles, Lisa came down on a summer tutoring program before the Sandinista uprising and has never been able to bring herself to leave. She has survived the siege of León and contra ambushes and come through looking like an advertisement for Jane Fonda's workout. Though she's not good at translating ground rules, she never falters in her account of Sandino's flight from the Marines. But this honorary Nicaraguan has also absorbed the Nicaraguan style—which dictates that militancy never get in the way of diversion. A nattering swirl of flirtation surrounds the *gringita*.

The UNAG officials who accompany us are hardly the image of toughened cadres, either. The easiest way to spot what might be called a Nicaraguan elite—that is, those who come from families that did not work with their hands—is to look for penny loafers and a chemise Lacoste.

The architects of this new society seem to be frustrated preppies. Though they show a predilection for the front of the bus, they're easy about allowing the back to be filled with ever-changing passengers. Everyone in the country wants to hop a lift with a bunch of ballplayers. Coffee growers in Stetson hats pay their fare in sacks of fresh Matagalpa grind, one pound to a player. Out of nowhere, a painfully thin adolescent squeezes into the half-seat beside the back door, holding an official Little League scorebook so dog-eared it may have been passed down for generations. I never figure out if he's asked permission to act as our official scorer and play-by-play man. His mop-haired younger brother totes a briefcase filled with coils of thick wiring and an antiquated microphone, probably the first public address system invented. The gizmo must weigh a ton. The two kids get their biggest thrill when Blue Jay or Jeff pass along their Walkman headphones so they can hear something "really radical." Our Apollonian surfers look twice the size of the teenaged Nicaraguans. The brothers admire our American swagger and gadgetry the way we would like to admire ourselves.

We've recruited two ringers to make our team respectable: a pitcher and a shortstop, of course. On a moment's notice, they left their families and gas station jobs in Boaco and grabbed their mitts. They get free chow two days, and one frigid night at La Selva Negra (the Black Forest), a mountain resort known to honeymooners throughout the country. At a rum-swilling party in one of the rustic cabins, we even teach them how to play charades. "First word...a Broadway musical...on the nose!" Did somebody say there's a war going on? Only toward the end of the tour do our two new teammates let down their guard. "Everything's fine if you belong to the party," one whispers after too many beers. "If we could, we would follow you home. Don't you need a pitcher for your team in California?"

Our most useful recruit is an Arizona agronomist named Circles. I never learn if this is his real name or one of those visionary monikers with which people anointed themselves in the '60s. Circles doesn't look old enough to have seen the '60s, but he perfectly embodies their spirit. This Harvard-style hayseed in tortoiseshell glasses and neatly pressed coveralls reminds me of the first volunteers for the Freedom Rides through the South. Now he rides with us, tackling inequality on a global scale. Circles fills our heads with more than we'd like to know about the redistribution of arable land to the lower and middle peasants. At last he settles down to the task of reeducating the pugnaciously reactionary Arnold. As our van rolls through disputed territory, this odd couple goes toe-to-toe over the free market system, Che Guevara's true intentions in Bolivia, whether there's really any more difference between Democrats and Republicans than between Trotskyists and anarcho-syndicalists. Both seem delighted to have finally met their match. Arnold hasn't traveled this distance solely to revel in his son's strong throwing arm. By inclination and training, he's a devil's advocate. And he's come to Nicaragua because he can't get into a scrap like this in the suburbs of Virginia—though he'll probably use Circles's very arguments to shock and outrage his colleagues. Each day, the rest of us grow more convinced that the Republican lawyer is undergoing a change of party affiliation—and equally convinced that we'll be the last to hear of his conversion.

Arnold gets more "brainwashing," as he calls it, at interminable meetings in airless rooms. The life of a ballplayer can't be all fun and games and we've got to suffer question-and-answer sessions that lead to hours of ponderous oratory. Commissioner Carlos Cuadra, the Sandinista placed in charge of baseball, demurs at first when asked for a summary of his background, then traces his activist lineage back three generations in an hour-long digression. Cuadra reports dryly how his grandfather was murdered by the first Somoza, his father was driven to Costa Rica by the second Somoza. As a child of exiles, Cuadra's thoughts were "with Nicaragua twenty-four hours a day. I loved it though I didn't know it." Expelled himself after becoming a student militant, Cuadra says he was able to sneak back into the country only during the chaos of the '72 earthquake. One hundred hair-raising escapes so he could become the Commissar of Hardball! Like so much else in Nicaragua, Cuadra's tale would seem slanted to provoke sympathy if it weren't true.

After a few such sessions, our squad begins to mutiny. The great ideological schism within Baseball for Peace occurs one breakfast over the question of whether or not to show up for a scheduled audience with Vida Luz Menenses, a prominent poet who's Vice Minister of Culture under poet-priest Ernesto Cardenal. The popular position, championed by the two teenage boys, is that a team practice would be more useful than a discussion of poetics. Some argue that we mustn't insult our hosts by failing to attend planned activities. The majority counters that we insult them more by failing to give them a good game. Besides, asks this action faction, what does baseball have to do with culture? I'm one of the few who goes to seek an answer from the vice minister. She's a severe woman in her forties, who lectures from under the protection of dramatic, gray-streaked bangs. She raised the only laugh by trotting out the standard joke about the Ministry of Culture's headquarters: "This used to be one of the Somozas' mansions, and it has twelve bathrooms. We like to say that this is because the Somozas spent a great deal of time washing their hands." When she outlines the new government's efforts to revive and preserve native expression, I'm amazed to find that she counts baseball among them. "Like North American music, baseball is a cultural influence that will always be with us," the vice minister declares. "All we wish is for people to become educated so they can make their own choices."

There seems little choice at all in Matiguas, an archetypal mountain village of loose donkeys and gully-washed streets. After wandering across the block from the town ballfield, I share a doorsill with a bubbly old coot in a cowboy hat covered with mock leopard skin. This farmer hasn't shaved in a week and looks like he's been on a bender for longer than that. As a conversation starter, he points to his crotch and wants to know how to make reference to the anatomical part *en inglés*. Before long, we're teaching each other introductory scatology. You say *"pendejo,"* I say "piece o' crap." A few buddies join us, acting all too merry in their involuntary indolence. The leopard man explains that they've all been smoking marijuana. He even says that there's *cocaína* for sale in these parts, a claim denied by Sandinista officials. This voice of Nicaraguan irreverence rubs his twinkling red eyes and asks the question I've been dreading all week. "Why do you bring us baseballs when we need spare parts for our Italian tractors?" For emphasis, he points toward a stalled rig in the middle of the street. "Do you know we haven't been able to lay irrigation ditches in a year? What good are bats and balls to people who are starving?"

The other men on the stoop nod. I can't tell if they're ranchers or winos. Maybe they're both. "We are slowly starving to death. There is nothing to be done about it." And they all have a good chuckle. "Tell your people back home that we are not Communists. The worst thing for farmers is Communism." But when I ask my stoopmate what he thinks of Somoza, he uses his thumb and forefinger to form the sign of the rifle. Like everyone you meet, he, too, claims to have fought with the *frente.*

After our squad manages its first triumph—whipping a makeshift collection of farmhands who haven't laid their hands on gloves or bats since last year's harvest—my stoned friend joins most of the other town luminaries for a chicken-and-beans luncheon in the town's single dank corner tavern. He, too, raises the long-necked bottles of Victoria beer high when the town's Sandinista mayor, who would look quite at home along the Pecos with his pointy boots and checked cowboy shirt, offers another round of barroom histrionics. "When the *frente* began, we were only a few. And look now! We have become everyone! Your presence here today proves it. Once we were few, now we are the whole world!"

But how will the dirt streets bear the traffic? Half of Matiguas wears an imported t-shirt that reads, "My Job Is So Secret—Even I Don't Know What It Is." A perfect explanation for the town's condition. But the locals want more Americana to bear on their chests, and we soon begin our ritualized swapping, our cross-cultural transvestism. Though the wind from a sudden rainstorm whips through the open pillars of the dirty bodega, I strip off my shirt reading, "Billy Ball—Oakland A's" for the chance at a coarse Spandex jersey hand-lettered, "los Criollos." A former pitcher for the Dantos gives me the top he wore at the World Amateur Championships in return for a cheap nylon windbreaker that he's been eyeing enviously. We leave with the names of a dozen Nicaraguan towns on our chests, while those who wave us off have become adopted citizens of every major league city. But the relative positions of privileged and underprivileged can't be traded as readily as our uniforms. We're still the good Yankee traders, getting the best of the deal.

Yet our group's obstinate loyalty to childhood pursuits dovetails perfectly with the Nicaraguans' own Catholic trust in the power of innocence. No, call it an embrace of the naïve. This upheaval supervised by priests and would-be-saints had been one of the least vindictive in human history—with fewer than forty of Somoza's hatchet men executed or murdered in acts of retribution. "The only way we know we're on the right path is that we bear no bitterness," says Daniel Núñez, the head of UNAG, whose brother had just been killed by the contras. "And that is what makes us so certain that, in the end, you will be on the same path with us." The Nicaraguan idea is that we should all be as children—until the corruption and power-lust that whirls and plots on all sides has exhausted itself. Until the other side takes its fancy gear and its fragmentation bombs home because nobody will play with them.

Baseball for Peace does not become a real team until our first day off in the schedule. Like a bunch of veritable jocks, we vote to skip the Museum of the Revolution and head for the beach. Poneloya is a half-hour drive from León on the Pacific coast. From the size of the type on our map, I expect a mammoth resort. In Nicaragua, as I should know by now, one abandoned hotel at the highway's dead end, all veranda and filigree work painted pink, constitutes a mammoth resort. Once the proprietor is found and awakened, he offers beer and, in an hour or two, lunch. Lisa's request for the local variety of sea bass elicits a long story about a group of village fishermen who've wandered too far out into international waters. They've been missing three days now. From the owner's deadpan tone, it's hard to tell if he thinks the fishermen have fallen prey to the sea or the contras. The war is just another excuse for being out of fish.

Not a promising start to our outing. Neither is the immense placard across the entrance to the beach reading *Zona Peligrosa*. There's more stenciled red print fading out underneath, but we get the idea. Cool yourself, gringo, at your own risk. Being gringos, we're willing victims of our own arrogance. Everyone plunges into the surf, a Marine amphibious assault going the wrong way. The breakers crest a good fifty feet out, offering a long ride in through coursing foam. Our group divides up between those beyond and those in front of the undertow. After ten minutes, one bobbing head seems a little far out into the inviting sea. Blue Jay has pushed his all-American indestructibility a stroke too far. The riptide will not let him return to Nicaragua's safe haven.

"A boat! ¡*Una barca*!" Silvio's impish smile indicates that, unlike us, he is not prone to hysteria. Sure enough, within a few minutes, the boy finds a current that takes him to where he can swim in with the undertow, not against it. Blue Jay's father and grandfather sprint along the sand, leading the rest of us, until they can huddle once more with their young. They hug and cry in the shallows, three pale but tough terrier bodies cast from the same genetic mold, clad in boxer shorts and baseball caps gone soggy.

When lunch arrives at last, the team hoists its Victoria beers with greater purpose

The baseball diamond on Mancarron Island is on the highest plateau of cultivated land, higher than either the village or the small hotel. Though the field goes unused for long periods, its base paths are marked by generations of wear. The backstop is chicken wire stretched over gray planks. The field is seeds and wildflowers that catch the wind and show their milky undersides, yellow and violet. There is no fence. The outfield slopes toward the water. From the pitcher's mound you can see the lake and, beneath the blue silhouettes of volcanoes, the solitary shapes of dugout canoes: fishermen at work.

On my last day on Mancarron, I walked up to the field and watched boys playing baseball. Ramón and Juan, in the jerseys my sons had worn, were easy to recognize. As was their father, standing at the backstop with the chunk of wood he had been carving.

It was now a bat.

—Randy Wayne White, *The Sharks of Lake Nicaragua*

than ever. The waves become larger with each telling, the tide stronger. Despite the alcohol and the heat, everyone has spare adrenaline. Our captain goes to the bus for his pants, his mitt, and his spikes. He corners one of the barefoot Poneloyans. "Is there a field in this hellhole? *¿Dónde está el diamante?*"

Before we know it, we're being led through a scraggly papaya orchard toward a clearing of baked mud. Nicaraguan oxen, placid as Asian water buffaloes, graze in left field. The right field line is your basic malarial swamp. Behind home plate, our distant backstop is the bluish, cold-eyed cone of the volcano Momotombo. The infield is rutted, the bases wherever we imagine. Here the team stages its only true practice of the trip. And everyone responds by making the plays with a crazed sense of affirmation. After each miraculous backhand stab, we whip the ball round the horn, hit the right bases and the cutoff men, back each other up the way it says in the how-to-manual none of us have ever read. Sweating and half-delirious from the heat, our khakis covered with splattered mud up to our knees, we revel in the crisp heaves and crazy hops. We stoop and pluck and toss how we've been taught by the dads here and the dads we carry with us. Captain Jay dubs this scabbed-over clearing of hardened chocolate pudding our "home field."

To be alive and pursuing the snaky twists of a hardball is consummate joy. A crowd of scrawny day laborers wanders over to watch the crazy foreigners. How can anyone play in the noonday sun? But this is not India and the natives are as mad as the mad dogs for the colonial game. Tiny, undernourished eight year olds dismount from tired ponies to take a turn with bats twice their size. Before long, we invite the Nicaraguans to take the field. Most of them outshine us. Though they've probably never played with such new balls or soft gloves, they're accustomed to the erratic bounces created by this ravaged, bursting piece of ground. *"Buenos manos,"* we shout, the universal baseball compliment. Having managed our own close escape, we're now more attuned to how the Nicaraguans live. In the midst of all this hostile lushness, the sight that pleases us most is our own survival. Having set our feet down at last in this looted land, the only landscape worth beholding is the human being.

Back on the bus, Captain Jay whips out his harmonica. He wants to teach us the turn-of-the-century tune sung by North American prospectors in Mexico which supposedly gave rise to the word *gringo*. As our van sloshes off into the sunset, we try a new version of "Green grow the lilacs all covered with dew." Our improvised lyrics begin, "We are the gringos who'll play ball with you...."

John Krich is the author of two widely praised non-fiction books, Music in Every Room, *and* El Béisbol, *from which this story was excerpted. He has also written a novel about the private life of Fidel Castro entitled* A Totally Free Man. *His travel and sports writing, reportage, and fiction have appeared in many publications, including* Mother Jones, Vogue, Sports Illustrated, *the* Village Voice, *and* The New York Times.

LEA ASCHKENAS

In Search of Zen

Self-discovery isn't easy.

CABAÑAS TRANQUILAS, ON THE PACIFIC SIDE OF COSTA RICA, LIES on a dirt road in an unnamed town between Dominicalito and Uvita. There are no telephones or electricity and the bus passes by only once a day. Cabañas Tranquilas is as much about the landscape (both physical and mental) which obscures it as it is about the cabins themselves. It is about mango trees depositing their overripe fruit in pockets of mud on the jungle floor, filling the air with the perfume of fermentation. It is about the steady downpour of a summer rainstorm mixing with and becoming indecipherable from the sound of the ocean. It is about the world at 5 A.M. when the sun first appears and the polished black surfaces that give night its sense of mystery are replaced with color and familiar textures, with edges. Cabañas Tranquilas is all this and the negation of it all. It is the absence of scent and sound and sight that occurs during meditation, the way, when you focus on yourself so intently, location ceases to exist. Cabañas Tranquilas is where I went searching for myself when I thought, by definition, being a wanderer meant you were lost.

It started with the settling in of routine in my life in Costa Rica where I'd moved after college for an internship. I was seeking out some fantastical image of how my life would be in the tropics. The script is a common one. It is the road trip gone international. Leave the landscape of the familiar and your life will be filled with adventure and insight. Often this did seem true, but just as often, the realizations I'd have on my weekend trips to the rain forests and volcanoes never made it through the office door on Monday. I wanted something to tie together and ground those moments, a way to hold onto them beyond the experience itself, a Zen of the everyday. I would wake anxiously at obscene hours of the morning obsessed with these thoughts. I would wake in a bed with no sheets, my body in strange, twisted yogic positions without any of the clarity that's supposed to accompany these formations. So, when I saw a sign outside a health food store in Plaza del Sol that read, "Vegetarian, tai chi, yoga, meditation center on the Pacific looking for help in December. Work/study exchange or salary. We use a holistic approach to living to achieve an awareness of the moment and sense of peace. We're looking for people interested in exploring this while working in our vegetarian restaurant, giving jungle tours or kayak lessons." I decided to put my insomniac yoga sessions to use. I called and arranged a weekend stay in exchange for helping out in the kitchen.

The bus from Dominicalito bumps its way along the potholed road.

"Are you trying to find yourself?" the driver asks when I mention Cabañas Tranquilas. "It's called *La tierra de los perdidos*," he tells me. "Land of the lost." I get an image of a Grateful Dead show translated to the tropics. Flower children in tie-dye sarongs smoking rain forest marijuana out of bamboo pipes and playing coconut-shell drums. But when the bus driver stops in the middle of this unmarked street and motions to me that I'm here, there is only silence and nothing in sight, not even a cabin.

"¿Aqui?" I ask.

"Sí, aquí," he says, spreading his arms as if to embrace the emptiness. And I stand, looking dumbly into the distance for signs of civilization. I feel a tap on my shoulder and, when I turn, see that an older woman is pointing ahead to a piece of driftwood on a stake.

"Oh," I say, just as clueless as before. "Oh, aha, right." I am ushered off by the ticket collector who hands me my backpack and smiles encouragingly. I step down into a muddy pothole, and the older woman and a little girl sitting behind her wave goodbye. The bus pulls away, leaving a mini-whirlwind of dust in its wake.

When I reach the sign, I can see the inscription "Cabañas Tranquilas—Vegetarian Restaurant and Resort" chiseled into it. And a bit farther along what's beginning to look like a path, there is a teenage boy cementing rocks together to form walkway steps.

"Hi," he says. "Are you Lea?"

"Yeah."

"I'm Rain." He reaches out a calloused hand to shake. "My mom's waiting for you upstairs."

I look above to a Swiss Family Robinson-type setup, an open-air bamboo tepee structure. Walking up to the tepee is like entering another dimension. The ocean spreads out below, turbulent and immense. A bamboo and seashell chime hangs over the entrance, echoing in the unenclosed space filled only with a table and a few mattresses and pillows laid out on the floor. Peace. Calm. I am here. This is me. A woman wearing an Indian print dress is stretching out on the floor. Even this high above the jungle, the humidity is intense and her dress clings to her, somehow delicately despite the sweat streaks.

"Hi, I'm Theresa," she says. "You're just in time for meditation. We'll be starting in about half an hour." Her voice is calm, almost emotionless.

"That would be nice."

"Julie can show you to your cabin first," she says, and as if on cue, a thin, pale woman with long black hair and bulging eyes emerges from a back entrance.

"Did you have any trouble getting here?" Julie asks as we climb back down the steps.

"Not really. I just caught a bus from Dominicalito."

"Oh, there's a bus?"

"Well, yeah. It would be quite a long walk. You usually walk to Dominicalito?"

"Actually, I guess I haven't left in a while. We're pretty self-sufficient here. There's a delivery man who brings groceries from San Isidro once a week."

"When was the last time you left?"

"Oh," Julie says, as though taken aback. "Oh, I don't know. Maybe a year and a half ago. Two years."

"But what do you do here? Is it usually very busy?"

"There's no one here now. Usually the rainy season is empty, but we've got eight cabins and after December, it really fills up quickly. I mainly just help cook meals and meditate now."

"Are you happy here? Is this what you'd expected?"

"Yes, but it goes much deeper than just a 'yes' or 'no' answer."

"Oh, of course." This is good, a lot to learn here. I inhale the salt air deeply and a bug flies up my nose. I sneeze and it flies off unharmed. Julie looks at me strangely.

"Well," she says, giving a quick glance at my nose before pulling out a set of keys. "Here we are."

My cabin consists of a bedroom with screen windows and a small bathroom in the back. In some corner, a cricket chirps. Julie is silent, perhaps contemplative of the peace she has found. She hands me a towel and turns to head back to the yurt/tepee.

From my screen window, I can see the sky becoming black, layer by layer. I take a shower and listen to the silence of non-existent highways and tropical bird calls I cannot identify. I feel the cold water saturate my hair and I imagine I am under a waterfall.

When I return to the tepee, I realize I must be late for meditation. The pillows are set in a circle and Julie, Theresa, Rain, and an older man are all sitting cross-legged. I suppose they are too deep into their meditation to notice my presence. But as I sit down at the one empty pillow across from Julie, I notice that everyone has their eyes open. Julie's eyes bulge out at me. I look back at her, but she looks straight through me. I turn around but there's nothing back there but the table and beyond that the omnipresence of the ocean. Calm, I remind myself. Beside me, Theresa sits shaping the outline of some sort of genie bottle. Her hands move as if under the direction of some master puppeteer. I close my eyes and time passes. In the way I'm often able to feel the sun burn into my eyelids on a hot day at the beach, I can feel it disappear even with my eyes closed.

At some point after the sunset, I can hear motion. I open my eyes and see the man, who introduces himself to me as Theresa's husband, Leonard, carrying lit candles to the dining room table.

Julie and Theresa bring out the food. During dinner, I can barely see. But still the taste awakens everything in me. There are garlic and spices and textures so smooth I cannot define them. The tea tastes of lemon, but also it's unfamiliar. I feel as is if we have just moved the meditation to the dining room table. As much as I'd like to ask what I'm eating, no one speaks during dinner and there's just the crunch of vegetables and an occasional spray from the evening storm. I concentrate so much on silence I nearly choke. I start coughing at one point but quickly swallow the tea which burns away the cough. We finish eating in silence, and Leonard begins clearing the table.

Time for eco-dinner arrived, so I was sat amongst the extended family on the porch with nothing more to fortify me than some watered-down guava juice. Gordon started on a monologue, and his two spotty kids would nod eagerly at each juicy fact. It was like staying with the Flanders family from The Simpsons. "Do you know what we're eating tonight?" Gordon asked the table.

"Yucca!" chirped one urchin.

"The staple food of…?"

"The ancient Maya!"

"And of course the modern Maya," Jilly corrected firmly. "They are the same people."

"Tony," Gordon turned to me. "Do you know how the Maya grind the yucca?"

"No, Gordon. Can't say that I do." He was in the process of explaining in graphic detail when a toxic stench wafted over us. "Skunk!" squealed one urchin.

"This *never* usually happens," Gordon assured me, as the table broke up in chaos. It was a brilliant opportunity to escape.

—Tony Perrottet, "Belize It or Not," *Escape*

"Whoa, dinner was powerful," Rain says to me. "A lot of energy, huh?"

That night I fall asleep to the hum of crickets and the mixing of storm and ocean water. I dream a fantastical dream of how my life will be here in December. I will wake early in the mornings, maybe when the sun comes up and enters my unshaded windows and I will go swimming in the ocean. In the afternoons, I'll help cook and serve meals at the vegetarian restaurant where I'll meet beautiful, intellectual, well-adjusted travelers. We'll share stories and have deep conversations. Before sunset, I'll go running along the dirt road. Then I'll hike to the waterfall. At dinner, I'll talk with Theresa and Leonard about my daily realizations and they'll share theirs with me. In the evenings, with a sense of passion and inspiration I had not known before, I'll write the book I've been carrying around in my head.

Although I went to sleep early and had been excited to see the sunrise, I am still in my dream world when Julie knocks on my door at 4:30 the next morning. "It's time for meditation," she says, pressing her face against the screen window.

"Uh, O.K.," I say, but drift off again. Ten minutes later there is another knock at my door.

"Lea, we're starting in fifteen minutes."

I pull myself up and tell her I'm coming.

Sometimes it is not until you wake up somewhere that you realize you really are there. So much in life is fleeting, vivid moments receding and vying for position in that overcrowded space, that dark corner of the mind where memories are stored and become foggy, that it often takes the disorientation of a morning in a foreign place for you to see the nature of where you are. The first thing that hits me when I wake this morning is the heat. It's so hot I don't even have to move for my pores to release sweat. Just being awake is enough. Even things I hadn't considered to be alive are sweating. I reach to put on a ring and necklace and they are as slimy as if I have fished them off the ocean floor.

I open my door. In the distance, the scenery looks artificial, almost man-made—the rocks farther out looking more like gray slabs of cement than the towering foam-covered ocean cliffs they reveal themselves to be up close. Meditation this morning is much the same as it was the night before except that, knowing what to expect, I close my eyes from the start to avoid the bulging-eye stare of Julie. I drift back into sleep and wake to the feel of sun on my eyelids and see that everyone else is at the breakfast table. The rules for behavior after morning meditation are different, I learn. Julie is holding a copy of *The Celestine Prophecy* and Leonard is responding, "Yes, I feel that."

"We didn't want to disturb you," Julie says to me. "We could see how heavily you were into the meditation."

After breakfast, I ask Theresa about writing an article on Cabañas Tranquilas for the newspaper I'm interning with.

"Well," she hesitates. "Not many people can fully understand what we're about. They can only see the surface. I'm doing tai chi this afternoon. Why don't you come join me, see what that's like, and we can talk more."

Julie tells me she'll give me a tour of the land and we can pick the food for the evening meal. Since there is no electricity or refrigeration, only a propane stove, the food is picked daily. This morning Julie seems to be in a better mood, more talkative and excited to have someone accompanying her on her daily gathering route. Right outside the house she picks a tall strand of grass and hands it to me. "Smell."

It is the lemon scent of our tea.

"Lemon grass," she says.

And as we walk through the ten acres that comprise Cabañas Tranquilas, like a child showing off her toys to a new friend, Julie opens up to me and rushes through the jungle in her knee-high rubber boots. I follow behind in my sandals and knee-high coating of red mud, amazed at the beauty and sustainability of this land.

The first cabin we visit has a loft with a bamboo ladder. Julie climbs up it and motions for me to follow. Reaching this mini-second story, I feel like Jack in *Jack and the Beanstalk* when he climbs above the clouds and discovers the giant's world. I can see the other seven cabins of Cabañas Tranquilas and the Pacific extends out from the jungle below, filling in the landscape like a half moon.

Julie lies back on a mattress. "Sometimes when there's no one staying here, I'll come up here to sleep at night," she says. "Or sometimes even in the day, just to think."

"That sounds nice, very peaceful," I tell her. "Where do you usually sleep, though?"

"Oh, now I have a cabin, but when the tourists come, I'll have to move, maybe to the meditation area or just a mattress in the kitchen."

"Does it bother you to not have privacy, your own place though?" I ask.

"What?" Julie seems disturbed, as if I've pulled her out of some deep revelation. "No, that's why I came here. To give up all those material notions of possession."

"Oh, right." I lie back down and just focus on the view. A bird cries out and I see a flutter of leaves on a nearby palm.

"A toucan," Julie says.

But this toucan is black. It looks nothing like Toucan Sam I've become so familiar with from Saturday morning cartoon commercials of my youth.

"Some species are black," Julie says. "But they call out to each other in the same way."

Descending the muddy hill, Julie points across the dirt road. "This was just built when we started up and on the other side is all the uninvaded jungle and waterfalls."

We cross the road in silence. I wonder, in one day how many cars traverse the road, if there's a Guinness World Record for the least traveled road, at what point solitude becomes loneliness, and when and how you cross back over.

In the jungle, I am amazed as Julie reaches up to pick nearly every fruit we pass and puts them in her cloth bag. There are papayas the size of watermelons, mangoes a tie-dye of pink, yellow, and brown, clusters of bananas so soft and ripe they break at the stem, falling into my hands when I touch them. Pineapples sitting awkwardly on short, palm-like trees are revealed like the center of a flower when its petals open to the sun.

Pink guava oil perfumes the air and the thump of falling coconuts echo my footsteps. And then there are fruits Julie must explain to me—a dried brown, shriveled football-looking one which is cacao. The insides, mashed with brown sugar, make chocolate. There is a Venus' flytrap-type plant which closes when you tickle the whiskers on its leaves, and then there is the waterfall, towering above and hushing out the chaos of the jungle.

"If you want, after we prepare dinner, you can come back here for a swim," Julie says.

The thought is so appealing I'm lost for words.

She laughs at my silence. "This is what life could be like if you lived here."

I know. This is a feeling I've been waiting for.

On the way back, I ask Julie how long she's been here. Her eyes bug out more. "Me? How long have I been here?" She looks toward the ocean as if I might have directed my question to it.

"Years," she says. "I've lost track, I guess."

Before dinner, I go to Theresa's cabin for tai chi. I've never done it before, and have trouble balancing myself.

"This is good to redirect your energy," Theresa says. "It forces you to focus on the moment. It's how life is supposed to be lived."

I hold my breath trying to maintain a semblance of balance.

"Don't you agree?" Theresa asks.

"Oh, yeah. It's good to slow down."

"Well not everyone understands. In life, there's not such a great separation between the physical and emotional as people would like to believe," Theresa says bending forward to touch her toes while one leg remains suspended in the air behind her.

I try to imitate but fail terribly, tumbling onto the wooden floor.

"Physical balance," Theresa says, "is directly related to emotional balance."

*

One hour and several bruises and scrapes later, I return to my cabin and change into a swimming suit. Even this close to evening, the ocean is warm. It is calm, no crashing waves, and it laps at my body in softness. I swim out to a certain point and watch its physical location in relation to anything else disappear. I am about to swim back to shore for the evening meditation but realize I don't want to. Since I've been here, I have seen both sunsets and sunrises through closed eyes and, on my last night here, I want to fully experience the sunset. It is eerie to be in the middle of the ocean when the sun disappears, taking all landscape and sense of location with it, leaving me with just myself.

For a brief moment, I am overtaken by panic, afraid I will not find my way back to shore. I think of the meditations and Theresa's bizarre arm movements and wish for a similar spell to ground myself, to move me back into the familiar. But out here there is no New Age philosophy to save me. I think I can't hold myself afloat much longer. But I do somehow.

Somehow I feel the waves and figure out which way is land. Somehow, on my own, I find my way back, feeling more refreshed than I have from any of the meditations. I arrive just in time for dinner. Leonard is sitting on the floor stretching as the others are bringing out food.

"Where were you?" he asks.

"Oh, I was enjoying the sunset. Very calming."

"Well, you've missed the entire meditation."

"I know. You weren't waiting for me, were you? Because..."

Leonard shushes me with his index finger to his lips. "No, we weren't waiting. Can't you feel the energy?" he asks, swirling his hands above his head.

"Well, no…"

"You can't? Sit down. Do you feel it now?"

"No, but well maybe it's because I wasn't here during the meditation."

"And why was that?"

"Why wasn't I here?"

"Yes, what else could I be asking?"

"Well, I wanted to see the sunset."

"No, see you're not on the right wavelength. If you want to be here, you have to get into this understanding. Have you read *The Celestine Prophecy*?"

"No."

"Well, it explains the subconscious. How if we focus in on it, we can all share the same energy. Others don't understand. They rush through their lives trying to grasp at meaning wherever they can. I've learned to tune into the real truth. It's about being one with your other body, blocking out the voices, letting life happen, understanding the history of your many souls speaking to you, purification through visualization."

"Do you feel a different energy depending on who you meditate with?"

"Why are you asking me that?" Leonard asks, picking up a candle and holding it close to my face. "Are you with them or us?" A flash of lightning, signifying the start of the evening rains, illuminates his face and gives context to the background.

Then like in a horror movie, it ends and everything goes into blackness. The candlelight flickers with a breeze but does not go out. It makes Leonard's face move in weird, distorted wavy motions when he speaks.

"Dad," I hear Rain's voice behind me but am afraid to turn. "It's time for dinner."

"I know," Leonard says. "But I'm having a discussion with Lea."

Turning back to me he says, "I asked you that because I'm not talking about energy now so I don't understand where that question came from."

"Well…"

"We are obviously on different wavelengths," he says and, sighing deeply, stands up and walks over to the dinner table. The candle flame wavers and blows out as if to accentuate his exit.

After another silent dinner, I walk through the rain to my cabin and think how I had come here hoping for some sort of epiphany, the type the Native Americans created in their vision quests by fast-ing until they hallucinated. I was looking for inner peace externally, and I didn't find it. And it's with less disappointment than I'd expected to feel that I realized I could not live here. The type of clarity I've been searching for would never come from community conformism.

I have trouble falling asleep. Too close to the reality of this place, I'm unable to enter back into my dreams of the past night. But I understand that the dreams will continue, whether or not they pan out. Just being able to envision them enables me to venture off to places I would have otherwise considered to be outside the realm of my reality. These fantastical images of the future are what brought me to Costa Rica in the first place. They're what carried me along the potholed dirt road to this nameless town and the beauty of nearly untouched jungle. And they will follow me onto the bus tomorrow as I wave goodbye to everyone at Cabañas Tranquilas.

Lea Aschkenas is a freelance writer based in Northern California. Her writing has appeared in Salon.com, Outside Magazine, *the* Washington Post, *and the collections* Two in the Wild, Travelers' Tales Cuba, *and* The Unsavvy Traveler. *She is currently working on a book on Cuba.*

CARA TABACHNICK

The Rainbow Special

What's in that soup?

It had been three months since I'd washed my hair, two months since my underwear got stolen off the laundry line, and six days since I last changed my outfit, so I felt sufficiently ready to attend my first Rainbow Gathering/Full Moon Party. It was to take place on the shores of Lago Atitlán in Guatemala. We were looking for Bob's tepee somewhere between San Pedro and Santiago. Because it was a favorite gringo hideout, it didn't take long to secure a boat at an astronomical price. As we approached the spot a giant tepee appeared with leaping figures dancing around, visible in the setting sun. Our friendly boatman's face quickly changed to disapproval.

"Gringos," he muttered as he paddled into the dock.

Appropriately insulted, my friend and I jumped out amid screams of "Sister, Sister, welcome!" Strange, I mused, I thought my sisters were back in the United States. Soon enough I realized this was the traditional way of greeting in Rainbow Land. Since I didn't have dreadlocks and couldn't name one communal van I'd lived in, I sat on the side watching the festivities.

It was nothing like I'd seen before, and I'd been in Central America a long time. About sixty people were dancing around to the beat of twenty people drumming, singing chants they all seemed to know. Some people were making out, others were spinning, and the rest were running around naked. Restless, I looked around for someone to make out with since naked running and spinning were out of the question.

That was when I was caught and enlisted to help the kitchen workers whip up a vegan dream for eighty hungry hippies. In a way I was glad; nothing makes me happier than slaving over an open fire at a party. There was a group of about eight of us and with our limited choices we dreamed up a menu of pasta. (I never said we were creative.) Then, as the saving grace, we added tortillas and hummus. Hippie Bob had an old-fashioned grinder attached to a piece of wood that served as the counter, preparation space, and table. I was assigned to the hummus. My team of three, including myself, got to work funneling garbanzo beans into the grinder. The conversation was quick and light with the usual traveler gab.

> Sunset Cafe is stuck on the lip of the lake, and it is one of several eating and drinking holes in "Pana" for travelers—American and European hippies, outdoor adventure types, Peace Corps workers, and even a few nefarious types peddling all sorts of "stuff." At this open air venture Drew ran into some other monolingual Brits and a few Aussies, and they argued and exchanged news flashes about home while deep in their cups. For several nights, after long hikes around the lake and launch rides on it, I absorbed this surreal quality to Guatemala, in my first real Guatemalan town, albeit primarily set up for expatriates and travelers. Vegetarian cafes, herbal stores, Buddhist enlightenment workshops.
>
> —Paul Haeder, "We Are All Refugees"

As the mound of light-brown mush expanded, the sounds from below grew louder. Someone had discovered an old sweat lodge and a fire was lit for a party sweat. People were preparing early for the event and had started stripping down, eager to enter. Our instructions were to have the meal ready after the completion of the communal sweat. Working away maniacally, adding some spices here, others there, the dinner was looking good. There was just one problem: the hummus. It was so dry and tasteless, that even I didn't want to keep on trying it. I tried to pass it off to someone else, but with no luck. My teammates had deserted me long ago for the greener pastures of naked bodies stuck together in one small room sweating together, so it was up to me.

What could I add to this? There was nothing except pasta. I considered it for a moment, then struck it off my list and at last in a burst of brilliant inspiration thought: water. Water is good. From childhood we are told to drink eight glasses a day. Water helps your skin, hair, and health, so I figured it could help my hummus. Now remember—we were in Central America where water isn't always the friend you know. There are two types of water: 1. Your best friend—Mr. Agua Pura (pure water). 2. Your worst enemy—Mr. Parasite-Filled Lake Water. Picking up the first jug I saw, I liberally drenched the food. Seconds later, Hippie Bob screamed across the way, "You didn't use the red jug did you, because that is the parasite-filled lake water!" Of course I did—what was he thinking, that I knew what I was doing? Everybody stared, shocked, the main staple of our dinner was now ruined and the animal-like sounds of hunger from below were growing more ominous.

"What should we do?" was the general worried question.

"Cook it!" came back the wise reply from the oldest and most experienced travelers in the group. So we did as told, and the hummus bubbled away merrily on the fire for about half an hour until the screams for food were unbearable. Dinner was served. As we approached the fire, varying travelers in a state of dress and undress were forming a large semi-circle around the glowing embers. All types of plates were brought out, from plastic ones that had seen their prime—to plastic bags and scooped out avocado peels.

Before eating, though, one last Rainbow tradition had to be performed—the meditation and thanks. We all held hands and against the background noise of drums, a flute, and a Tibetan meditation bowl, we started singing chants of thanks. Usually I don't believe in this crap, but I must say even I was moved by the beauty of the occasion. With a last "buen provecho," servers started walking around dishing out generous portions of the hummus, pasta, and tortillas. I didn't want to take the hummus, but then I decided if everybody went down I would too. Gingerly, I spooned the first bite into my mouth—and God it was good! From the murmurs I could tell other people were in agreement. Relaxing and flushed with my success, I began to truly enjoy the evening. I even tried playing the drums and made new friends. When I closed my eyes hours later enclosed in a fluffy sleeping bag, surrounded by unwashed hair including my own, my last thoughts were that I had done well.

Hours later the first groans of pain rose from the floor somewhere near me. Soon the groans got louder and were joined by others as people made their way outside to join the ranks squatting in the bushes. Instead of people dancing in the dawn, they were crouching on the lawn. My rhyming stopped as the pains began to seize me, and I soon became one of the many. It turns out that everyone in the gathering had gotten the travelers' fun and feared friend—giardia!

I had poisoned the peace-loving group. With daybreak the softer travelers snuck out for the easier comforts of flush toilets (myself included). As the tepee receded in the distance, I watched from a fetal position in the boat and made myself three promises: 1. I would always use bottled water for everything, including brushing my teeth; 2. I would never eat off the street again; 3. I would never cook for anyone I didn't want to poison.

These resolutions reached, I smiled, looking forward to my next gathering and the story this would make for my grandchildren. I never did follow any of those promises, though, and I try to poison people on a daily basis with my cooking, especially my immediate family.

Armed with her savings and a backpack, Cara Tabachnick spent two years traveling around the world and returned safe, sound, and a whole lot wiser. Born and raised on Long Island, New York, Cara currently lives in New York City where she concentrates on writing, art, helping other people, and just being a better person, which is the best lesson traveling can teach.

RANDY WAYNE WHITE

An Evening with Croc Poachers

Shortly after the U.S. invasion, some local operators look for opportunities.

WHEN IT COMES TO ECO ETHICS, I TAKE A REAR SEAT TO NO ONE—certainly not to reptile poachers. But Panama challenges ethics as naturally as it dismantles virtue, so, morally speaking, folding like a cheap tent not only is acceptable, it's a tradition. Even in these days after Manuel Noriega.

Panama is as fun as it is beautiful, no matter who's in charge, and all the invasions in the world aren't going to change that. The country's possibilities are varied and often strange. One minute you're roaming the streets of Panama City, hunting for Pepto-Bismol, the next minute you're in a dugout canoe with two strangers hunting crocodiles. It can happen. It happened to me.

On a Friday morning in Panama City, I purchased a small meat dish from a street vendor. The meat dish was still with me Friday afternoon, gurgling like an eighth-grade science project. It wasn't serious, nothing that required dipping into my drug reserve of Lomotil or Septra, but I still wanted some relief. Plus, I like Central American pharmacies. They're stimulating. They keep you on your toes, for one never knows what chemicals one will walk out with.

Typically, customers file up to a window and hand the pharmacist their needs written on a piece of paper—any paper will do, it doesn't have to be a prescription. Then the customer flies to a neighboring window, where he is given some medicine that has been wrapped in butcher's paper or sealed into a plastic vial. If the customer's Spanish is good, it's probably the medicine he wants. But if the customer's Spanish isn't good, the results can be interesting. Once I asked for time-released cold tablets and left with birth control pills instead. When I tried to exchange the pills, the pharmacist smiled diplomatically and passed me a brown paper sack. There were condoms in the sack. Communication became increasingly confused. So did the pharmacist. So did the people waiting in line behind me, most of whom seemed unconvinced that I needed a condom for every hour of the day.

But finding Pepto-Bismol was no challenge. I walked from my hotel past the Papal Nunciature where Noriega took refuge during the U.S. invasion, and turned east along shop fronts where security guards idled in the shadows, their automatic weapons slung like guitars. These omnipresent security guards were the only symptoms of unrest in Panama, which came as a surprise because I had been following U.S. newspaper and magazine

> Panama's image abroad is defined by the Panama Canal, which the United States formally handed over to Panama at the end of 1999. But the Isthmus of Panama is also a land bridge, linking North and South America. Oddly, the foreign powers that dominated the country—first Spain, then France, and then the United States—neglected to build a route that would open this land bridge to traffic. Today Panama has no highway or railroad running its entire length. The so-called Pan-American Highway, a hemispheric network of roads that includes our national highway system and those of other countries has only one missing link from end to end—in Panama's unruly 6,400-square-mile eastern border province of Darien.
>
> —Benjamin Ryder Howe, "The Forgotten Highway," *The Atlantic Monthly*

stories about the country. They had painted a lurid picture of a crime-crazed nation teetering on the ledge of anarchy; a place where all Americans were despised. Instead, I found a lively city nearly unmarked by the recent war, where people were unfailingly friendly. Indeed, recognizing me as an American, Panamanians often introduced themselves on the streets and wished me a pleasant stay.

As a result of the bad publicity, many Panamanians go way out of their way to be kind to visitors, particularly American visitors. Which is why I wasn't surprised, upon perusing the shelves of a nearby *farmacia*, to hear a pleasant voice behind me say, "If you got the craps, it's not the Panamanian water. They got good water here. But if you've got a hangover, it could be the Panamanian beer."

The man, whom I will call Ben, was an American expatriate in his late sixties who said he had come to Panama when life in Louisiana became too tame. "'Bout twenty years ago," he said, "and I wished I'd come about two wives and one prostate operation before that." Ben was in the *farmacia* with his partner Angel, a grinning Panamanian man. The t-shirt I was wearing had rallied their attention: Save The American Crocodile, Skin A Developer.

"Say—you really like crocodiles?" Ben wanted to know. Angel wanted to know, too, judging by the enthusiastic look on his face.

Sure, I told them. It wasn't my t-shirt—I'd borrowed it from a friend and had no plans of giving it back. But I liked crocs well enough, and was alone in the city and happy for the conversation.

Coincidentally, we moved off down the same aisle (they needed duct tape and bug spray) so the conversation continued.

Would I like to see some crocodiles? Some Panamanian crocodiles?

At first I thought they meant they could recommend a local zoo, but then I saw by their expressions that they meant something else. What, I wasn't sure, though Ben's questions, "You're not too sick to travel a little? You feel O.K. to do a little work? Can you *swim*?" piqued my interest.

Outside, they told me: The two of them were headed for a river about two hours' drive, and they could use another hand because they were going to catch crocodiles. The guy who was supposed to help hadn't shown. "Catch the crocs alive," Ben said. "Small ones.

Tape their mouths and put them in the back of the truck, that simple. It'll take most of the night."

It is always unwise to accept invitations from strangers, especially in a foreign land—and why I do it so regularly is anybody's guess. But what were the alternatives? Sit alone in my hotel room, listening to my stomach gurgle? Hang out in the hotel bar watching the U.S. pilots in their flight suits, faces still flushed from crossing the Caribbean at Mach II? I hate being alone in a hotel room, and I hate hotel bars, and exchanging these two bleak options for a night on a jungle river seemed worth the risk.

I squeezed into the truck cab with Ben and Angel—Angel drove—and we were nearly an hour out of Panama City before I knew for sure that I had fallen in with poachers. Before leaving Ben had assured me that Angel had a government permit for taking twenty crocs. They seemed proud of the permit, for they said they were going to sell to a nearby reptile farm that was strict about buying only legally captured animals.

"They're all strict these days," Ben said. "Everything's gotta be tagged. Everything's gotta have a permit. Even in Panama. Never thought I'd see the damn day."

I wouldn't have become suspicious, but the permit was mentioned so often that it clearly was a novelty—they were used to doing this work without permits, and now they were enjoying a night of respectability. Or were they? I wasn't so sure when I learned how fate and good fortune had brought the permit into Angel's hand.

"One thing about wars," Ben told me, "they tend to cause a lot of confusion."

I could only agree and wait for him to explain.

We were driving northwest on a lean asphalt trail that seemed to be guided by the jungle that dominated it; a great green presence, cool to the nose, that steered the highway through partitions of light and gloom; sheer walls of vine spotted with bright bursts of color: butterflies and iridescent blooms, and then fireflies as it got darker. I rode along, arm out the window, listening.

Finally, Ben said, "Another thing about wars is, government workers won't go anywhere near their buildings. If there's no war, you can't pry the lazy bastards out of their offices with a crowbar. But start dropping a few bombs, and they scurry. 'Fraid they're gonna get blowed up."

"*Sí*, true, true," agreed Angel, grinning, always grinning. "I go looking for a permit at the very bad time. Right during the war, but nobody in the permit office. They all hiding. So I give myself a permit. It's legal. I signed it myself."

Ben looked on in admiration. "Choppers flying all over the place looking for Noriega, but it was business as usual for ol' Angel there. He went into the municipal building looking for opportunity, and he come out with that permit for twenty crocs, plus a certificate that says he's a state-bonded plumber, and picked himself out a chauffeur's license to boot." Ben leaned across me to say to Angel, "And you don't even own a car. You shoulda got a liquor license! We could have done something with that. Wars don't happen along every day."

Thieves, I thought to myself. *Poachers and thieves*.

Ben leaned back and added, "But it's like I always say: If a person can't profit from adversity, he damn well deserves to suffer."

Suffering is a condition inevitably shared by all indigenous creatures, human and otherwise. The shape of the pyramid is well established, the lines of injury long ago formed. Just as all the invasions in the world won't diminish the beauty of Panama, all the Earth Days and hip eco-cartoons in the world won't dent a more compelling reality: To a community of hungry people, wildlife isn't a resource, it is table fare. To a community of poor, wildlife isn't a natural wonder, it is chattel to be eaten or sold. The same with rivers and rain forests. Photos of teary-eyed seals and gnawed rabbit legs aren't going to change that—nor should they be expected to. People have as much right to exist as otters and dolphins, and if the crunch was really on, even the most self-righteous would elbow their way toward the drilling fields. No one can argue that American groups now so passionate about animal rights are dominated by descendants of the same affluent class who pushed wading birds to extinction because they fancied egret feathers in their

Sunday hats; a group that once generated the same faddish enthusiasm for raccoon coats and safari shoots that members now display at Save the Whale rallies.

To people surviving on the precipice, criticism from the terminally trendy carries little validity and less weight. Modern times create modern ironies. Fifty years ago, "backward" nations were characterized by a dearth of industry but a wealth of natural resources. Today, many of those same nations have nibbled those assets to the nub, have sold their future piecemeal with as little foresight as stray dogs pissing on fire hydrants. In some places, now the crunch really is on.

On a trip through the rain forests of Sumatra, I was astonished by the realization that some of the most remote jungle rivers in the world had almost no fish, and none of size. Zero. America's worst industrial rivers supported more life. The river fisheries had withstood a thousand generations of netting, but they could not survive the combined assault of car batteries and hand-crank telephones that local people used to shock the fish, or the poisons locals used to stun them—nor the suffocating turbidity created by clear-cut logging. Confronted by such techniques, the fish were as helpless as rhinos and African elephants sprinting from machine guns.

The destructive—and just plain addlebrained—behavior of driven people is tragic enough, but when profiteering is added to the equation, the straits become desperate. But with all the new regulations worldwide and the manpower devoted to enforcement, it's getting tougher to make a living as a poacher.

Ben had said that—it's getting tougher. Which was why he and Angel were so pleased with the permit to capture and keep twenty American crocodiles (*Crocodylus acutus*), which is now one of the rarest reptiles in the Americas.

"You shoulda got a permit for a hundred," Ben said more than once. "This river where we're going, I can get you a hundred. Two hundred if you want. I haven't been there for about ten years, so they should be thick."

Prior to my visit, when I thought of Panama, I pictured the canal and the military bases, and not much else. I did not expect to find a biological wonder, a rich land of rain forest and jungle and remote rivers. But that's what Panama is. Ironically, though, Costa Rica and Belize attract far more tourists—which is good for those of us who prefer to make our own paths. In Panama, you can make a path easily enough once away from the city.

"Wait 'til you see this river," Ben kept telling me. "If you like wild places, you're going to love this river."

After more than two hours of driving, Angel turned onto a dirt road, past some concrete block houses, past some bamboo huts with thatched roofs, and Ben directed him to a clearing where he said a friend had hidden a boat for them.

The moon was up now, the night was clear with stars, and we found the boat in the moonlight, a long open *chalupa*, or dugout canoe, with a motor. We had to push and carry the boat more than a hundred yards from the road to the river, which is why they had recruited a stranger to help—the thing must have weighed four hundred pounds, and neither Ben nor Angel were young men.

"That was a regular hemorrhoid tester," Ben hooted when we finally got to the water. "Bastard's heavier than it was fifteen years ago, huh, Angel?"

Maybe so, but Angel was still grinning. And he kept grinning while he and I wrestled the hand-hewn hulk into the water.

Mosquitoes had found me, I was soaked with sweat—and Ben wasn't far wrong in his assessment regarding hemorrhoids. Even so, it was a pretty place. A nice night to be out. The river was a gray void in the moonlight, a narrow clearing that evaporated into the forest gloom. I could smell the rot of hardwood leaves, but there was a hint of mangrove, too; an odor of salt and sulfur, and I knew we were not far from the sea.

Ben steered. I sat on the wet floor in the middle of the *chalupa* and Angel took the bow, holding a long pole with a rope noose at the end. Ben had a spotlight, and he shined it high into the trees to preserve his night vision as we ran. The beam of light was like a column of yellow vapor through which giant moths and bats darted. Over the noise of the engine, Ben promised we'd see our first croc around the next bend, and he swung the light down the river bank.

There was a pair of amber eyes, but it was a mammal, not a reptile.

"Gato negro," Angel said over his shoulder. Black cat. But it wasn't a cat, it was a martenlike animal I had never see before. Ben followed it with the spotlight as it twisted off into the bushes.

"There'll be a croc around the next bend," Ben promised again.

But there wasn't. Nor did we find one in the next hour. But we found several sloths. We saw four or five peccaries. We saw more bats, and there was a moth that, with its wings open, looked just like the face of an owl.

"Someone musta hunted this place since the last time I was here," Ben admitted finally. "Cleaned the place out." But he knew a branch, he said, where there would certainly be crocs.

"We got a permit," he reminded us. "And we got all night."

Randy Wayne White is the author of the best-selling Doc Ford novels, and a contributing editor to Men's Journal *and* Outside *magazines. He was a skiff guide on Sanibel Island, Florida, for many years and now lives on Pine Island where he has given up fishing to play baseball. This story was excerpted from* The Sharks of Lake Nicaragua: True Tales of Adventure, Travel, and Fishing.

MARTIN MITCHINSON

Dancing for Centavos

Many years later he really did run off and join the circus.

WHEN I WAS A CHILD I DREAMED OF TALL SHIPS AND CIRCUSES. I ran over open fields, swung on ropes across ravines, and I told far too many lies.

Now in my mid-thirties, drifting along the coast of Honduras, I join a circus and can finally appreciate the wisdom of a child's dreams.

It is a poor circus, an open-air circus with scrap-lumber bleachers and torn tarps for walls. A circus with no tent to house the show, no truck of their own to move locations—only tin roofs over two-by-fours for sleeping, canvas flaps for privacy, pots of watery stew cooking over a wood fire, and an abundance of children wading about in the tall grass of a vacant lot.

I only just stumble upon the circus as I bicycle along the Caribbean coastal road. As a lone traveler with an open schedule, my trips seem to either thrive with vitality or die with a fizz and a trail of smoke. At the worst of times, I am overwhelmed with isolation and self-pity, secluding myself in some village pension and writing endless letters home describing my lonely, detached observations on local culture.

At the best of moments—those rare moments—I trip and stumble forward, falling through side doors, learning to revel with each unexpected detour until eventually I come to embrace discomfort as a motivator and a mode of transport.

"What would you think," I ask Renaldo, head of El Circo Emperador, "if a gringo wanted to join on and work with you for a while," proposing that I might photograph something of their shows and daily life.

Renaldo is thirty-eight. He's trim and strong and handsome in the manner of a gypsy. After my proposal he studies me with an expression of muted dismay, a lack of comprehension evident in his gaze, as if I were speaking in Hindi, or had committed some outlandish faux pas.

I wait. I consider rephrasing my broken-Spanish request, but instead I just wait.

"Explain to me again," says Renaldo after the pause. "Why would he—this gringo…" he asks, speaking slowly and looking straight into my eyes. "Why would he want to travel with us?"

I struggle with that. My Spanish falters; but in the end I tell a half lie that is likely almost truth, explaining that as a photographer and artist I want to document the lives and work of other artists. Renaldo accepts that as a valid reason. When he gathers the others together to ask their support, I can see them nod when he mentions, "well, he's an artist, like us."

El Circo Emperador is a family circus with thirty-five members—thirty of them relatives—mostly children, heavy women, a few old men, and Jenny the transsexual dancer. It is a world in a bubble, floating and bobbing from Nicaragua, through Honduras, into El Salvador and Guatemala. It is a string of 100-watt bulbs and a floodlit ring with a rotted picket fence in a region best known for poverty, desperation, and civil war.

"If we had a tent…" Doña Lydia starts to tell me. She is in her late fifties, and is queen of the circus, ruling from a rusted-steel bed frame and a straw-stuffed mattress. Her eyelids are puffy from the heat. Her words form slowly. "Yes, if we had a circus tent of good strong canvas…and a truck…"

Her voice trails off and she seems to have tired of the story, as if she has been saying these same words all her life. "With a truck and a tent…then we could move as we wished, and we could work every night, even in the rainy season."

But they don't have a tent, and a truck can't be imagined. Even the next meal is often a question.

"Renaldo is my oldest," Lydia tells me. "He isn't like my husband was. There aren't circus men like that anymore, but my son will find something for us. He always does. We always eat," she assures me.

On the Caribbean coast in May, when I'm sleeping on a cot in a dirt lot—even with a fan blowing directly on my body—I begin perspiring heavily by six in the morning. By ten A.M. I abandon any hope of appearing composed, and I follow along footpaths behind Renaldo. He looks like the Pied Piper with a trailing line of star-struck children carrying dirty laundry, pots and pans, and empty sacks. He fishes in private ponds, casting his net for fifteen minutes until a security guard threatens us with a machete.

"Get out of here, you whore," shouts the guard. "I told you last year to stay away."

Renaldo apologizes, as he has done many times before, and we file away with the sack full of fingerlings, wandering back to dirty rivers in the time of cholera. A dozen children trudge along behind, trying to skip and pirouette while dragging their bundles to a deeper bend in the stream. Our soft-focus lethargy

> The heat in northern Honduras was a tangible presence I organized the day around. I learned not to walk in the streets at noon when the sun radiated in waves off the tarmac like hot rocks in a sauna. I learned that if I took a cold shower, the only kind I had, just before eating, I could finish a meal without having to change my sweaty clothes. I learned I could make perfect yogurt on the kitchen counter, which stayed a uniform 105 degrees all day long.
>
> —Lani Wright, "Honduran Heat"

slips away to water fights, swimming lessons, and afternoon naps. The river water washes off the blanket of salt and dust, and the furnace heat. We welcome the breezes in the shade of a giant ceiba tree, washing pots and pans and clothes and diapers.

Renaldo slips back onto private property and scrambles up a knotted rope to steal mangos. He dances from branch to branch in a fifty-foot tree, dropping fruit while the children scramble to catch them in the folds of empty flour sacks.

In the late afternoon when we gather our belongings, there are a hundred pounds of mangos, and four watermelons to cut and sell at the nighttime show.

I'm not a clown by nature. I love laughter and good humor, and I've been known to hog the limelight; but slapstick overacting, oversized shoes, and a sponge nose have never been a natural part of my character.

"Yo no sabo nada," says Limonada, a third-generation clown, now approaching his fiftieth birthday. He patiently instructs me in the art of speaking like a gringo who knows very little Spanish—horrible accent, faulty grammar, and a certain expression of bewilderment when the clown teacher asks me questions in the classroom sketch.

"Yo no ***saaaaabo*** *nada,"* he repeats, emphasizing the grammatical errors and pronunciation. This should come naturally to me, but I've come to learn that there are some gaps that are difficult to bridge, subtleties that only a circus clown can discern; a true, natural-born, circus clown.

The mimicking, braying, and bellowing continues for another half-hour in his tent before he declares that I'm ready. I think I exhausted his effort. He has a hard time looking me in the eye.

Limonada is gruff and gnarled, and looks as if he were born in a cantina. He travels with four miniature dogs, and performs a rude marionette skit. He plays the roughhouse drunk in clown acts, and he stands on his head alone, swinging upside down on a low trapeze, his arms outstretched while drinking down a bottle of Coca-Cola, the bottle clenched between his lips and teeth. "God, that really hurts," he says to me as he leaves the ring, and the announcer asks the audience, "Is it in his head or in his stomach? Only the Great Limonada knows for sure."

Limonada joined Emperador earlier in the year to be with his son Sebastian, and his only grandson, now five months old. In the afternoon, the three generations sit in Sebastian's tent, a soap opera on the black-and-white television while they cut up sheets of pink and yellow foam, tacking pieces together with contact cement, and then drawing designs and faces with colored marking pens. In between acts at the evening show, they will parade along the bleachers, hawking goofy hats and foam clown puppets along with candies, watermelon slices, and stolen mangos. Every centavo earned is precious.

Not every member is so endearing. Sixty-four-year-old Salazar seems forever bitter.

"Such shit for food," he complains about the fish soup. "And we get paid a joke here. I could just leave this circus," he tells me, "leave these cheap assholes behind."

With his bowl of soup he walks off to the side to sit on a wooden box and stare out at the empty ring, stomach hanging over his trousers and rope belt. He won't leave. He's old. He's been with the Emperador since the days before they had bleachers and tarps and a ticket booth, since the time when they would arrive in a town and knock on doors to rent a living room. Three clowns, a juggler, and Doña Lydia the dancer.

I wonder if it was all about art in those days.

On most afternoons, Salazar passes away the hottest part of the day in his tent room filled with boxes and wood-crate furniture. He wears a pair of bikini underwear and sits on the dirt floor—a whiskered man with cards in his hands, beads of perspiration rolling slowly down his sagging breasts and over his stomach. He plays poker in the shade of his tent cheating those precious centavos from the children, women, and fellow clowns. He isn't well liked, and in the late afternoon he paints his face alone in his tent and waits for the event to begin.

I love the build-up to an evening show. Crackled voices blare from the pole-top speakers, Renaldo's taped message shouting away in a static madness: "Dancing Women! Clowns and Laughs! Tingo the Bird Man Defies Gravity! The Giant Clown, Twenty-Two Feet Tall!" announces Renaldo's amplified voice. "Only ten minutes till show time! Get your ticket and move inside!"

I love the flow of people arriving, the bleachers filling with unruly children, drunks, and local machos with their shirts unbuttoned and chests stuck out, whistling and catcalling at passing women. And I feel for the penniless boys trying to slide past the barbed wire fence, past the security boys armed with wooden clubs.

My role in the evening is minimal. They pay me a little more than a dollar a night, along with three square meals, to speak Spanish like a gringo, and then beat upon me with a wooden paddle while we dance around the ring. The remainder of the show I run around with my cameras trying to capture the performance and the life around the ring.

I climb up a rickety ladder with the Bird Man when he dives out on the trapeze lines, the crowd gasping as Tingo releases and flies through the floodlit night, relying on a net that is so disgustingly narrow, so obviously short, that Edwin stands at the end trying to align a "rebound rope" in readiness for a mishap.

I lie on my belly and shoot upward with a wide-angle lens as the seven-meter clown performs shaky dances on two-by-four legs overhead. And only once do I fire a flash photo when Alberto throws knives at an audience volunteer. "No problem," insists Alberto when I ask if he minds. But I can hardly stand to watch while he humbles the drunken macho standing spread-eagled against the backstop.

A lesson learned: Never swagger and attempt to steal the show from your knife thrower. He demands respect.

The first two knives slam into the backstop on either side of the man's head; then one beside his waist; one below his crotch, and then another again even closer to his crotch—just to let him know.

As that final act comes to a close, boys run shouting and wrestling into the vacant ring, the bleachers empty, and friends leave laughing, arm in arm. The evening humidity passes into a nighttime shower, muffling voices, and dampening the dancing torches and paste-on glitter. The children roll up the tarps and unplug floodlight cords. A tide of heaviness descends on this dirt-lot world gone suddenly quiet. All that remains are paint-streaked faces, frilled costumes of shiny beads, and a tiny whisper of madness.

Renaldo's woman, the mother of his youngest child, runs through the blackness, tripping over ropes and pegs, screaming and crying, hiding in the darkness under the wash table until Renaldo approaches, coaxing her, pleading with her, then locking his hands with hers and slowly pulling her out from below.

His face is still half painted, and his tears mix with rain. He bands his arms around her body, absorbing her kicks and blows, holding her tight to his chest, speaking her name until she quiets her rage to heavy sobs, letting him carry her limp body across the camp, back to the privacy of canvas walls, so that only shadows and forms are seen.

I'm alone at that moment. Others look out from their doorways. Knowing glances pass from one to another before they slip back behind tarp flaps, into that precious sleep that will bring them into yet another day. I'm alone.

Only Limonada, the tough one, is still outside. His posture tells me that he knows that sometimes the clown has the saddest life.

"I'm fine," he says quietly. "I'm fine."

On those nights after the circus closes down, when he stands under the streetlight on a muddy road—baggy sweatpants and an open shirt—his eyes look sad and lost, a heavy weight pulling his shoulders down.

"I'm fine," he says again. And time slips away through the haze of heat and humidity, between the dust and the mud, the fleas in the mattresses, and the holes in tin roofing. And I know that this will never be my home.

Six months later at my home in northern Canada, the temperature has dropped to below zero degrees. We sit around the wood stove, and it's wonderful to be with family again. In some ways it was only half of a journey. My father hates to hear that when they asked me to stay on long-term and learn the trapeze,

I had to wait three or four days before I could decide to decline the offer.

On the twenty-third of December, surrounded by a world of snow and ice, of family and friends, I feel nothing but elation when the telephone rings with a collect call from Renaldo, the static hissing and pops like a worn vinyl LP of your favorite music. We shout back and forth to be heard and exchange greetings and wishes from two separate worlds until the line goes dead, as it invariably does in Honduras. But for that briefest moment I can smell and taste and hear all of El Emperador. I can see the children playing, the heavyset women dancing, Jenny's warm smile, and a tent full of Latin clowns trying to teach me to speak like a gringo.

Martin Mitchinson has traveled extensively for the past fifteen years, concentrating much of his time in Latin America while working on writing and photography projects. Currently he splits his time between his mountain home in southern British Columbia and a transient base aboard his thirty-six-foot sailing vessel Ishmael. *He also contributed "I Hear Voices" in Part IV.*

JOSEPH DIEDRICH

The Lady Who Lassoed Jaguars

An unusual opportunity comes and goes.

IN PAST YEARS, THE WAY THAT GOVERNMENT WORKED IN MOST OF the little countries of Central America was for one gang to get in power and then steal absolutely everything that wasn't nailed down. What was nailed down they passed laws to take and expropriated.

After a while, if they managed to stay in power long enough, it worked fairly well. The currency was solid, the streets were safe, nobody was running around shooting people, and after they had stolen everything that they could steal and had found out how nice it was to be on top, the gang in charge would begin to worry about staying there and do a few things to keep the common folk contented. Those who weren't content, at least those who weren't content and tried to do something about it, had a way of disappearing.

The trouble with Guatemala was that nobody seemed to be able to stay on top long enough to calm down. When one gang would take over they barely had the time to shoot the required number of people and to send whatever was left in the treasury to their Swiss bank accounts before another gang picked up their machine guns and machetes and chased them out. The various gangs had various names: Liberals, Conservatives, Communists, the Army, even a faction who claimed to be Protestants, but they all were essentially the same. They all wanted to muscle in on the act.

The only thing which never changed was that the native Indians, who were the majority of the population and who only wanted to be able to live in their villages in the hills and be left alone, always took it in the neck. One gang would come into their village and threaten to shoot them if they didn't help them and then the other gang would come into their village and shoot them for having done so.

Despite this, I liked the place. It was Pan Am's hub in Central America and I was there quite a bit. When they weren't having a shoot-em-up around the Presidential Palace, Guatemala City was nice. The people were sort of laid back about things. There was a little man with a sidewalk stand near the main plaza who sold nothing but patches to put over bullet holes in plate glass windows. He did a good business.

When they did have a shoot-em-up, teenage peasants in lumpy army uniforms would appear on the streets, nervously fingering the triggers of machine guns. Then you stayed inside for a while.

I was stuck in Guatemala on one of those days. Everyone had seen this revolution coming and stayed away. Even Pan Am had heard about it and rerouted its passenger flights. My cargo flight had been told to land anyway. We had a lot of fun getting into town from the airport and there wasn't any chance that we could get back for another day, at least. In Guatemalan revolutions they were quite prompt about shooting the guys who lost. Things were usually back to normal in a day or two.

I was the copilot. The captain of my flight was a religious fanatic, the first officer seemed to have sleeping sickness, there weren't any stewardesses on cargo flights, and the streets were dangerous. Somehow, I lasted until late afternoon before I headed for the hotel bar, a dimly lit old-fashioned place that smelled pleasantly of limes and rum. There was one other customer, a girl sitting on a stool at the far end of the bar. The bartender was standing there too so I walked over and sat down one stool away. The girl watched me as I ordered my drink.

"Do y'all mind if I talk to you?" she asked. Her accent was from Texas, I thought.

"Please do," I answered, turning toward her to get a better look. She was quite pretty in a sort of Country and Western way; small, slender, blonde hair cut short, no makeup that you could notice. She wore a cowgirl outfit and Texas boots.

"Kin I set next to you?" she asked.

Before I could agree she had moved over, sliding her drink along the bar. Then she picked it up with both hands and downed most of it in one gulp. Her hands were shaking and her fingernails were bitten down to nothing. She set the drink down and drummed her fingers on the bar. I remember thinking that I had never seen anyone so on edge in my life.

She saw me looking at her hands. "I'm sorry I'm so damned nervous," she said. "I only git this way afterwards."

"Afterwards?"

"After I've caught my cats. I'm never nervous while I'm doing it."

"I don't understand," I said.

"Oh shoot. Course not. How could you?" She gave me a pretty smile. "What I do is I fly down here from Los Angeles in a little Beechcraft I own and I catch jaguars in the jungle with lassos and then I fly 'em back to Los Angeles."

"You catch jaguars in the jungle with a lasso and then you fly them back to Los Angeles in a Beechcraft?"

"Uh huh. I kin only take two, though, 'cause the plane's so little."

"Live jaguars?"

"Sure live. Lassoing don't hurt them none."

I thought about it and figured what the hell? "I can see why that might make you nervous," I agreed.

"Well it surely does and I'll admit it," she said, smiling at me again. A very friendly smile. "Now let's have another drink. I'll buy." And she did.

This time she picked up her drink with only one hand. The other hand she put on my thigh. And squeezed. Her hand was surprisingly strong.

"It sure does make me nervous," she said again. "And I surely hate being like this. There's only one good way I kin get over it."

"What's that?" I asked, thinking that I already knew the

answer. The hand on my thigh was moving north.

"Makin' love ever' way that I can for just as long as I can." The hand that had been on my thigh had now reached its destination. Happily, it was being considerably more gentle.

There are times when I handle things pretty well, I think, and there are times when I don't. This was one of those. The bartender, who spoke English well enough to understand exactly what was going on, was watching in fascination, not even pretending not to eavesdrop.

I wondered if she could be some sort of escaped lunatic, but I was nearing the point of not caring. Lassoing jaguars wasn't her only talent. The hand was now displaying real virtuosity. I knew that I had to say something, but I couldn't decide what.

"Come on up to my room with me," she asked before I could. "Please. I really need it bad."

Part of me wanted to go ahead with it—by this time it wanted to very much indeed—but the rational part of me wanted to think things over when I wasn't under pressure. Gently, reluctantly, I took the hand away. As soon as I could, I stood up.

The jaguar was a god to the ancient Maya, and today's Maya still revere this mysterious, elegant creature. When this story was written, jaguars were still being hunted, but today the world's third largest cat species is endangered throughout its range. The world's only jaguar sanctuary is located in southern Belize, a 150-square-mile area of tropical forest that is home to some 200 jaguars, the highest concentration anywhere in the world. The Cockscomb Basin Wildlife Sanctuary was created through the efforts of individuals and local and international conservation organizations. It was first established as a forest preserve in 1984, then in 1986 a portion was set aside as a jaguar sanctuary, and in 1990 the sanctuary was expanded to include the entire park.

—LH & NP

"Sure," I said. "What's your room number? I'll go up to mine for a few minutes and then I'll come over." I never told her my room number. She hadn't even asked my name.

In my room, I debated what to do. How many times in your life does a pretty girl pick you up in a hotel bar, ask you up to her room to make love with her, and ask you please? Usually they ask you for two hundred dollars. Still, the whole thing seemed extremely strange. The cowgirl was certainly a neurotic and probably a nut.

Pilots are trained to be cautious. I stayed in my room and had room service that night. The next morning the shooting had stopped and we left for Miami.

In those days a bilious, pot-bellied, middle-aged Irishman who used to be a sports commentator had the most popular show on U.S. television. His name was Ed Sullivan, and his show was a mixture of a talk show and a variety show. People came on it who wanted to make it in show business or who wanted public exposure for one reason or another. Sullivan, who looked as if he had a perpetual hangover and probably did, wasn't very nice to his guests. To boot, he had the personality of a dead codfish.

I didn't like Ed Sullivan and I didn't like his show, but I had a girlfriend who did. She had other qualities which more than made up for her taste in television, so once in a while I found myself watching the thing. It was on the TV in my living room one evening about a month after I got back from Guatemala. I had gone into my kitchen to mix a drink.

"And what do you do for a living?" I heard Sullivan's voice ask.

"I fly down to Guatemala in a little Beechcraft that I own and catch jaguars in the jungle with lassos and fly them back to Los Angeles."

I ran back into my living room. There was the cowgirl on the *Ed Sullivan Show*, but this time she didn't look like a cowgirl. She was dressed in something expensive and she looked absolutely sensational. I watched, open-mouthed. She really did those things. She really caught wild jaguars with a lasso in the Guatemalan jungle and flew them to the U.S. trussed up in the back of her little plane. She didn't do it for a living, though. Her daddy was a real estate man from Texas who owned half of Southern California. She lassoed jaguars for the thrill of it, she said, and then she liked to relax afterwards.

I groaned and turned away.

"What's the matter with you? What happened?" my girlfriend demanded.

"Nothing," I replied, telling the miserable truth.

I have found as I get older that I can usually live with the memories of things that I have done that I should not have done. It is things that I did not do that keep me awake, sometimes, in the middle of the night.

Joseph Diedrich is a retired Pan Am pilot who spends his time sailing, trekking, and wandering to offbeat places, which are in ever-diminishing supply. He and his wife live in Mallorca, Spain.

VICTORIA SCHLESINGER

When Water Bends

The world of the spirits is close at hand.

I WOKE UP TO SUNLIGHT PUSHING THROUGH THE SLAT-BOARD cracks of my hotel room and falling in bars over my face and the red woven blanket pulled up under my chin. Climbing from bed, I looked out bleary-eyed onto the slow twisting Mopan River: a ribbon of reptilian green that skirts the line between Guatemala and Belize. It's a river so lazy you can't tell which way is upstream and which way is down. Morning vapor rose from the riverbanks and then dissipated. Those banks were tangible. They defined sides, while the thick, green vein of water between them seemed ambiguous—a corridor where the definite loosened into fluid. Situated on the Belize bank, I was just a stone's throw from the rest of Guatemala where I had spent the previous months. The water inched by, and I pondered the opposite shore from this new point of distance.

For the past few months I had lived in Tikal National Park and worked for a Guatemalan man named José, whose family owned one of the three hotels within the national park. I first met José during a short visit to Tikal with my mother. We pulled up to the hotel late in the evening; he greeted us at the front desk, and then helped carry our bags to our bungalow. He ended up joining us for dinner, and it wasn't until halfway through the meal that José let on that he oversaw the place for his parents. We joked and laughed about travel, Guatemala, the United States—he had gone to college there in the '70s. The next morning José offered to lead us on a walk through the Maya ruins. It was somewhere around Temple IV that he turned and asked if I'd be interested in helping him write a guidebook to the ruins of Tikal.

He'd been thinking about it for years, he said, but needed someone to get it down on paper for him. From my just-out-of-college perspective, it was an offer of a lifetime. At home I was pulling espresso shots for the already wound-up residents of Mill Valley, California, and looking desperately for any sort of writing job. I didn't stop to think about why José would choose to hire me—someone with little publishing experience who knew nothing about Guatemala. But while riding a bus toward the Belize border, after having worked with José for months, I was thinking about it a lot and grappling with what had rolled in all directions away from me.

I didn't know quite where I was going on that bus, all I knew was that I wanted to be near water. I wanted to watch it reflect sunlight, peer into its murky depths, see its currents slide over one another like layers of skin. When the bus reached the Belize boarder we all got off for Immigration, and there I noticed the Mopan River wending its way through the little town of Melchor de Mencos. I grabbed my bags and asked around for the nearest hotel.

That night, nestled in bed, frogs from the Mopan chorusing, I opened a book my mother had sent me. Over my life she's given me hundreds of books and probably thousands of clippings. Since that trip to the border I read everything she sends me, but previously, I just as often did not. This particular book, whose jacket cover I had not even glanced at, somehow made it into my bag. I began to read *Sastun: My Apprenticeship with a Maya Healer*. It was about a woman named Rosita Arvigo, an Italian-American from Chicago, who had spent the past several years studying medicinal plants with an old Maya healer in Belize. Looking at the map in the front of the book I realized that this woman was within twenty miles of my hotel. I fell asleep chanting, "I'm coming tomorrow, Rosita. I'm coming tomorrow, Rosita. I'm coming tomorrow…"

"Are you ready to go?" the hotel owner, a Swiss giant at six-foot-seven, hollered to me from his small office.

"Yes," I called, turning from my water musings and gathering my things.

He gave me a lift through town and down the empty, dusty road to Ix Chel Farms, and then left me waiting for Rosita in the shade of the visitor's gazebo. Travelers come to Ix Chel to hike the Rainforest Medicine Trail, learn about the healing properties of tropical plants, and buy small bottles of tinctures with names like Immune Boost, Belly Be Good, and Female Tonic. I wandered around the gazebo reading labels and the backs of books, unsure of what to do next, or if I was even in the right place.

Two men, local canoe guides, lolled on a bench under the gazebo waiting to paddle visitors to San Ignacio. They asked where I was from and what I was doing in Belize. I said I was taking a break from my writing in Tikal where I had been working with José. One of the guides began to laugh. "Oh man, those motherfuckers are crazy. Those boys are madmen." He was genuinely laughing and glancing at me through teary eyes. "They're my friends. I know them. I know them…and they are mad. Didn't turn out like their father wanted them to at all." He shook his head until his laughter settled into the occasional snort and a smile. The other guide, named Felice, asked if I was waiting for a ride. I said no.

"Are you sick?" he asked.

"No. It's, um, the other kind," I replied.

He nodded, then looked at me for a long while. "Does she know you are here? You're lucky you know, she's not usually here in the mornings." He stood up and walked out from under the gazebo and into the wall of jungle.

Rosita and others set up the Rainforest Medicine Trail and shop to support ethnobotanical research and the work of traditional healers, but her primary work continued to be as a healer to many people in the area. I knew my asking to see her was a little bit nervy.

After I waited about a half-hour and read the ingredients of all the tinctures, Rosita's assistant beckoned me from the gazebo and led me to a patio shrouded in greenery. I took a seat; the mounting heat and hum of the midday insects lulled me. My mind drifted back to one of my first days in Tikal.

I had waited, equipped with pens, paper, and tape recorder, on the porch of my bungalow, for José. We were going to begin interviewing, and he was going to tell me about his family, how his father had been the foreman of the excavations of the world famous Maya ruins and how they had lived in Tikal before there were roads. José grew up as mounds of jungle were stripped away, and the thousand-year-old ruins were exposed. He and his three brothers helped build bungalows for the archaeologists and catch lizards and tarantulas for the herpetologists and entomologists. Eventually I learned all of this, but not during that first interview. That day I waited twenty, thirty, forty minutes for José before he finally emerged from his bungalow and climbed up the steps onto my porch. His hair was wet, shining black. He gestured slightly toward the empty chair.

"Sit down, please," I said with a smile. He sat slowly and let go a low, wind-like sigh.

"You want to learn about spirits, Victoria?"

"Sure," I piped up, as if he'd just asked me if I wanted a piece of gum.

"Are you sure? Because they will meet you if you want. They are here. You may think you're just humoring me, but they are here. One just hit me, POW, hit me with its presence while I was in the shower." They came to him all the time, he said. Spirits came like a bat swinging and left him shaking for hours. As he began a story about a spirit that tormented his friend Miguel, he reached into a paper bag and pulled out two bottles of red wine.

Before I could introduce myself, or stand up for a handshake, Rosita strode onto the patio and said, "So, what's going on?" Black wiry hair twisted away from her face. She looked at me with steady, dark eyes. I was so relieved to be talking to someone, to an American woman, that without plan, the words and stories tumbled out, and I began describing the night in room 16A.

"We were in there waiting for spirits," I started. Everyone at the hotel in Tikal knew that a few spirits lived in the fringe bungalow 16A. Everyone knew. Except me, of course, who knew nothing at all about spirits other than that this guy who'd hired me to write a book had been talking about them since the day I arrived.

That night, just after the sun had gone down, we opened the door to Room 16A, which had the usual two beds, a dresser, and a bathroom. Tourists stayed there all the time. I wondered if they noticed any spirits. José was slowly walking the length of the room, looking up at the rafters. His eyes were wide open, and he explained in a low voice that he wanted to ask the spirits about the ancient Maya, that he was inviting them to come speak with us. We sat down on the beds to wait. I tried to relax but struggled between deep fascination and wanting to tell José to knock it off. At some point, I lay down and without realizing it, I fell asleep. I couldn't help it. My eyes and body felt as if they weighed thousands of pounds. As if I were at the bottom of the sea. I dreamt about being in that same room, in 16A, about lying on the double bed with its white, wind-dried sheets, and sleeping. José slept next to me, holding my hand. A spirit came to the foot of the bed and I woke up. It sort of gooed over me, pressing into every crevice. It was heavy and thick like congealed liquid. So heavy that I couldn't move or yell, although I tried.

José was right next to me and I yelled for him to wake up. He started to mumble, saying he understood what was happening. I dug my nails into his palm. He told me to stop. And then the spirit stopped its squeezing and pressing. It peeled back and was gone. We got up and left the room. I was annoyed at the spirit for thinking it could trap me. It seemed mean (dare I say spirited?) to prevent José and me from speaking. I did not feel threatened but confused, taken by surprise even. Sitting in the hotel's dining hall, I saw a friend from college. It made no sense at all... I woke up. I did not know what room I was in or what bed. José was not next to me. I felt like clear sky.

"José?"

"I'm right here." He answered from the next bed. Leaning forward with his forearms on his knees, he stared at me. "You haven't moved in a half-hour. They were here."

I glanced up at Rosita. I'd been playing with a bead on my bracelet, trying to center it perfectly between two other beads, as I told my story. Rosita simply nodded and listened. She didn't appear to think I was crazy, even if I thought I might be crazy. That was reassuring. It wasn't that I was closed to the idea of spirits and other worlds. It was that I was open. I was ready to embrace whatever the world threw at me. But these spirits, José's spirits, turned the back of my neck cold, made the thousands of hairs on my body prick to attention. I wanted nothing to do with them. I told Rosita about the guidebook, but that I didn't know if I could go back to Tikal. I was out of my league.

She shook her head and said that what people say about spirits being in Tikal, about the ruins being some sort of mecca, is crap. The Benevolent Spirits left when the archaeologists came. I had to agree. Telling me to wait there, Rosita stood up, and in two quick steps was off and absorbed by the green swirl of jungle. I looked at the palm fronds crowding to fill in the clearing around the patio and thought about the many hundreds of thousands of people who walked through Tikal in a year. During my time there, I had found only one quiet spot. It was the northernmost building in the park and part of Group H; getting there entailed a long walk through jungle. The first time I explored the temple I climbed up its steep stone steps and wandered into the three inner chambers. Some anthropologists say the rooms in the tops of temples were meant to replicate caves in the side of a mountain. Maya priests sat in these sacred rooms and let blood from their bodies, allowing it to collect in small fig tree paper bowls. They burned the blood mixed with leaves and copal resin, and as the smoke twisted and rose, a giant serpent emerged in front of the priests. The serpent's jaws split open and out leaned an ancestor, there to guide and counsel.

Inside the first chamber I found a handmade ladder propped against the wall, leading up to the roof. Rungs, fitted into crude notches on the frame, were bound with *botan* vine and wire. I placed hand above head, and climbed up the gray, dry wood onto the roof of the temple, which lay flush with the jungle canopy. I visited there most days during my stay in Tikal. On four occasions I watched a mother spider monkey, a baby clinging to her belly, feed on figs in a nearby tree. A mealy-headed parrot often roosted in some of the branches that leaned in toward my limestone perch. From up there I could look south and see the six temples of Tikal poking up through the green canopy. I could see the sun and moon for the split second of the day when they faced each other.

Rosita reappeared almost suddenly, as if the jungle had coughed her back up and landed her on the patio. She was laden with bundles of green plants and small packets. Into one of my hands she pressed a bundle of rue, the smell bitter and sharp. In the other hand she placed a bag of copal. Rue

I sat on the temple's summit [in the ruins of Yaxha, southeast of Tikal] without a thought for my friends. The sun set over the lake chain, a more continuous system of small creeks and ponds than I had seen on any map, sprawling to fill a shallow depression between low heights. Geography had preserved the ancient continuities.

To the east behind me, the headwaters of the Belize, Sarstoon, and Mojo rivers rose just out of sight, running to the Caribbean. The geographical and historical connection was as clear, unambiguous, and fated as the Champlain-Hudson corridor of home. The route followed the lakes directly below, visible from the temple for eight or ten miles. It was easy to imagine laceworks of canals and raised agricultural beds in the low-lying margins and intervening wetlands, and the creeks and wetlands, separating larger waters canalized for navigability, all visible from here.

—Christopher Shaw, *Sacred Monkey River*

is an herb with small, round, blue-green leaves that I had heard of time and again in Guatemala being used for calming the nerves.

"Give me your necklace," Rosita said. It was an uncut piece of jade about the size of a human eye. It was bound in thin silver wire and I wore it on a black cord around my neck. José had given me the stone. He kept a burlap sack, which probably weighed twenty pounds, full of jade stones of various sizes. Every night as he moved to a new bungalow, he brought the sack with him. José lived at the hotel, but had no room; he simply stayed in whichever one was unoccupied that night. Besides the jade, I think he kept a few boxes of clothes and a camera, all of which maids ferried daily from room to unoccupied room.

One evening we sat on the porch of his bungalow, talking, gazing at the black shapes of jungle. Lianas draped like rope between the tree crowns. Overhead cracks in the canopy opened onto leagues of night sky; more stars, it seemed, than space. José held the bag of jade on his lap and rummaged through it, sometimes picking out a piece and holding it up to the porch light.

"I am looking for your piece of jade, Victoria; the perfect piece. I'll know it when I see it, when it has the right light."

I began to examine the pieces he had set out, laying them in my palm, feeling the texture, thinking how different this jade was from anything I had ever seen. "I like this one," I smiled, holding the jade out.

He swiped the stone from my hand. "You cannot choose! This one is not right at all!" he barked.

Adrenaline ignited fires through my arms, stomach, the back of my skull. Icy silence. He flung the sack into the corner of the porch and slumped in his chair. My eyes focused on a hairline crack in the concrete floor. Suddenly, he blurted, "Can I borrow some film for my camera?"

I said of course and pulled several rolls out of my backpack for him to choose from. He leaned over and scooped all three out of my palm.

"I can feel them. They are here," he said and disappeared into his room. I sat on the porch and listened as he took photogragh after photograph.

I handed Rosita the jade pendant. She took the stone and began murmuring prayers in Spanish, speaking to the four directions. Nine times she repeated each prayer over the necklace. As she murmured I looked at the plastic bag full of copal in my hand. In Tikal I had seen copal trees oozing sap like thick tears. It was the same resin the Maya gathered to burn in their ceremonies. In the past they called it *itz*: an excretion of life, a medium through which the gods spoke.

Rosita finished saying the prayers and sat back. Her look into my eyes was unwavering as she gave me her instructions. She explained that copal smoke cleanses a person and can help protect them from a Malevolent Spirit. She said not to feel fear because it's what the Malevolent Spirits feed on, it's their door in. Sleeping with a fresh sprig of rue under my pillow and chewing on bits of it throughout the day would help keep me calm. The Benevolent Spirits never try to scare people. They only communicate in ways that won't frighten a person. I asked how exactly. She replied that they come in

> One day, out of the blue, Panti said, "It's time to do a *Primicia*, Rosita. I want to introduce you to the Maya Spirits."
>
> I was surprised and honored. The *Primicia* was an old Maya ritual that had all but faded from modern daily life. The purpose of the ceremony is to give thanks to, worship, and ask favors of the Nine Maya Spirits…and God.
>
> "People rarely honor the spirits anymore," continued Panti sadly as he stuffed the leaves in his sack. "They have no respect for the Lord of the cornfield. If you ask them to honor the Lord they will only laugh at you and say, 'What Lord of the cornfield? I'm the only lord here. I don't believe in your old Spirits, old man. We don't need them anymore.' But now look at the ugly corn they harvest and the droughts. They need the Spirits more than they know."
>
> —Rosita Arvigo with Nadine Epstein, *Sastun: My Apprenticeship with a Maya Healer*

lots of ways, but dreams are common. "Don't try to save José, as women have a tendency to do, Victoria. Of the nine Benevolent Spirits, five are female." She also warned me not to try to learn about the spirits with José, because he didn't know what he was doing. She said to go write the guidebook, that it was a good opportunity. Handing back my jade pendant, she smiled and wished me well.

That night, back at my borderside hotel room, I went for a walk along the river. I searched for a place to build a fire, but every piece of wood I found was wet and I couldn't get them to catch. I wanted to burn the copal.

As I began the walk back to my room, thinking that maybe I could just burn the resin in a dish and forget the rest, a slight spiral of smoke caught my eye. Near the edge of the river was a rock fire ring, with embers smoldering amid bits of trash—eggshells, cornhusks, pineapple cuttings. Scraping a few of the orange coals together, I poured a palm full of copal granules onto the mound. I crouched over my tiny offering and blew. Sweet smoke billowed and rose above me, clouds like round faces, swelling and falling. The bunch of rue was in my pocket. I took it out and placed a sprig of its lobed leaves under my tongue. My eyes watered at the earthy, almost bitter taste. I began to call silently into the smoke, letting it wash over me, asking for some sort of sign, some sort of map for crossing rivers.

Victoria Schlesinger is a freelance writer who believes that home is wherever pen, paper, and a nice, solid writing surface can be found. She has lived out many adventures in Central America and is the author of Animals and Plants of the Ancient Maya: A Guide.

PART FOUR

In the Shadows

JENNIFER K. HARBURY

Everardo

During the Guatemalan civil war,
a journalist meets her fate.

IT IS HARDLY A MATTER OF LOVE AT FIRST SIGHT, IS IT, EVERARDO? You think I am a CIA agent, and I, half-blinded in the sun, think you are an adolescent standing over there, almost frail-looking, in the shadows of the forest. We will laugh about this later on when we become inseparable, amused by the perils of first impressions. We will marvel at how our true selves, let alone our intertwined futures, could have been so invisible to each other. It is as if we passed each other by, oblivious, then turned around for a second instinctive glance, a glance that would fuse us together against all logic for the rest of our joint lives.

It all begins a few weeks earlier, when permission finally comes from the Guatemalan underground for me to climb the Tajumulco volcano and interview women combatants for my book. I am thrilled, for I have waited two years now to enter a combat zone, contenting myself instead with interviews in various safe houses and clandestine clinics scattered discreetly throughout the region. The stories and the people I encounter in these furtive meetings are quite extraordinary, but I must see the *frente* for myself. I must understand how it operates, who is up there, and why. I must see it with my own eyes or the book, for me, can never be valid. The comandancia has always deemed the trip too dangerous until now, for they will risk no foreign lives to chance skirmishes or ambush, but at last I receive the terse message, the small green light. I may spend thirty days in the Luis Ixmata *frente* of the Revolutionary Organization of the People in Arms [ORPA]. I should prepare to leave at once.

> The Guatemalan civil war was the longest armed conflict in Central America, lasting thirty-six years from 1960 until the signing of a peace accord on December 29, 1996. In the end some 200,000 Guatemalans were killed, 45,000 "disappeared," close to a million lost their homes, and some 400 villages were destroyed. The vast majority of the victims were indigenous people, leading some to call the war a campaign of genocide against the civilian population. The peace has been imperfect, with the government failing to comply with many of its commitments, including increased social spending, guaranteeing indigenous rights, and substantial funding for housing. Common crime has increased significantly, but at least the fighting has stopped.
>
> —LH & NP

I outfit myself carefully and in accordance with their instructions. All clothing must be dark green or black, including underwear, gloves, and scarves. Even the smallest item drying on a makeshift clothesline could be visible from the air and cause a bombing raid or aerial attack. I should take a lightweight pair of boots, the hollow rubber kind that I remember so well from my previous years in Guatemala, the kind that glide across the sucking mud holes like snowshoes across the mounding snow. The pack itself must be small and easy to run with. I should take a small plate and cup and a tin spoon, a sturdy flashlight with batteries large enough to last, but not the shiny metallic type. No more than two changes of clothes, but plenty of socks, the cheap nylon kind that dry quickly in the sun. A few toiletries, a dark sweater, and perhaps a few tins of food and a bit of chocolate for the compañeros. I add several thick notepads and extra pens, and after consulting with some friends in an underground clinic, I pack some hard candies, spices, and cartons of cigarettes. For my arrival in customs, I add some bright-flowered hippie-style skirts as camouflage. These I will leave at a friend's house once I'm safely across the border.

I stay quietly ensconced in a small room for a few days, receiving last-minute instructions on codes and maps. Then word comes that it is time to go, and a curly-haired youth with crooked teeth and a good smile appears with an aging car. We drive through the deepening shadows on a remote, ever-curving road for several hours, chatting pleasantly as if on the way to an afternoon tea instead of a dangerous rendezvous. I hold the map in my hands and we check off the kilometer points together and swap stories until we reach the fork in the road that signals we are ten minutes from contact. It is time to be serious now, very serious, and I follow his instructions to watch our rearview mirror without turning around. He slows slightly, for we are rather early, and precision in arrival could mean life or death. We both know well enough what happens to any person, foreign or otherwise, caught by the army while approaching the "subversivos." At the five-minute point, my friend tells me to put on my boots, and I take off the black cotton Chinese slippers I am wearing and quickly pull on the boots. At two minutes I put on the dark jacket. Then we roll down my window and watch for a villager carrying the correct bundles in the correct hand and wearing the shirt with certain designs on the sleeves. We find him almost immediately, strolling down the roadside with a relaxed gait. We slow, but he does not look up until I speak, reciting the lines I have been given. He turns his head cautiously toward us then, wary of my accent, and in the half-light I make out the open face of a villager with dark, intense Mayan eyes. They lock with mine for a moment, exchanging silent confirmation; then he recites his own coded lines and swiftly pulls open my door.

In a few seconds I am out of the car with my pack and he has me by the arm, pulling me into the heavy foliage and down a small rocky trail. We come to a large tree surrounded by enormous vines and shrubs that conceal us completely, and he quickly strips off his shirt and pants, revealing olive green fatigues beneath. Then he bends to retrieve a heavy rifle from the brush. We say nothing, but he communicates with his eyes that all is well and pulls a small walkie-talkie from a tangle of green vines, whispering several code words into it. There is a crackled response and a sudden clattering of boots; then four other compañeros appear in the shadows. They look quickly at me, evaluating my readiness, then give me welcoming hugs, calling me their sister and telling me that they are glad I have arrived safely. The older one scoops up my pack and moves on ahead of us to scout, and we stride off at a fast pace behind him. There is no time to waste, for we are deep within army territory. I worry some about the small huts in the distance, wondering if we are visible, but the others smile and tell me not to worry. These are the homes of friends.

For many hours we move at a half run through the darkened forest, skirting around open fields and jolting down steep, rocky paths. The young compañero just in front of me holds his flashlight pointed straight down so that the light skims the terrain about my feet. His fingers are positioned just over the bulb, keeping the pinpoint of light soft and dim. He and the others call to me in low voices to warn me of pitfalls and slippery spots, taking gentle hold of my wrists to help me over particularly bad terrain. Together we cross river after river, stepping across moss-covered stones in the cold rushing water. Inevitably I fall in, soaking my socks and the bottoms of my dark jeans, and end up wading across, smiling as they try desperately not to laugh. They cross so effortlessly, like gazelles, that my wild thrashing is preposterous to them, but they do not wish to hurt my feelings. Instead they help me wring out my socks and smooth my hair, murmuring words of encouragement. By late that night we know one another well enough that when I slip and splash we laugh out loud in unison. During our brief breaks, I learn that the sweet-faced one is named Daniel and that he has been in the mountains now for nearly fifteen years. The older, sturdy one is Abram. The three younger ones are Eloy, Carlos, and Antonio. Perhaps in their late teens, they are rosy-cheeked and playful in the cold shadows, but also wary. Their dark, ever-alert eyes, like those of so many villagers, suggest they are old beyond their years.

As the hours pass, I grow used to the rapid pace and catch my second wind. It is beautiful here, the sharp black outlines of the volcano etched against the night sky with its scattering of brilliant stars. A rich silence envelops us, for we are far from any sounds of roads or towns now. There is only the murmur of nearby streams and the rush of the wind through the thick branches above our heads. Carlos and Antonio take turns mimicking the coos and trills of wild birds to amuse me, and I notice that we have begun a difficult climb. When Daniel calls us to a halt, I look at my watch and find to my surprise that it is nearly two o'clock in the morning. We are out of the military's grim reach now, and it is time to rest. We are safe here.

Abram and Daniel throw some heavy canvas wraps on the ground and smooth them out, and we curl up together under yet another layer of canvas and lightweight blankets. Eloy takes the first sentry shift and the others quietly agree among themselves as to who will take the next turns, so that everyone will get some rest before dawn. Then we lie down to sleep, fully dressed, boots on, a neat pile of rifles within easy reach. They have learned the hard way always to be ready for surprise events. For a while I am wide awake, far too amazed by my new surroundings to fall asleep. But as I grow warmer beneath the covers, the exertion of the last few hours overtakes me. When I open my eyes again, it is dawn.

Daniel and Abram are already up and about and cooking some wild roots over a small fire. Later, they explain, it will not be safe, for the flames will be visible from the air. We must eat quickly now in the pale light and then move onward. Antonio hands me a small portion of the boiled roots and I chew them slowly, surprised by their sweet taste. More than anything I am thirsty, as if all the fluids had been sucked from my limbs the night before. The others seem to intuit this, for a tin of cold water mixed with powdered milk and sugar appears, and I drink it down gratefully.

Soon we are off again, the tarpaulins rolled neatly into Daniel's pack, the fire out, and the ashes scattered so as to leave no trace that we were ever here. Eloy takes a fallen pine branch and gently sweeps away the vague imprints that our bodies left on the ground as we slept. The others look quickly about for mislaid scraps of paper or other telltale signs. No clues can be left for random army scouts, no signs that this is a trail used by the compañeros. Such errors lead to ambush and certain death.

Today the hike is more difficult, for my legs have stiffened during the night and we are no longer running across the low, uneven ground of the coffee farms. Now we are climbing so sharply that I keep grasping for vines and rocks above my head to pull myself upward.

Even the flatter stretches are difficult, for the earth is soaked through with the daily rains and gives way under my stumbling feet. The trail is very narrow, and we skirt around and around the hairpin turns of the green mountainside. Carlos and Antonio hover close, ready to take my arm or hand if I totter too near the edge of the cliffs, and they banter back and forth with each other to distract me from the climb. Their voices are soft and somewhat singsong, with the birdlike accents of Mayan highlanders, and as I listen to them I realize that I am indeed back at last in Guatemala.

The thought makes me giddy. I have been miserably homesick for this land that I was not born in. With the faint light, the lush scenery is fully visible to me now, the enormous lily-like leaves covering the slopes below, together with the twists and turns of thick vines, wild shrubs and grasses, and short angular pines. The entire valley is incredibly green. As I gaze downward, I see the pale morning mist drifting slowly up the mountainside toward us from the dimly lit villages below. For me this is home. I cannot stay away.

Gradually the sun emerges, and although the winds continue to chill, I begin to grow wildly thirsty again. The compas stop frequently to give me sips of water, warning me not to drink too much. As we hike upward, the muscles above my knees begin to throb, and I curse myself for not thinking of running hills instead of distance in preparation for this trip. I am nearly forty now and irately note the changes in my once-sturdy body. Daniel and the others encourage me gently, promising that the upward climb will not last long, that soon a downward stretch will come. They are right, but the shift downhill does little to alleviate the pain growing throughout my legs, for the slopes are so sharp and jolting that my muscles are worked even harder by the descent. They know this, and soon a soft voice begins to reassure me that the downward part will not last long, that in just a bit we will be climbing again. And so they encourage and cajole me as we climb farther and farther up the cliffs of the volcano, stopping in shady clearings here and there for short rests and drinks of water. The younger ones have lost their initial shyness now and pull at my braids and tease and throw their arms about me, villager style, as if I were some long-lost cousin just arrived for a visit.

At last we reach the upper volcano ridge and cross a ravine. The trail becomes dangerously narrow now and a thick rope is bolted to one side of the cliff, with heavy knots for handgrips. We cross step by step, hanging on to the knotted rope, then climb through the last cluster of pine trees. Out of nowhere a sentry calls softly to us and Daniel waves his rifle and calls back the password, adding a joke in Mayan that provokes a smothered giggle from behind the screen of giant leaves and vines.

We walk a few more yards into the sunlight, and suddenly we are in a small clearing with a campfire and low wooden stools made of tree trunks. To one side is a small shelter with a well-camouflaged roof of interlaced pine branches and flimsy green and black sheets of plastic. Inside are cooking supplies, a clothesline hung with sundry socks and shirts, and small benches. A cold, clear stream encircles us just a few feet below and I see two young men on their knees down there, scrubbing their laundry on the rocks and splashing each other.

As my eyes adjust, a large, sturdy man hoots out a welcome and sweeps me off my feet, whirling me around. It is Marco, my friend from one of the underground houses so far from here. I interviewed him long ago when he was recovering from a bullet wound, and he made me roar with laughter and weep over the stories he told of his many years in the war. It is strange to see him now in uniform, his rifle slung easily over one shoulder, and I remember that he is second in command here, a man of responsibilities, despite his relaxed manner. I cling to him, happy and surprised to see him, and he sits me down on one of the tree stumps and hurries to bring me a pan of cold water. Daniel and the others tarry for a moment, then, quite untired by the climb, they move off to their different tasks of chopping wood, gathering water, and teaching reading and writing to the new combatants. Marco gives them their assignments in a quiet voice. Then he explains that many of the women I have come to interview are still away on a mission but will be back in a few days. Meanwhile, I can interview as many other compañeros here as I wish; he will make all of the arrangements. I must be very tired from the climb. Have I any blisters that need attention? Any torn muscles? Jorge, the doctor, will be returning this evening if I need anything. At night I will be staying with Emma, a sassy-faced woman bending over the cooking pot. She looks up and sends me a humorous smirk of welcome as he tells me this, and I immediately like her. Short and robust, she is in her thirties perhaps, with a shock of unruly black hair, bold eyes, and curved lips set at an impish angle. She is so roguish and at ease, I can't help smiling back.

Marco puts an arm around my shoulders and points out the different faint footpaths. That one leads to my tent, up there behind the boulders. Emma will show me which one later on and help me to set out my things. I mustn't unpack completely though, for up here one never knows what could happen; we must be ready to move quickly, even in the middle of the night. The trail over there leads to a small swimming hole for bathing. Up there is the communications post. I can always find one of the officers there if I need anything—Celia or Emma or Comandante Everardo. That's him, in fact, to the right at the edge of the trees. Marco points up the slope and I see a young man in olive green standing motionless in the shadows of the pines. He is neatly proportioned, with short, sturdy arms and legs, and he stands very straight with his rifle in hand. He waves politely as we look up at him, but his face, though intriguing, seems impossibly young. It is very wide at the cheekbones, with fierce black eyes and full vulnerable lips. His smooth gold-colored skin shows not a line or wrinkle. Surely I am looking at the wrong person. I glance about, searching for someone else back there in the shadows, someone older, more grayed and stooped under the weight of such responsibility. The young man watches us for a few moments, his head up and his eyes sharply alert, and I have the sense of being scanned and evaluated, read like a book. Then he turns and walks off into the forest with a silent, catlike gait, without so much as a backward glance.

And so it is, the first moment we meet, Everardo. You are wary and I am confused, looking for someone utterly different. But I remember this first glimpse of you, with your fierce eyes and lithe mountain walk, as clearly as if it were yesterday. I will remember it always. There is no detail about you, no fragmentary image, that I could ever forget. These memories, at least, the years cannot take from me.

Jennifer K. Harbury later married Everardo only to see him disappear in the ongoing Guatemalan civil war. After years of pressuring the U.S. and Guatemalan governments for information about Everardo—eventually by going on several hunger strikes—she moved U.S. Congressman Robert Torricelli to reveal that Everardo had been abducted and murdered by CIA-sponsored Guatemalan officials. Harbury is an attorney and human rights activist and the author of two books, Bridge of Courage *and* Searching for Everardo, *from which this story was excerpted.*

YAEL FLUSBERG

Deceptive Moonrise

Even in paradise, darkness resides.

YEARS LATER, A FRIEND TOLD ME THAT THE ISLAND HAD BECOME built up like the others. I preferred to keep it as it had been in my memories. Green. Abundant. A place with reggae in its crevices, where easy smiles were as full as the mangos that fell to the ground. Where the only tourists carried their homes on their backs, and each one of them had a story that made them more real than the people you had known your whole life. I can still feel the trade winds on my cheeks, and the sand between my toes. Yet, after my time on the island, I no longer had faith in the oasis. I could no longer believe that refugees ever found refuge any more than survivors wholly survived.

It was the first time I skipped winter. The first time I had even heard anyone talk about a moonrise, I knew that it was going to be as worthy of spectators as a match between the Brazilians and the Italians in the World Cup. It did not disappoint me. It rose slowly out of the Caribbean, taking half the horizon with it. I had never seen the moon look orange before, or the hue of yellow that followed its upward trajectory. Then again, I had never seen aquamarine waters that were clear in my hands, and deep blue beyond the reef.

From my front row seat, on an old but sturdy pier where the

boats arrived from Belize City daily, I thought of the other full moons I had seen in my life. Sitting on the tar roof of an abandoned punk club in Long Island City. Sneaking out of the Air Force barracks in Anacostia at three in the morning. Watching the night turn to day on a Roman ramp, deep in the Israeli desert.

Years would pass, and I would carry in my dreams the curve of that moonrise, the spell it cast me under. The light hitting earth from a Caribbean moonrise was more supple than anywhere else in the world. Brighter, but with a golden hue that softened its blow. The moon took on the warmth of the water, the rhythm of the people who watched it rise. In American cities, few people even notice the occurrence of a full moon; when they do, it's to joke about urban werewolves, to rationalize eccentricity and simple horniness. But there, on a tiny island off the Central American coast, life stood still before a moonrise. Grown men tried to restrain their excitement at the moon's forthcoming display and planned special rendezvous with her. Composed serenades. Choreographed poetic heartbreak. Some say the moonrise was spectacular precisely because of the sheer number of people who participated in the show. The lack of a good audience could sabotage even the most extravagant display of natural existence.

My whole life, I've shared a secret with the moon. I've understood that its power lay in its utter femininity, just as my strength stemmed from the waning and waxing of my life. Adapting to what is bestowed, as water does to the shape of a glass. To adapt is to survive, to invite courage into uncertainty. To be afraid of losing the self to which you have grown accustomed, but placing yourself in situations where you may well lose your old self anyway. I know from watching the moon that in the world of nature, there is an order against which resistance is fruitless. Yielding in this world is not submission. It's a recognition that there is a way to do nothing and get someplace at the same time.

When the moon rose, I silently watched how it lit up my companion's face as well as any bonfire. Lost in my thoughts, I had forgotten that he sat beside me, lost in his own reverie.

"Do you overstand the meaning of His Royal Majesty Haile Sellassie?"

"Overstand?" I asked.

"You're still speaking the Queen's English. Dead language!" he spat.

"Me? The Queen's English? Man, I'm a Queens native. What other kind of English you expect to come out of my mouth?" I laughed. He did too, and tried his hand at speaking like a New Yawka, until we were both clutching our stomachs with laughter.

"Man, listen up," he said seriously, wiping wetness from the corner of his eye. "I mean, did ya eva realize how much death in the English language there is? Negativity. Making deadlines and getting out of deadlocked situations, trying not to look deadpan."

"So, you're saying that an entire language that people live, breathe, and express love in can be negative?"

He nodded.

"Hmmm." Made me think of a neighbor who "forgot" German, the language of his youth. Even a two-week trip back to the fatherland couldn't restore his memory. I scratched my left cheek, found the solitary hair that always sprouted in the same spot. Damn, and the tweezers in my Swiss army knife had fallen out. Where was I going to get tweezers around here?

"I'll take it one step further. A negative language has the power to corrupt a righteous soul. Babylon begets Babylon." He carefully unfolded a torn piece of brown paper bag and spread the contents, picking out the seeds.

"You want to roll?"

"Can't roll for shit. Major life skill I should acquire."

He shrugged his shoulders and gave me a knowing smile. He licked the semi-sticky part of the paper, rolled the joint between his thumbs and index fingers, and passed it to me. I examined his work for a few moments, then grabbed the lighter I had inadvertently taken from the bar the night before, and lit up.

"So, are you saying that I'm Babylon, that you are too, just because we happened to be born in a place where English is spoken?"

He smiled. "My sister, at this point, this is the language we have come to be comfortable in. I'm not about to tell my sweetheart that

I love her in a language not my own. But you know, that doesn't mean we can't change the negative words to our advantage. Just because we get the Queen don't mean she have to get us!"

I sipped my beer, thinking about Creole and Caliche, Ladino and Cockney, Aramaic and Ebonics. I lay back down. Tried to touch the small of my back to the pier, stretching out the residual soreness caused by over-strenuous snorkeling, or sleeping in a hammock, or thinking too much. Somewhere in the distance, a stereo played Lord Rhaburn. I listened to the waves roll in, watched the moon distance itself from the ocean it touched only minutes before, and scale the firmament.

Camacho was a Belizean native, and a religious Rasta. We had met within a few days of my arrival on the island. We shared a common pleasure: walking. The only time that I can think, or empty my mind of all thoughts, is when my feet fall into a long, easy stride. Meditation in motion. Camacho and I walked the length of the island together often during my weeks there, a twenty-minute hike on a slow day, to where another islander, the self-proclaimed Belizean national poet, had built himself a brightly-painted house high up in the trees, and where the fishing cooperative was housed.

"How come there's no other houses on this side of the island?" I asked Camacho. It seemed strange that folks lived crowded together when the island was at least the size of a few football fields.

"With the way the trade winds move, there are too many damn sand fleas, and a limited supply of 'Skin-So-Soft'," he laughed. "It's the only thing those critters won't eat." By the time we got to "our" side of the island, I counted 100 little red bites below my knees, and swore to find the Avon lady soon.

I was attracted to his carefree attitude, and a keen intelligence that showed in his continual curiosity. I knew little about him other than what I chose to see. A fisherman, a tour guide, a jack-of-all-trades. He worked to live, and what he did mattered less than taking his time to enjoy the smell of the wind under a coconut tree, the feel of his muscles when he pulled anchor and set the sails to rest, the sharpness of his mind when he thought about God. He danced like a teenager, with complete lack of awareness, even though he was old enough to be a grandfather several times over. Camacho's partner was a middle-aged white woman from New Jersey named Debbie. She had fallen in love with the island years before, brought in money by serving hungry thrill-seekers tropical fruit crepes and other breakfast delights. Debbie possessed the cynicism of someone who had surrendered the prospect of financial and marital security when she learned the secret that kept most of her childhood friends enslaved in suburban palaces, chained to the corporate life and a passionless partnership: the myth that stability begets happiness which begets inner peace. "If peace is what you're after," she reasoned, "then start there."

I was in Central America hoping to figure out what to do next. I had actually made it through college. Now I had no goals to occupy my mind, occupy my time. Breakfast with Debbie and Camacho quickly became a part of my morning ritual during my foray on the island. I lingered often, ostensibly for a cigarette and another cup of coffee, admiring the life that they had created, trying to figure out how I could create my own functioning paradise. I wanted to trade in my life. For a while, theirs became my point of reference.

The moonrise was a big event in these parts. Some fellow backpackers hurried off to Guatemala, to Tikal, to sleep on Temple V under the stars. Tikal's magic is strongest with the full moon, and many of those living in a state of self-imposed exile felt a need to be touched by magic before returning to strip malls and Top 100 radio stations. I decided to stay put on the island, mostly because I couldn't imagine leaving. We walked down to the longest pier on the island to watch the moonrise, Camacho and I, not wanting our vista abridged by artificial lights. Debbie didn't join us. She rarely ventured out at night.

There were other spectators enjoying the lunar ballet on the pier. From the edge of the dock, we could see the lights from the bar, hear a muffled strain of dancehall reggae. We stayed for a long while, soaking in the protective cloak of the moonlight, talking softly to each other while looking at heaven. I thought about the sound of water, wondered how I could stay here, what kind of work I could make up. I thought of my encounter with a nurse shark surrounded by purple and yellow striped fish the day before, the way the red coral reflected the sunlight, the taste of fresh conch soup with cilantro (the trick to soften its meat, I was told, is to beat the hell out of the conch before cooking it). I thought of everything and nothing, until I could no longer think of anything better than a beer that had been properly refrigerated.

That night, on a pier that extended out beyond the groves where the mosquitoes bred, the moon tested me. Its fullness tricked me into a false serenity. Made me think that in a place like this, nothing could touch me but the warm waters surrounding the island. I had forgotten that sharks lurked below the turquoise surface, and it was only a few degrees of hunger that protected me from them.

I asked Camacho if he was ready to return. Looking around, I saw the others had already left, perhaps with the same idea as mine, to go to one of the island's two bars. Were there others? The evening seemed to contain an entire lifetime of thoughts, and after the herb, I couldn't recall who else had been on the pier glowing in effervescent moon rays.

"I'm going to kill you." It was a factual statement, calm like the sea after a storm.

I flashed him one of my you've-been-watching-too-many-werewolf-flick smiles. "You're gonna kill me," I teased. "For what?" Shit, I thought, I can play moon games too.

"I'm going to kill you so that you understand what it's like to die."

His voice was a flat, blunt instrument, speaking of my death as his precious everlasting gift to me. I knew, in the instant when I felt the chill of the tropical breeze climb up my spine, that this was no joke. I stared hard into his eyes, trying to see if I had misread their intent, while quickly scanning my physical environment for a way out. Soulful in our philosophical strolls, his eyes now were a vacant lot of madness. Something within him had snapped.

I struggled to maintain my composure, knowing that it would be easier for him to kill a sniffling American idiot, a weak female. I needed for him to see me as a human, not a sacrifice to the moon. I tried every excuse I could think of to get off that pier, to pacify his ego, to force him to remember what we had spent all evening talking about.

Snapping was familiar to me. My mother had snapped too, but in a different way, thinking it was wartime all over again, that the Nazis were looking for her. But where she had snapped into fear, this man, the one that I found myself alone with, snapped into a fury that was directed at me. This same man who peppered his conversations with words like lifelines and lions and *niyabinghi*, could not stop talking about death. My impending death. I couldn't seem to talk my way out of it. Logic doesn't work on the insane.

I felt his hands, the same hands which expertly had tied ropes around his boat's mooring as we lay anchor and went fishing past the reef, wrap around my neck. He pounded my back into the wooden planks of the pier. At one point, he stopped. Started to unzip his pants with one hand.

"You deserve to be fucked. You little tease. Pretending interest in Zion."

I tried some of the moves I had learned in self-defense class, but none seemed to work as well as they had in the church basement auditorium. Exhausted from the struggle, I half hoped he would just rape me, and forget about allowing me to experience death firsthand. I'd learned how to separate my mind from my body, allow myself to float away, like at the dentist's. Calmness becoming your best friend. Preferable to float than to become shark feed, to die in this place, alone, with no one to remember me and bring crimson gladiolus and offerings of frankincense and fresh figs to my goodbye service.

Just as suddenly, he shifted gears, wanting to toy with his prey. Sounds escaped my throat, carried out to sea on gentle breezes. His hold on my throat strengthened. I lost my breath, saw the darkness setting in. At the last moment, I felt a sudden release.

This is it, I thought. *Judgment day.*

But it was only Camacho making the game last a bit longer. He loosened his calloused hands, looked at them as though they belonged to someone else. I thought I saw a window opening.

"Camacho, forget this shit, man. I ain't telling no one what happened. Let's go get a beer. You don't really want to do this."

"Bitch."

Shit, I thought. My trying to stay cool only made him angrier. He returned his hands to my neck, tightened his grip around my throat. I allowed myself a silent prayer.

God, I don't know how I got into this damn mess, but get me the fuck out.

"Camacho, please man, I'm in love with you," I forced myself to spit out. "Don't do this. Let's work it out." The lure of love was an option worth trying. I had no others.

"Liar," he screamed, tightening and loosening and tightening and loosening his hold.

I sucked in the air, my last supper. Only somehow, I could breathe again. He started telling me about his near-death experiences, all self-imposed. Failures, I screamed to myself. If he had died, I wouldn't be here begging for my life, begging him to go with me to my hotel, so I could show him just how deep my love for him was. I didn't have it in me to be a compassionate listener, when all I could think was how the hell I was going to make it off that pier alive. Bullshit artistry was the only thing that could save me.

But I already knew that logic doesn't work on the insane.

Nothing to fear but fear itself? Like most women I understand the philosophical concept, but less how to send fear running to its damp, dark closet. And I know I am not alone in this. At some forever-to-be-remembered point in the lives of all women they will lock arms with fear and dance a deadly tango. And it will not be just ordinary fear they pair with, but fear that can undo lives and lay barren the core of the self. Call it the enemy. Some women will size it up. Some will try to deny it. Some will take it dead on. And it will not be a matter of strength or weakness who is victorious, but who in its grip surrenders fastest, and in that moment of surrender glimpses the barest fragment of the thing fear fears most—faith.

—Jessica Maxwell,
Femme d'Aventure

After a while, he seemed to become bored toying with me. Maybe whatever had snapped in him was now trying to mend itself. He let me go. Generously agreed to accompany me to my room. We held hands as we moved toward the shoreline, lingering to glimpse at the moon, now brightly shining directly above our heads. My heart pounded in my ears, but I feigned boredom. I walked with him, my hand in his, trying not to run, wanting to fly away.

It didn't work. He sensed my agitation. I was disgusted by the thought of my left hand touching one of the hands that might have killed me.

"Where are you running to?"

I inhaled deeply and made my voice deliberately light and joking.

"Shit, what do you mean running? This is regular pace for me. You forget where I'm from. It's an island too man, but that's where the similarities stop." I disengaged my hand from his while I lit a cigarette, and took one last look at the night sky. Then realizing what I had to do, I placed my hand back in his.

He laughed. "For real. I lived in Flatbush for a few years."

We came to the spot midway between the pier and my hotel, about 100 feet from the bar, when my legs made an instantaneous decision to bolt. I yanked my hand free and lunged toward the safety of people. Spotting an Australian backpacker I had met earlier in the day on Camacho's boat, I stopped.

"Stay on my fuckin' ass."

He complied. I silently thanked God for the globalization of American movies. Otherwise, this guy never would have understood what I meant. Inside I found the island's only cop, one of Camacho's many cousins, enjoying a cold drink. I quickly joined him, telling him what happened, asking him to check on Debbie to make sure he didn't go home riled up and looking for a fight at all costs.

I couldn't prosecute Camacho. It would mean weeks spent in Belize City, dealing with a corrupt bureaucracy that was as slow as a manatee's rising aggression. I couldn't get off the island the next day either. Instead, I borrowed snorkeling equipment and searched for the prescription glasses that Camacho had pitched off my face and into the water during our struggle. My body hurt. Soft purple bruises covered my spine and neck. Camacho was ordered by his cop cousin not to leave his house until I could leave the island. Debbie, however, did roam out of the house, and found me in the home of an artist who preferred winters on the caye to the New Mexican cold. She looked me in the eye.

"If you're not off the island by tomorrow, I personally am going to wring your little neck."

"What?" Stunned as much as if she would have started prophesying the end of the world, I noticed for the first time how her mouth skewed to the side when she spoke.

"You've been after him for two weeks. Don't even have your own man. You think you can strut down here and get mine?"

I wanted to lash back, to say that I had no sexual interest in a man twice my age with a missing tooth and, obvious to me now, missing screws. But the words didn't come. I could only return the stare, try to figure out how this woman could be defending—and seconding—Camacho's threat on my life. When she stomped out, I crawled into a corner and cried, listening to the artist in whose home I had sought refuge.

"Evil exists even on balmy islands. There is no paradise, except for the one we re-create every day."

I knew in my head that strangers in urine-stained alleys did not hold the monopoly on evil's existence. But in my gut, I wished for my childhood. The childhood that I was sure I must have had once, cloudy images of a protective bubble. I wished I could hold onto the simple belief that evil has a geographical preference, just like my grandmother preferred rural hovels in Hungary to comfortable immigrant digs in New Brunswick, New Jersey. Just like colds prefer rainy days. I learned, that night on the pier and the next day despite myself, that none of us could ever escape it. Not even the ring fashioned for me by the artist who sheltered me that afternoon, a simple, glorious ring made of malachite with a turquoise ball suspended by silver that I wore on my third finger for years, protected me entirely. Seven years later, I gave the ring to a man who held me up at gunpoint. I hoped, at least, it had been pawned for food.

I have since gotten over my initial feelings of betrayal by the moon. I have come to feel that she did protect me that night, just as sure as she pushed Camacho over the edge. I remember learning in third grade that the moon appears full only because she gets out of the direct path between Earth and our sun. It is the sun whose rays transform light into food, that makes our cheeks flush with healthy glows of spring. The moon is nothing more than a degenerating planet whose ebbing beauty is a mere whisper of finer millennia. She could not have helped me on this branch of my journey. I thought I was backpacking to discover a new life. Had I succeeded, I would have killed my old one. Maybe Camacho was just helping out. Maybe the magic of the moonrise held him back. The natural order of things required that I continue this journey with my own life, one that occasionally bores and bugs me, but which is brimming with authenticity.

The day after searching for my glasses, the day after seeing the hate in Debbie's eyes, I fled the country that had seemed so full of promise. At the time, I knew that there was some critical lesson to be understood, but I didn't quite know what. I found myself taking a boat to a van to a pickup truck that delivered me to the Guatemalan border, where I boarded a converted school bus heading to Peten, to Tikal. Half an hour into the ride, the driver let me and two European backpackers ride on top, as long as we promised to hold on to the metal beams meant to hold luggage in place. I closed my eyes and fantasized I was a sailboat riding the trade winds to open seas and freedom. I wanted to be cleansed by Tikal's magic. I hoped to be healed enough to continue my trip; there was no way I would admit defeat now and head north. It would be months before I was ready to head back to the land of commercials promising the good life with a simple purchase.

I walk often down city streets, by myself, late at night. If my parents were around, they would either protest or praise the bravery of their daughter.

"When I was her age, I had a little more respect for all things unknown," my father would say to my mother as she stirred the contents of various pots with a wooden spoon.

"Sha!" my mother would reproach. "You wanted a scaredy-cat, you should have raised her differently."

On the nights when I can see the moon clearly through the urban haze, I find myself talking to it, giving thanks for its protection, promising not to give away the secret to those who aren't yet ready. When I was a little girl, I once asked my father where God lived. I couldn't believe that God would choose to live in our rundown synagogue, and the churches I had gone into didn't seem cozy enough. He searched his mind for a while, maybe about what his own father had told him, or maybe trying to reconcile his scientific interests with his religious roots.

"God lives in the sun and the stars and the moon. That's why they're always around looking over us, looking out for us."

When my friend told me that the island was now developing rapidly as a popular eco-tourist site, I found myself walking at midnight to a twenty-four-hour bookstore cafe down at Dupont Circle that carries Central American guidebooks. There, in fine print, my attacker's name was listed as "a reliable native who will take you out to the reef, and cook fresh fish on his boat while you snorkel." No mention was made of his obsession with death. I thought about writing them, telling what I had learned the day after I felt his hands around my neck. About the time he had jumped off a water tower in Belize City only to escape death with a broken leg. About the other time he snapped and charged a fellow islander with a machete. I thought about writing them about the time he almost killed me. I thought about it, and then I decided to think about other things. My need to swallow pain, like the man at the circus who swallows torches. I left the bookstore, went home and dreamt of an awesome moonrise instead.

Yael Flusberg is a Washington, D.C.-based writer and activist who has never been content to stay within expected borders. Her travels continue to inspire a vision that, despite the cruelty in life, goodness does, and shall always, prevail.

MARTIN MITCHINSON

I Hear Voices

A traveler tries to understand the realities of post-war El Salvador.

"WE CAN'T GO ON LOOKING AT THE PAST. IT'S CLOSED..." SAID ARENA party member, Rene Figueroa, responding to demands for investigation into human-rights violations and assassinations that occurred during the civil war.

I try to keep moving in downtown San Salvador. I don't linger with my camera, or stand idly on a crowded street.

First arrival in the nation's capital is like stepping in front of oncoming traffic, that momentary suspension of time before impact occurs. The initial denial. The peripheral awareness of decommissioned soldiers armed with shotguns and 9mm pistols scattered about in storefronts and McDonald's restaurants. The tangle of cargo trucks and buses and cars and push carts with wood-spoke wheels and a skinny, shirtless man straining uphill. Fruit stands and greasy, sugar-coated pastries; tables of shirts and shoes and toothpaste and live chickens cluttering the sidewalk and spilling out into the street like the worst of Los Angeles with its sewer smells and deep fry, rotting fruit and back-alley garbage, but poorer, filthier, and brasher. As if mufflers were unfashionable. As if the drivers agreed to disregard traffic lights and one-ways and painted lines on the road, so that everything grinds to an angry, motor-revving, carnival parking lot: a sad-clown circus of decorated buses with Che Guevara portraits, and tax-software CDs hanging like holiday tinsel, for ten blocks square, while I sit on the bench seat of my city transport, hemmed in all sides by a thousand lonely buses slipping their clutches and pumping the brakes, jerking our way across town, inch by painful inch. I look out my side window, my eyes squinting and burning from exhaust, look out through the haze of smog that I taste in my mouth, wiping the film of soot and sweat from my forehead, look out through my side window, through the bus trapped next to us, and the bus next to that one, beyond the passengers. I can see through five filthy windows two lovers on the distant sidewalk, pausing as they greet in the storefront eddy, slowing for a soft embrace, every passenger watching and longing through sideways glances as her hand touches the nape of his neck, and their lips press together. Her red, red lipstick the only smudge of color in this gray and black world, on my first day in town.

I hear voices when I travel. I listen to radio broadcasts, and read newspapers and magazines. And contrary to mainstream media and presidential statements, it appears that the past is not yet finished with El Salvador.

Parking meters, according to *El Diario de Hoy*, are the key to understanding peacetime El Salvador. They are front-page news, and an insult to Salvadorans.

Eight years since the signing of U.N.-brokered Peace Accords formally ended a civil war between U.S.-supported government forces and FMLN guerrillas—a war in which 75,000 Salvadorans lost their lives—the international press has long gone home, and news-story triage has been left to the judgment of local media and publishers. For three days running, headline news in the nation's largest daily paper focuses on the mayor's decision to install parking control in the city center.

When I read these articles, I wonder whether the editors are expecting me to be swept up in the outrage; whether they hope—even while every promise and intent of the peace accords is being distorted beyond recognition, while legislators are firing bullets at police agents, and an ongoing crime wave has elevated kidnapping to growth industry status, and police officials have been filmed taking part in armed robbery, and the office of the Human Rights Ombudsman has been transformed into an empty title through political maneuverings, and the president insists that history, known and unknown, be settled with a hasty amnesty rather than through investigation—that I will come to believe that the parking scandal is the cornerstone of El Salvador?

> Apprehension came to color the entire Escalón district for me. I recall being struck by it on the canopied porch of a restaurant near the Mexican embassy, on an evening when rain or sabotage or habit had blacked out the city and I became abruptly aware, in the light cast by a passing car, of two human shadows. One shadow sat behind the smoked glass windows of a Cherokee Chief parked in front of the restaurant; the other crouched between the pumps at the Esso station next door, carrying a rifle. It seemed to me unencouraging that my husband and I were the only people seated on the porch. In the absence of the headlights the candle on our table provided the only light, and I fought the impulse to blow it out. We continued talking, carefully. Nothing came of this, but I did not forget the sensation of having been in a single instant demoralized, undone, humiliated by fear, which is what I meant when I said that I came to understand in El Salvador the mechanism of terror.
>
> —Joan Didion, *Salvador*

When I arrive at the Hospitalito Divina Provedencia, the former residence of Oscar Arnulfo Romero is crowded with middle school students standing silent and attentive while Sister Rosa recounts the stories surrounding each photograph and article displayed in Romero's honor.

"Major D'Aubuisson [founder of the ruling ARENA party] went on television and threatened Archbishop Romero," says Sister Rosa, "saying that the same would happen to him as had happened to the other priests who talked too much." When she tells the story it is easy to forget that this occurred twenty years ago. For her, nothing is closed or distant about the past.

She fixes her gaze on my eyes when she talks, ensuring that I understand her words. "But Monsignor Romero continued to speak his words as a true saint," she says, referring to the posters on the wall, printed with his portrait and the demands he broadcast on the 23rd of March, 1980, on the night before he was assassinated.

"I beg you," he said in his radio homily. "I ask you…I order you," he commanded, directing his exhortations to the military and paramilitary death squads that were murdering any opposition to the status quo. "Stop the repression."

When I read these words, and see his photo with the long, oval face, the myopic gaze, and faint smile, and I put them into context of the early part of 1980 with its escalating death squad activity, kidnapping, and repression, I have to believe he was aware of the table he was setting; aware that this might be his final homily, that in the morning as he was preparing to say mass in the hospital chapel, he could expect the gunmen to enter; that they would fire their weapons at him and the bullets would rip holes in his flesh. Perhaps he even anticipated the bullet that would pierce his heart; and that the Sisters would come running in vain to his side, gathering up his limp body, wrapped in blood-soaked vestments, carrying him to be laid in the back of an open pickup truck for a journey that would never arrive.

"…that my blood might plant a seed for freedom…that my death might be for the liberation of my people," he had said in an interview three weeks earlier.

Juana Mendoza is forty-nine years old, and lives nearby in a scattered village of brick houses connected by muddy footpaths through the scrub trees and waist-high weeds. She didn't vote for the ruling ARENA party in past elections: not for President Francisco Flores in the 1999 elections, nor for the ARENA candidate in the 2000 legislative elections. There is a faded paper FMLN flag taped to her porch wall. When we arrive, she is standing in the smoke of her outdoor cooking fire, stirring a five-gallon pot of corn *atole* with a rough-carved wood paddle.

"Everything is fine here," says Juana as she sits down in the hammock to talk with the El Salvador Commission for Human Rights [CDHES] workers. Her muddy feet are squeezed into plastic loafers adorned with tin buckles, and her calloused hands begin shucking ears of corn.

Like Rosalina, her greatest concerns are for others. Her twelve-year-old son suffers from epileptic seizures, and Juana believes that the condition was triggered by trauma while she was pregnant with him, watching as soldiers captured her pregnant neighbor…"stabbing her," Juana tell us, recounting the incident, "and then opening her up with a machete. That might have been what caused this problem with my son."

The doctor asks Juana whether she suffers from persistent stomach pains or headaches—symptoms of depression. "Well, of course there is that," she answers. And she mentions that at times she has nightmares over losing her husband and four brothers during the war—all killed or disappeared as suspected guerrillas.

When her youngest child, an eight-year-old daughter, returns from school, she squeezes into the hammock with Juana, glowing with her mother's praise, and showing us her notebooks from math and writing class.

Juana describes the loss of each family member, her hands still cleaning ears of corn and passing them off to be roasted for us over the fire. She then settles back into the hammock, and draws her daughter in close.

"Mostly we sleep peacefully here," she says in the end.

"Students today don't care about politics. They don't care about ideals," Martin, the CDHES attorney, tells me during our return to the city, crouched in the back of the pickup truck, bracing ourselves against the swerving, braking, and the clatter of potholes. "They don't want to struggle against an unjust system. They just want to learn to survive within it," he says, raising his arms in a shrug of helplessness. Martin is a short, thin, bespectacled man who uses sweeping hand gestures, so that sometimes the words seem larger than his stories.

He recalls an incident, while working for the FMLN guerrillas during the 1980s, when shots were fired in the air, and he was lying face down on the university pavement. A soldier was kicking him in the ribs, and only by holding up a bible that he had grabbed from one of the students was he able to convince the soldiers he was a church worker ministering to his flock.

"Fucking priest," said the soldier as he marched away.

"They don't want to see the university shut down again," he says. "They want cars, cellular phones, and a profession that will earn a good salary."

Martin laughed when his cap blew off in the wind, bouncing over the tailgate and tumbling into the darkness. Amidst all the frustration, he was smiling, and he continued talking about his work, about political corruption, about the collapse of the Human-Rights Ombudsman's office, and the failure of the FMLN's political strategy. He continued talking even while we were stopped

---

Ceci dances around the table in the priest's courtyard where the group and I eat. We reach out to tickle her as she flits past. "Cecilia, you're breaking my heart," Peter sings. "You're shaking my confidence daily." She covers her mouth with her hands and laughs. Carmen is more somber. Her parents were killed by government troops in a massacre at the Rio Lempa. Ceci's mother, Telma, whose husband was also killed, has informally adopted her. In the heat of an afternoon, Carmen retreats with me to the shade of plantain leaves. We sit close together on a rough-hewn bench holding hands. I attempt simple conversation, but she doesn't understand me. She gazes somewhere beyond the courtyard, her thoughts impenetrable. Absent-mindedly, she strokes my hand. She sighs. Pats my hand like an old woman. Her tender palm is cool, refreshing.

—Marguerite Watson,
"Salvadoran Vignettes"

---

between other trucks and buses with open windows at city red lights. I felt uncomfortable. He remained animated.

The University of El Salvador (UES), where Martin once posed as a priest, is a natural setting for a Hollywood disaster movie.

The campus is a clutter of collapsed buildings, concrete rubble, and makeshift rows of classrooms. There is a mountain of broken desks tangled outside the repair shop. The shells of burned-out vehicles with windows smashed lay scattered in various degrees of disassembly. Plastic bags, dry leaves, and scraps of paper blow about, skidding over cracked sidewalks and coming to rest in the patches of overgrown grass.

Little has been spent to repair the damage since the 1986 earthquake; since the guerrilla/military clash of November 1989; since the students greeted the arrival of then President Duarte with a volley of stones and angry protests against the murder of student and labor leaders.

On the upper floor of the Medical Sciences building, where the guerrillas held their base during the '89 offensive, and pipes and wires and broken fixtures hang lifeless from the ceiling and walls, students sit in front of an empty window opening, using the outside light to study.

"We talk about politics," responds one of the three students by the window at the end of the hall. "If something big happens, and it's in the news, we'll talk about it." But when I ask them about student reaction to growing voter absenteeism, giving the ARENA party control of the Legislative Assembly with only 14 percent of eligible voter support, and about recent poll results suggesting that more than half of the population would support a military coup if the Government/Police could not control the wave of criminal violence, they seem more curious about my interest in their country than in the situation itself.

Briseida, a second-year journalism student, is surprised to hear about the 67 percent absenteeism rate in the last elections. "During the campaign the parties promise you everything including the stars and the moon," she tells me, trying to explain the apathy. "But after they're elected, you'll be lucky if you end up with even a light bulb."

Estela Blanca's children will never study at the National University. Her husband went on a journey eight years ago when Estela was seven months pregnant, leaving her with two growing children and a promise that he would be joining the 15 percent of El Salvador's population now living in the U.S. and collectively sending back a million dollars daily to their families in El Salvador. Estela tells me that she cried and cried when he walked out the door. And she never heard from him again.

"I've been thinking about this for quite a while," she tells me, obviously nervous about sharing her plan. "If I could get hold of a map so that I knew where to get off the bus in Guatemala and Mexico before the border crossings," she explains, "...then I might try to move my family to the U.S."

I could give her my map, but I don't want to encourage her. I don't have the heart to tell her about the immigration check points she would face long before and after the border zones have been cleared. I

Violent crime remains high in El Salvador, in many cases because of youths who fled the 1980s war as children only to be deported from the U.S. in the 1990s after absorbing gang culture on the rough streets of Los Angeles. The irony of this ramification of El Salvador's civil war was captured by Scott Wallace in the August 2000 edition of *Harper's*: "In the 1980s, the fugitives roving Guazapa were Marxist rebels fighting for social change, and the names, like the Revolutionary Army of the People and Popular Liberation Front, succinctly captured their ideals. But the triumph of capitalism has spawned a breed of outlaws who have more immediate imperatives and a whole new nomenclature befitting their current sources of inspiration: Los Millonarios, The Fat Ones, The Power Rangers, and Hatchet Face."

—LH & NP

don't even want to consider what would happen to a single mother without money or documents, traveling with young children and a newborn baby, attempting to bluff her way for 3,000 miles and across three international borders.

There was a time when Estela worked in the office of then vice-president Guillermo Ungo. Today she ties a rope between two lampposts to display the clothing she has sewn, staking her ground in the shadows of a Blockbuster Video, Burger King, and Happy Land amusement park, sitting in the shade beside a graffiti painting of Monsignor Romero, protector of the poor.

Her fat-cheeked, six-month-old child is healthy and wrapped in clean blankets and clothing. He sleeps a child's sleep in a cardboard box with contented sighs and his tiny fingers curled into upraised fists, while Estela's eight-year-old daughter walks car to car selling flowers, and the eleven-year-old son washes windows at each red light pause.

Estela is well aware of her failures as a mother. Her children are clean and polite and hardworking, but they are not in school. And despite recent government pronouncements concerning the number of new schools built and textbooks purchased, Estela knows that she will not be able to offer her children even the level of education her parents made possible for her.

As I prepare to leave, I offer Estela some small bills to help with her family's bus fare home that evening. She seems perplexed, refusing the money while aware that it is needed. And as I walk away, I wish that I hadn't tried to put a band-aid on a gaping wound.

At the planned starting hour of a youth festival billed as "Politics of Youth and Adolescents: Now Young People Have Their Say," the stage crew saunters in to assemble backdrops. The sound equipment arrives through the door shortly thereafter, and the technicians begin rolling out lengths of speaker cable, stopping to visit with friends, shaking hands, and performing endless sound checks, *"Uno, dos. Uno, dos,"* amid static pops and the painful hum of feedback.

Two hours later, with the room temperature rising, my shirt stuck to my back, my sandaled feet perspiring and the smoke levels topped off by a cluster of youths two rows down, the show finally begins.

In the first presentation, the two child actors and their on-stage mother are superb in a seamless portrayal of a family living in an urban hovel—without sufficient food or hope, with the family patriarch returning home jobless, penniless, drunk, and abusive.

The audience is captivated. They literally fall from their seats, belly laughing and clutching their sides as the scene evolves to where the father, in a drunken rage, chases his children around and around the confines of the stage set. Moments later, with the head of the family flailing his arms in the air in an unsuccessful bid to stab his wife with a bread knife, the stage family unites for a climax scene in which the mother fights back to defend herself and her children, beating her husband on the head with a rolling pin, and chasing him out the door.

The crowd passes beyond the point of recovery. No one appears bothered by the subject material. No one seems aware of how art mimics life. My seat neighbor, tears rolling down his cheeks from the slapstick comedy, looks over to share his enthusiasm. And I have to hope that my own tears might be mistaken for laughter.

Like so much of the international press coverage in post-war El Salvador, the follow-up scenes—the extended monologues by the children, the struggle for survival and solution, the father's entry into an A.A. program, and the nursing of the family back to health—are far less riveting. Audience members filter out through these sections, and conversations start up between neighbors while the play continues to its conclusion twenty minutes later.

Many in the crowd appear surprised by the final applause.

When the festival M.C. regains the microphone, she thanks the young actors, and then apologizes to the audience for the lengthy second section, which, she concurs, was a little bit boring.

It's raining in San Salvador this morning, dampening down the fog of exhaust, dulling the endless traffic din, and leaving the taste of wet pavement and dust. I wanted to visit the Jesuit-run University of Central America (UCA) today, but I awoke fatigued.

My body has conspired with an infected ear, with back problems, and an unexplained paralysis in my right shoulder, to give me a morning's rest. And now I lie curled up, alone on a sagging single bed, listening to the muffled barking of the neighbor's dog, and allowing the drumming of rain on tin roofs to calm my impatience. I watch as water streams down the inside walls of my salmon-pink room, forming puddles along the perimeter of the floor while I ruminate over gathered materials.

I'm lying on my side, in my traveler's home—a budget hotel cubicle littered with news clippings and magazines, university publications, State Department releases, camera gear, a tape recorder, and half of my wardrobe hanging in vain to dry on the glass slats of the venetian window. Fleas are biting my ankles as I listlessly read through last week's newspapers, waiting for the rest and medicine to begin their healing process.

Later, in the afternoon drizzle, I board a #44 bus and ride across town to the Jesuit university. A security guard waves me through while inspecting the identification of the Salvadoran students around me.

Unlike the government-funded National University, the grass and hedges at the UCA are trimmed and tidy. Uniformed boys play soccer on the lush, green sports field, and workers are sweeping sidewalks and cleaning out gutters. Unlike the UES, the garbage cans are not lying on their sides with the bottoms rusted out. The windows are intact. The walls are free from graffiti. There are no piles of dirt, or collapsed buildings, or shells of rusted out cars. It is a peacefully privileged world on the surface, masking over the undercurrent of discontent.

Impunity built the museum at UCA's Monsignor Romero Centre. The bricks and mortar were inspired by injustice. Without the culture of violence, without the tradition of closing the door on the past, and the directive to never look back, there would have been no reason for the glass cases filled with relics and memories from the 16th of November, 1989: Father Elacuria's brown night robe and blue pin-striped pajamas with the collar torn and ragged; the green terry cloth house coat, the sleeves ripped at the shoulder;

the mangled slippers; the sleeveless undershirt cut open for an autopsy, and a bullet hole at the right side of the chest: all of the clothing worn by the six priests, stained with eleven-year-old blood and ground-in dirt from the outdoor patio where their bodies were discovered.

In the final room there is a collection of photographs with the victims' faces crushed and distorted, noses torn sideways, teeth fractured off, lips swollen beyond recognition, and their skulls split open so that the innards spilled out onto the ground.

Obdulio, the gardener, was the first to arrive on the scene that morning. He found the bodies of four priests outside on the patio, and two more inside the residence. And then he came upon his wife Elba, and their sixteen-year-old daughter Cecilia, locked in a final embrace, shot full of holes, lying in a pool of their own blood, Elba's face cracked wide open, as if to murder was not enough.

Obdulio lived for five more years after that night in November. He lived to see the Peace Accords signed, and the war come to a formal conclusion. He worked until the end as a gardener on the university grounds, planting a rose garden on the spot where he had discovered the bodies. A ring of eight red roses—one for each of those who died, and two more yellow roses in the center representing his wife Elba, and their daughter Cecilia.

No charges were ever laid in the eight murders that occurred on that November night in 1989. And now the courts are upholding ARENA's amnesty law, refusing UCA's petition to reopen the case.

No one was ever charged for the assassination of Monsignor Romero, or for the 900 villagers corralled together near the village of El Mozote in late December, 1981—forced, in small groups, to enter a one-room building and then shot dead by government troops, their bodies buried in a mass grave and the dirt piled over while at the same moment U.S. President Ronald Reagan was preparing his stamp of approval for El Salvador.

On January 29, 1982—six weeks after the slaughter at El Mozote, with *The New York Times* and the *Washington Post* just then headlining their eyewitness accounts of the aftermath, and two days before the murder of nineteen Salvadorans by government troops in

Now she began to disentangle the bits of ruined fabric: "Shirt, light in color, fragmented, with buttons...Belt of brown leather, metal buckle...Pants, light in color, with patches of blue and green color in the posterior part...In the pants pocket...ah...um..."

The strong voice took an odd slide downward and stopped. Over her shoulder, I saw her staring at something in her palm, then heard her swear in a low voice: "*¡Hijo de puta!*" She turned and opened her hand to reveal a tiny figure: a little horse of bright orange plastic. #59 had been a lucky child, had had a family prosperous enough to provide a lucky toy.

After a moment, the anthropologist Mercedes Doretti said, "Ordinarily, we could use this for identification. I mean, even after eleven years, any mother would recognize this as her kid's, you know?" She looked back at #59 and then at the brown rubble. "But here, here they killed all the mothers, too."

—Mark Danner,
The Massacre at El Mozote

the capital city, these new victims found with their hands tied behind their backs, and witnesses testifying to the rapes of children by military personnel—President Ronald Reagan sent off to Congress his "certification" that the Salvadoran allies were "making a concerted and significant effort to comply with internationally recognized human rights," insisting that military aide be continued.

A week after my visit to the University of Central America, I ride a bus along a winding highway, scenery slipping by outside my window. An evangelical couple in the seat behind plays a video recording from a recent gathering, reminiscent of every village experience during this past month—a peaceful setting shattered by a pair of broadcast speakers so that a half-dozen people in a large hall can spoil the mountain tranquility on any day of the week, at any hour of the morning, afternoon, or night with their off-key singing, and passionate appeals. *"Padre mío, Espíritu Santo,"* the crying and praising, the shouting and banging on drums, and obnoxious, rhythmless guitar strumming.

Turning in my bus seat, I'm greeted by smiles that only melt away when I ask if it might be possible to "please, please," turn the volume down, or, better yet, wait until their return to Nicaragua, *"por favor,"* or borrow my single set of earphones, *"por favor,"* because I just can't bear to listen to any more of that unbridled enthusiasm over and over and over again.

I ride a bus along a winding road, leaving El Salvador in the same manner I arrived: the long, senseless lines at border crossings, waiting for a rubber stamp, and paying their undocumented tolls (because it's the weekend, or after 4 P.M., or during their lunch break, or one of the village saint days, or some such excuse) until nothing is left but my bagful of books, my scribbled notes, the loose cassettes, and this gray-cloud sky above us; these storm clouds over a volcano; this egret perched upon the back of a sagging cow feeding on garbage in the ditch; this filthy Gulf of Fonseca; this broken-down bus; these three-wheeled bicycle taxis with shade umbrellas; these solid wood wheels on a cart pulled by a pair of oxen that make me want to cry. These voices. These faces, these eyes, these cynics, these fatherless children, this woman alone, these mothers full of despair—so clear in my mind. These voices I hear...these voices.

Martin Mitchinson also contributed "Dancing for Centavos" in Part III.

RIGOBERTA MENCHÚ

Return to Laj Chimel

A Nobel Peace Prize winner makes a pilgrimage to her hometown.

AFTER I WENT BACK TO LIVE IN GUATEMALA IN 1994, I REALIZED there was one more step to take. Without it, I would never be happy. I had to go back to Laj Chimel, the village where I was born. Just imagine, if I was afraid of going back to Guatemala, I was even more afraid of going back to Laj Chimel.

There had been so much violence, so much death, and so much disintegration within the armed struggle itself. No one ever knew who killed whom, or what had happened where. It is a place which holds many mysteries, secret graves, people eaten by animals...

Everyone took justice into their own hands. Some people used it to act against their neighbors, because of land, or women, or for jealousy, and for all kinds of problems. Three or four communities had title to the same piece of land. They all claimed it had been held by their ancestors, and they fought over it. Chimel was probably the place where the first seeds of revolutionary consciousness were sown, the seeds of struggle, of democracy.

The problem of land is not just being aware of not having it, it is being aware of the need to fight for it. On top of that, there was the issue of impunity. There was no hope that a person guilty of a crime would ever be punished or brought to justice. If the judicial system doesn't work anywhere else in the country, what chance would it have in this little village?

Chimel is a very magical place. The land is rich in so many varieties of trees, animals, birds, flowers, lianas, and fungi. The rain forest is "misty and mysterious," one of the few left on earth, one of these places they call the "lungs of the planet." It has become even thicker since the repression. These gigantic mountains and forests sheltered thousands of internal refugees and displaced people.

I was very afraid. I didn't know what had happened to the murderers, to the *judiciales* who were paid to bump off catechists or to wipe out other groups. Many landowners' sons became assassins, killing in broad daylight. Their parents taught them to hate poor people, humble people, especially in the municipality of Uspantán. Fear of them sowed terror in the streets, you did not know whom to trust.

Fear of so many memories is tragic too. However much we say we never had a childhood, there must be some trace, some remains of it left, not only in Laj Chimel and in Chimel, but also in the town of Uspantán. "The only thing to do is to steel

Rigoberta Menchú was awarded the Nobel Peace Prize in 1992 for her work on behalf of indigenous rights and social justice. Involved in social reform activities in Guatemala from an early age, Menchú fled to Mexico in 1981 following the torture and murders of her father, mother, and brothers. There, she continued organizing against oppression in Guatemala and helped to found the United Representation of Guatemala Opposition (RUOG), which promotes human rights in Guatemala at international forums such as the United Nations. In 1984, Menchú dictated the story of her life for the book, *I, Rigoberta Menchú*. The book and Menchú's ongoing campaign for social justice brought international attention to the conflict between indigenous Indians and the military government of Guatemala.

—LH & NP

myself and go back incognito," I said to myself. My husband always encourages me, and he pushed me into taking the step. He is a positive man, he finds a generous answer to everything.

So we went, and a few days before leaving, I dreamed of my mother, and of the house where I grew up. They hadn't changed. I was overcome by sadness. I kept getting a big lump in my throat and crying. I didn't feel hatred for those who had destroyed my community, my home and my family. I just wanted to cry. I missed the past, when I was a girl, and the home that I can never have again. The heart always feels great pain. We talked a lot about my mother and my father during that time, and of the many sorrows I had thought time had erased. When something irreversible and irreparable happens, our strength as human beings is put to the test.

My first surprise was that the journey wasn't the nine hours it was when I left Laj Chimel. In those days, we walked for hours and hours, up and down the hills, those interminable bends! I remember each drop of sweat. But people had worked tirelessly to open the road from Uspantán to Laj Chimel, so we only had to walk for four kilometers. We didn't get to Chimel, it was a few hours further on.

We must have arrived at about ten in the morning. I was surprised at how small the place was. It was a miniature Chimel. It seemed like a different place. Most of the rivers had dried up. The marshes, the swamps, and quicksands we had been so afraid of—the places where we hid for fear of snakes and mountain animals—these had all shrunk. Small, too, were the mysterious rocks. When we were children, we thought snakes might be asleep on them or other frightening things, or, worse still, *nawaals*.

Now we were there with my sister Anita, my brother Nicolás, my sister-in-law Juana, and others who had lived in Chimel before. My husband was with us too. All of us had been born there and we were all surprised at how tiny Laj Chimel had become. That's where the name comes from. In K'iche', *laj* means little, something precious in a very small space, something small that is full of surprises.

"This isn't the land I left," I said as we walked along. "Where are our mountains?" The land now belonged to landowners, and they had cut down our precious trees. Part of the hillside was bare. We remembered having played as children in the great ancient forests, and many of them had now been cut down. The rivers, too, had dried up.

A small community of twenty-four families was living on my father's land. My brother Víctor's house was still there, so was Nicolás's house and Marta's house and my father's house. The people there were so neglected and hungry that I felt sad for life itself.

"This is the birthplace of a winner of the Nobel Peace Prize," I said, "who is much loved and respected. But didn't I grow up among worms and poverty too? How can people love me but not these children, these women, these sick undernourished people? It's as if what happened to me belongs in the past, and today it is different."

I felt so sad. The people were like skeletons. They had a sad, hard life. Yet even so, they went to find a chicken, and we ate it. We were sorry we hadn't brought anything with us. We came from a city of consumption and waste. It's not just in the developed world that food is wasted, but in ours as well. The families who lived there were very poor. Fifteen years after I left, they were even poorer than before. At least we used to have straw houses with wooden planks. It was something, not a lot. It certainly wasn't this type of misery. We had more to eat then.

The fact is that when the repression started, the majority of the inhabitants of Chimel were killed. Many were killed in Laj Chimel itself. The army, the corrupt mayors, and the regional office of the state land agency (INTA) acted fraudulently with respect to the land left by people who died in Chimel. The way corruption and injustice worked in this area was to pretend that the former owners had sold their land. Since the majority of them were dead, the title deeds were falsified and the signatures faked. According to the deed, my grandfather Nicolás Tum had arrived, at the age of 130, with a group of thirty peasants from Chimel, to sell the land in Laj Chimel to a certain Reginaldo Gamarra. In those days Laj Chimel was the center of the community of Chimel.

The contract of sale was recorded as was the fact that Don Nicolás Tum could not read or write. He left his fingerprints mixed up with those of everyone else. I couldn't figure out which was my grandfather's. The officials said that they had sold their land voluntarily.

When I finished reading the contract, supposedly drawn up legally by a notary, I said, "This is an injustice." And I went to investigate the names that were there. I found the families of several of these people, and they swore that their relatives had died before the contract of sale. The only way to prove that an injustice had been done was to go to the registry office, to find the death certificates of my grandfather and the others who had supposedly sold the lands at Laj Chimel. We soon discovered that all these documents had disappeared. All trace had gone of anything that could prove that my grandfather was already dead when he apparently sold the land. Yet how could he have lived to be 130? My grandfather did live to be 117. I don't think he ever reached 130!

When we eventually came to Laj Chimel, the people were fearful. The new landowner was a bad man. He didn't let anyone work, or cut firewood, or walk through his land. He didn't even let them cross his road, so they had to live from what was available in the village. They were afraid of him, not just because he was a *ladino* and a landowner, but because of his contacts with gangs of murderers and *judiciales*. He was well know for having stolen land.

Some of the former mayors of these areas had gone to prison, thank God, and when we arrived, we swore on the memory of our parents that we would fight for the return of that land. My brother Nicolás had been fighting all along, but he could not win against people with so much power. I never thought that the deep spirit of struggle my father taught us would well up again in me, but it did. I said, "We must fight for it, whatever the cost. We must get our land back." Everybody was very happy and we spent several good hours together.

We had arrived at ten o'clock. By eleven, they had prepared us a meal, and by twelve we were starting to relive our old memories of this little patch of earth. We wondered why the rivers had dried up, why the marshes were smaller. Was it only our perception? Was our land really bigger in those days? Or did our sense of belonging with our community, with our people, make it seem bigger? Who knows what had happened?

We went to find one particular tree, a *cuxín*, which we had all dreamed about (not only me). My sister Lucía once told me that she always dreamed of that *cuxín*. So did my other sister Anita. It was big and beautiful, and bore a lot of fruit. We used to eat its fruit. I remember, from my dreams over the years, sitting under the *cuxín*, or walking beside it.

We found no trace of it. I asked my brother Nicolás what had happened to it. He replied sadly, "It died a long time ago." "Why did it die?" I asked. It was a huge tree, and very old. It was there when we were born.

Why did it die so soon? Other trees had been cut when we were children, and their trunks are still there. Nicolás said that many of the inhabitants of Chimel had been hanged there and shot. Their blood had splattered on the *cuxín*. It lived for only a few weeks after that. It died by itself. It withered and fell, and its roots came out. It quickly decayed. Not a trace remained, nothing. We were amazed. The tree we had dreamed about so often was no longer there.

There was another tree near the house where we were born. They say a neighbor called Don Gerónimo Poli, a *compadre* of my father, was hanged on it. Another man was hanged there too. The same thing happened. It was a sturdy tree, an evergreen oak. Mountain people say that when these trees are splattered with human blood they die straight away.

We found many bones in the fields and under rocks on the hillsides. Nicolás said, "So many things happened here and so few people are alive to tell the tale." During the repression, most people were not buried. Bands of dogs formed, and, when people died, the dogs tore off their flesh and took the bones away to gnaw. There was a plague of dogs hunting for the bodies of the dead. They say there was a time when people were afraid to pass the village for the dogs had become so used to eating people. The army was continually laying ambushes; people seeking refuge with their families died, and so too did many guerrillas. That is why there are so many bones strewn over the land.

After that, Laj Chimel was settled by the new landowners. They brought their cattle to graze, but they didn't stay long. The cattle started dying in droves. They would go to sleep and not wake up. Many seemed alive but they were dead. The dogs became increasingly ravenous for meat. They tore the flesh off the cattle as well. And ate them. So human bones are now confused with animal bones.

My brother looked at the sky in silence, as if asking the Creator for permission, then he said with due respect, "I had a dog that was pregnant. She joined a band of man-eating dogs. When her puppies were born, they had the eyes of humans, the expression of humans. They looked at me as a person would. I had to kill them one by one. I hope I haven't committed a crime before our Creator." Only the Heart of the Sky knows. For how can we distinguish between a human bone and a cow bone?

When we saw all this, we remembered the six or seven groups of people who had passed through this blessed land. Nothing of them remains. They left quickly because they were afraid. The spirits in the village are very active. People believe that all those who were murdered there actually now inhabit Laj Chimel and Chimel, and are the real owners of the village and the lands. They guard it.

In the circumstances, very few people could bear to live there. They quarreled among themselves and left. The new landowners again began selling off pieces of Laj Chimel, and dreamed of becoming rich from the vastness of its natural resources. Many of the more ambitious ones dreamed of logging and selling the fine wood of the ancient trees. What a wealth of flora and fauna is hidden in that great misty rain forest. For more than ten years so many people have wanted to exploit that land.

Our visit was not all sad and tearful. Once again we were able to breathe the unforgettable smell of Chimel. We remembered the times when we had been happy there. We remembered our games as children, the places where we took our sheep to graze, and the things that scared us. We imagined wonderful things for Chimel again, as well as for Laj Chimel. But first we have to recover it, and to get tenure of our land again.

Rigoberta Menchú used the money awarded by the Nobel Committee to establish the Rigoberta Menchú Foundation, which works to promote peace, human rights, and development, especially as it concerns indigenous people. The sixth of nine children in a Mayan Indian family from El Quiche province of northwestern Guatemala, she saw her village razed to the ground by the Guatemalan military and its population reduced from 400 to 12. She fled the terror and went into exile for twelve years in Mexico, returning in 1994. She currently lives in Guatemala City with her husband and son. This story was excerpted from her memoir, Crossing Borders.

PART FIVE

THE LAST WORD

HENRY SHUKMAN

In the Land of the Cunas

Time, and a little help from a shaman, heals all.

IT'S HARD TO EXAGGERATE THE STRANGENESS OF THE SAN BLAS Islands, a society where money consists of four coconuts tied together at the stem and where politicians are elected for their ability to make you laugh. A world without electricity, where all day long the village chief sings about your favorite hero, and at night the men troop off to smoke in their clubhouse while the women get down to some serious work. Where no one eats or drinks anything that they haven't caught or grown. Where, when the village wants to get drunk, you brew the beer together, then drink yourselves blind until it runs out, thereafter lying around in hammocks, groaning ensemble.

This is Kuna Yala, land of the Cunas, a group of some 40,000 Amerindians who over a century ago were driven from the mainland to the relative sanctuary of Archipiélago de San Blas—a string of tiny islands littered along Panama's northeastern coast. Beginning in 1918 their sanctuary was threatened by the Panamanian government, which wanted to force the Cunas into a Western way of life. The Cunas staged a revolt in 1925 and since the 1930s have had their own autonomous region within Panama, the Comarca Kuna Yala, a strip of mainland 130 miles long, as well as the offshore islets.

Here they live traditionally—in one of the last pieces of pre-

Colombian America that has miraculously survived 500 years of traders, slavers, miners, and soldiers. Their life makes an anthropologist's mouth water: night-long recitations of myths, panpipe dances, shamans on every corner, puberty rites for girls, longhouses, home-chewed sugarcane wine, dugouts.... This is the real thing, an ancient lifestyle sweeping back into prehistory, into the immemorial origins of man.

> There are few times in my travels when I have sensed the absolute blending of man and nature and heritage and philosophy. The Cuna concept encompasses and recognizes the mutual complexities of man and nature and their utter symbiotic state. I had planned to leave the following day. But I didn't. I stayed on and continued to see and learn and, I think, understand why the Cuna are regarded by many as (dare I say it) a prototype for evolved man—perfectly harmonious, an integrated blending of spiritual and material selves into a balanced whole that contains the very essence of The Golden Time—a state that our world is desperately needing.
>
> —David Yeadon, "The Golden Time of the Cuna"

My plan had been to get to one of the more remote islands and live for a quiet week or two just like the Cuna. As far as I could see, the Cunas had out-Crusoed Crusoe. They had generations of desert island living behind them, and I wanted to see how native desert islanders did it.

After various enquiries, in Spanish and Panama English, I headed for an outlying island some 400 yards wide called Chichimen. Population: 20.

King of Chichimen is Don Ramón. For twenty years he worked as a chef in Panama City, then came back to claim his patrimony.

"My father died, and I came straight back," he tells me. "I haven't left this island in seventeen years. Not a single day. All my brothers have died now," he adds, raising a hand from his cane. "*Soy el último.* I'm the last."

He is a small old man with a permanent smile and three sturdy pegs for teeth in an otherwise empty gum.

His niece Buna lives in the hut next door, a middle-aged woman with a short haircut, gold nose ring, and colorful blouse of all Cuna women. Just up the beach lives her husband, Muchacho. "Boy." He is getting a bit old for the honorific. In his fifties at least, with a face like varnished oak, he walks with stiff determination as he tends to his duties, which are liberally showered upon him by Don Ramón. "Boy, fetch fruit…Boy, cut coconuts…Boy, fish."

Boy rides a dugout that looks like something out of *The Flintstones*—a hefty bole with a sizable shark bite out of the stern and a lump of lava for an anchor. Every morning he shoves it down the beach and paddles out into the lagoon, pausing to bail with half a coconut. I see him bobbing out there near the reef, fishing as the sun climbs up.

When he paddles back in at noon with his catch, another member of the island entourage, Eulogio, meets him on the beach. Eulogio loads the fluttering snappers onto a broken clock face that must have once washed up with a tide.

The matrimonial situation is a little strained. Buna lives with Eulogio rather than Boy. Yet Eulogio is not her lover. Far from it. One indication is the clear-cut Cuna dress codes: men wear shorts or trousers; women wear wraps and blouses decorated with textiles called *molas*.

They also daub bright pink rouge onto their cheeks. Eulogio, a rather young man with long wavy hair, uses the rouge and wears a pink singlet and a towel wrapped around his waist. He is an *omegit*, a man-woman. You see them around, stitching *molas* like the women, shuffling about in flip-flops in a tribal parody of camp. The Cunas make no attempt to get them to conform. In fact, they say they make the best *molas*.

Don Ramón sets me up with a half-built Cuna house—a thatch roof, partially finished bamboo walls open to the waves.

The only intrusions in this Paleolithic paradise are the pots, the machetes, and me. It's a wonderful thing to live in the midst of natural things, but it's hard to say exactly why. Something happens.

At first I just feel this is a nice place. The first night, sleeping in the open wind is a stirring, restless experience. But I wake at dawn excited and ready to give myself to the island. I walk around it, explore, go fishing with Boy. I can't help but imagine living here. After a day or two, a warmth spontaneously arises within me. All my reasoned defenses melt in the heat. Nature is rearranging my body and mind, performing its subtle surgery on my soul. The rocking of the dugout, the swing of the hammock, the constant sway of the palm fronds—nothing stops moving here.

I begin to notice patterns: first in the palm fronds; then in the pelicans' endlessly repeated glide and plunge, glide and plunge; in the grasses that sprout in long straight rows from underground runners; and in the starred perforations of a sand dollar. I begin to wish I, too, could be infused with a similar pattern, then realize that I am—I'm just unschooled in seeing it.

Beneath the veil of civilization I begin to glimpse a different person: simple, brown-shouldered, strong. A man who would take pleasure in beaching his own dugout, in hanging up bleached driftwood for a shelf, in bailing his craft with a gourd. A man for whom money—coins, bills—would be funny and interest-

> One of the things I learned in El Coco, Panama, was simplicity. What is really necessary for me to live an enjoyable and fulfilling life? What, like a sculptor, should I chip away as unnecessary to my vision?
>
> I also learned about generosity. Freely giving of whatever you have, with no thought of reward or gain. The other lessons are things I cannot explain to you. The joys of sitting on a step in the tropical heat sipping from a coconut. Swimming and splashing in a turbid jungle river with friends. Gathering around a campfire eating fried plantain chips, quietly soaking up the sounds of the night. These things bypass the intellect and imprint directly upon the heart.
>
> —Ryan A. Murdock, "Living Wisdom of the Painted Men"

ing, mere objects, and for whom paper would be more precious than clothing.

Half a mile away the reef roars constantly, like a train. Sometimes I see the black faces of breakers rising above the horizon, unfurling like mirages. I hear there are no sharks in Kuna Yala: forty years ago a powerful shaman sent them all away. Hurricanes stay away, too, ever since the same shaman banned them. The Cunas say hurricanes are like bad drivers who have gotten lost. When one approached a few years ago, all the Cunas started shouting and banging pots, so it could hear them and get its bearings again.

Panama may be called a banana republic, but this is a coconut culture. A handful of ways to use the plant: 1. Drink the coconut water. 2. Eat the meat. 3. Chip off a piece of husk for a spatula. 4. Dry the husks to smoke fish. 5. Grate, soak, and sieve the meat for milk. 6. Roof with the fronds. 7. Convert the trunks to house posts. 8. Use the logs to roll dugouts into the water.

The pleasure of being here is akin to looking at a model railway: seeing a whole universe, replete with its spirits and Creator and ancestral sages, its own indigenous technology.

Eden is an inappropriate analogy. There is toil here, plenty of sweat and uncertainty, as well as innocence. We suffer from millennia of indoctrination that innocence must be lost, paradise left behind. But that now strikes me, swinging in the firm embrace of my hammock, as a falsehood. Here, innocence is not negotiable.

My plan meets with a hitch. The wind shifts from sea to land, and I understand why mine is the only house on Chichimen's northern shore. In the island's lee, the wind dies completely. The ground becomes as hot as a skillet. All the insects God has raised against man wake up. The hut becomes an entomologist's fantasy. I slap six dreamy mosquitoes on my legs in as many seconds. Horseflies circle my head menacingly. Houseflies dart around my face. Now and then a sharp prick has me searching leg or arm, where I find a microscopic life-form, a mere grain that crumbles when I brush it away, far too small, surely, to deliver such a sharp stab.

I sweat. I itch. I fan at the marauders, wondering how so many man-molesters can coexist in one place.

I make a dash for the sea, arriving just in time to see a dugout filled with an entire family sail by. The sail is a collection of rags stitched together. They stare at me, bewildered. I return to the hut, wrap in a sheet, pray for wind.

Buna brings over the evening meal: rice, plantains, and fish, all served on an old, sea-delivered Frisbee. She greets me with her usual smile, puts down her load, then raises her eyebrows, emits a whoop of surprise, and takes hold of my arm.

I had not noticed, but it is covered from wrist to bicep in an angry rash. The other arm too, and now that I take a look, my legs also. Sunburn? Salt rash? Prickly heat? A medley of insect bites?

She strokes my arm and says something in Cuna.

I have a troubled night. The cocktail of sun, salt, and insects makes my skin boil. Not only that, but a storm approaches. I sit on the beach watching it come. Out of the black sky sudden cloudscapes of gold and mauve erupt. Half a minute later, long grumbles interfere with the reef's even roar.

It is quite a storm. It spreads around the island. Clatters of firecrackers echo from the sky. I retreat to my hammock. Minute by minute the flashes encompass more and more sky, the thunderclaps grow. For five minutes the wind drops completely: all is quiet; a sucking through the hut, hissing in the palms. The rain arrives with apocalyptic decisiveness. I hadn't been this scared of a thunderstorm since I was a child on my first camping trip.

It's hard to say how long it lasts. The lightning flickers silently long into the night.

In the morning Buna pays a visit. What a storm! she says. What *relámpagos*, *"Luz-boom! Luz-boom!"* she explains, in case I don't know what *relámpagos* are, throwing her hands apart like an explosion on each boom.

The rash worsens. I feel as if I'm wearing clothes one size too small, and they're all made of canvas. When I pull on my shirt, my sides itch. At the same time, my mind slows down, numbing itself to the oversensitive flesh. My instinct is to keep to the shade, to be cool, to rest.

Help arrives in the form of a friend of Don Ramón: Henry Harrison, a Cuna who worked in the Panama Canal Zone for twenty years and speaks a garbled, half-remembered English. He passes by in a dugout with a small engine on his way to Isla Tigre, some forty miles away, partway to Colombia.

Henry wears thick glasses, and a ballpoint pen protrudes from the breast pocket of his shirt: an intellectual. He is conducting "investigations" into his people, he tells me. But he's hard to follow.

"Yeah, when I eight," he says, "I got a big dream. A man with a beard come and tell me I live to a hundreds and meet peoples from all over the world. A cargo boat take me to Panama. I cry and cry."

His conversation skips from autobiography to philosophy to Cuna culture and back. Henry had visited most of the Cuna islands and launches into a speech on the wisdom of their healers. Before he jumps onto some other topic, I jump first, presenting him with my left arm. Does he know of a healer who could heal this?

Indeed he does. Isla Tigre, the very island he is heading for, is home to the best Cuna medicine man.

It is hard to leave Chichimen. The island has become my own *cuna*, or cradle. But soon the waves have taken hold of my dreaminess. We tip and loll through the waters. The many little islands trundle back and forth along the horizon, like beetles rearranging themselves. Just when I think I know which is which, I realize I have no idea at all.

Rio Sidra, our first stop, is covered in palm-thatch houses and threaded with alleyways. Four boys kick a soccer ball around the plaza, while naked toddlers play a game of tag, freezing when they are stranded in the middle of intense play.

We are to spend the night here, in the longhouse of Señor Jorge Carpintero—George the Carpenter—the mild-mannered man who slings up two extra hammocks in his longhouse and goes fishing for our dinner.

I join him. Soft spots of sunlight float over the blurry mosaic of the sea's surface. Across the water come the noises of settlement—voices, the knock of wood on wood, the gurgle of distant laughter, a child's call—*Nini! Nini!*—like a faint mosquito whine. These are the sounds of a village without gasoline or electricity.

Cuna men live with their wife's family. When we return with our fifteen little fish, all the women of the household come out to greet us: Jorge's mother-in-law and four sisters-in-law. One of them attempts to haul in a sheet drying in the breeze, but it floats away like a kite. Everyone roars with laughter. Jorge rescues it with the poles of his sardine net.

Later Jorge kneels on the floor of the longhouse in front of a kerosene lamp. First it emits clouds of black smoke, then a single yellow flame envelops the whole thing, until it settles down into a dazzle of white light, leaving most of the longhouse in blackest shade.

There's nothing like night in a longhouse. This one must be all of forty yards long, twenty feet tall. Its rafters are completely filled with children's clothes, which hang folded over the beams in great long rows, carefully organized: underwear here, blouses there, trousers up above. Some fifteen kids run around, periodically flocking to the table where Jorge, Henry, and I sit. A feast arrives: lobster, fish, fried plantains, yucca, coconut rice…and Pepsi-Cola.

Later, in the dark, kerosene light tiger-stripes the interior, shining through the bamboo slats of the walls. The structure groans with the weight of filled hammocks. Soft chatter continues late into the night. Two or three houses away you can hear two girls laughing, their laugh becoming a long dreamy moan of sleepiness, a final note for the day. The entire village is permeable, each house a soft-walled cell breathing into its neighbor.

I wake up itching in the middle of the night. The darkness is heavy with slumber.

The next morning Henry and I are on our way again. The engine is not well today. As we churn along, the waves slosh over us so that in a matter of minutes we are drenched. The motor occasionally interrupts its roar to break into a series of moans: *No no no!…no no!…no!* it pleads. Soon it can take no more.

For a while we drift in silence, relieved not to be bucketed by the waves. The rest of the journey we limp along at quarter speed. Every time Henry tries to increase the revs, the outboard gasps and dies. What should have taken an hour takes four.

Isla Tigre is another village adrift in time, not anchored to any century. (How long has mankind been making dugout canoes and palm shelters and scraping out fields in the jungle?) We coast up to the dock. Henry becomes his busy, nervous self as soon as we are on dry land again.

It's like arriving in the middle of Chapter 21 of a Graham Greene novel: a scene of desolation. A dilapidated Colombian boat creaks at the dock, draped with supine peddlers dozing amid piles of knickknacks and sacks of fruit. A concrete quay opens onto a concrete plaza where four or five individuals rest in the shade. A woman, apparently a friend of Henry's, charges me three dollars "island tax." She goes into a room with a table and chair, extracts a receipt book, and painstakingly writes one out for me. Without the breeze of motion, the heat seems intolerable.

We idle away the afternoon in a shop, drinking orange sodas. I work out that the shelves above contain 15,000 cigarettes in unopened cartons—every single one of them a Doral menthol.

Visiting a healer is not a simple matter. You don't just make an appointment. First you have to see the village chief.

When darkness falls Henry conducts me to a giant longhouse, where I can make out rows of benches with men sitting here and there.

Up at the front two men sway in hammocks, one of them keeping up a stream of high-pitched emphatic chanting, punctuated every so often by a decisive note from the other: *"Nabiri!,"* or something like it, meaning, "That's right!"

"He is telling for the history of Cuna peoples and culture," Henry tells me, making no attempt to keep his voice down. I suddenly realize a low babble of chatter fills the house. Apparently no one is expected to listen too closely to the lengthy recitation of myth. It forms an aural wallpaper to the assembly room, a Cuna Muzak, a backdrop at the fringe of consciousness, just where history should be.

Sweet tobacco smoke fills the room. A hurricane lamp hangs in one corner, making the whole scene look tender.

One man with a big belly—rare here—slouches on a bench. On seeing Henry, he leans across to shake our hands. They start talking, ignoring the solemnities a few feet away. Then Henry tells me this is the *sayla*, the chief, and I may present my petition: "He speak Espanny."

I get a sudden attack of shyness. Another old man, his face glistening like walnut wood, lights up a pipe of aromatic tobacco, softly sucking, half-listening for what I will have to say. After an elaborately formal greeting, I express my hope that I may be treated by one of his village's far-famed healers.

The *sayla* tells me to take a seat. I hope I'm not committing a sacrilege by sharing his bench. Without moving, he speaks out loud into the empty darkness ahead, addressing no one in particular, then lights a cigarette.

Immediately a man somewhere behind us launches into a musical speech. His voice glides, swoops, plunges, climbs musical stairs toward some emphatic point. He cannot possibly be talking about me. How could I occasion such spellbinding rhetoric?

Finally he stops. Beside me, Walnut Face's pipe draws softly. He seems to be enjoying the performance. Then he pulls his pipe from his mouth, leans back, and starts to talk, softly and thoughtfully, though humorously, too, it seems. Soon the whole longhouse erupts in laughter. I can feel the bench shaking as the chief rocks back and forth. The old man, warming to his theme, rises to his feet and keeps up the show, his old voice sounding muffled.

Then once again the chief delivers a short and decisive speech.

Henry says, "O.K., O.K. Let's go."

I follow him into the street.

"So you haves to pay five dollars, and you can't carry photograph," he says.

"Carry photograph?"

"Right. We go to the *igar wisid* in the morning for seven clocks."

An *igar wisid* is a healer.

⋆

A muggy, sticky dawn outside, an aluminum pan hanging on a wall catches the sunlight like a bronze gong. The bathroom, just off the longhouse and concealed by a plastic curtain, is cool. It's a straw cubicle open to the sky, a floor of pebbles so the water can drain, and several tubs of well water, a gourd floating in one of them. I wash off last night's sweat and yesterday's salt. My skin is rough as sandpaper.

Henry takes me to a yard by a cooking hut. An old woman with a giant gold nose ring and a face wrinkled by decades of smiling has me hold my hand over a metal bowl full of cold black tea. She scoops up one palmful after another, bathing my arm in it. It feels cooling, like camphor. The itch I woke up with disappears.

A little crowd of family members watches her at work. She lets out satisfied grunts as the black fluid trickles down my arms. Occasionally she chats to me in Cuna, and one of her sons, a man in shorts and an orange baseball cap, translates for her.

"This medicine is very strong," he says. "If it touch your tongue, it kill you dead. You have to wash your hands before eating."

The woman's grandson stares at me from behind a toy plastic plate, with which he shields his face. I can see he is grinning. He is two years old, and a special child—a shaman. Shamans are born, not made. They come into the world already possessed of such power that their mothers sometimes die in childbirth.

I have had no breakfast and am relieved that this lotion seems to be the entire curing session. I had imagined a long smoky séance. I'll be back at the longhouse eating fresh rolls, drinking thick, sweet chocolate, before long.

It turns out the real session has yet to begin. The old woman leads me into the longhouse, where against the bamboo wall, I see bowls of dried roots, powders, rocks, boxes of flutes, knives, pots, and, most conspicuous of all, a great entourage of *nuchugana,* wooden puppets or dolls. They range in size from five inches to a foot, and many have little bowler hats. Spirits live in them. Some have red paint on their cheeks, indicating they are fierce.

The woman leaves me to her husband, Don Ignacio, a small, lithe old healer. He brings a little pile of coals balanced on a palm frond, tips them on the floor, then fetches a gourd of white cocoa beans. He starts chanting on a high, even note, inhaling noisily between phrases, accompanying himself with a rattle.

I grow hot. A sticky oppressive heat fills this longhouse.

But the old man's voice is pure and sharp like a boy's. He begins dropping beans on his bed of coals. A bitter smoke fills our corner, with only a hint of the familiar smell of chocolate. The smoke is the food for the dolls: he is nourishing them for the work ahead.

He gives my hammock a push, lulling me with the easy motion, and with the rhythm of rattle and voice. Something changes in me. I feel unaccountably safe, inexplicably carefree. I could be in my childhood home with a sunny day unfurling outside and nothing to do except swim in the river with friends. Gold light presses on my closed eyelids. His voice is a stream high on a Scottish moor. I wonder why I feel so at home. I am sure I will rise from this hammock into unalloyed happiness.

I don't know how long the performance goes on. At one point the old man leaves me rocking and returns with a hardcover ledger. He scans through the pages. Someone has covered them with rows of symbols, some hieroglyphic-like, others full-scale paintings of animal figures, all done in bright watercolors. In my suggestible condition they look wonderful, and strongly but unidentifiably familiar. Where have I seen sunny images like these before?

Though I understand none of Don Ignacio's song as he sings, its beneficence is palpable. Later someone tells me that the stuff of his narrative was a journey he and his troop of spirit-helpers made up the River of Life to the land where the spirits live. The spider spirit had apparently stolen part of my soul. After a long battle, and much diplomacy, Ignacio managed to persuade the spider to give it up.

Had there been a spider among the biting marauders?

Afterward the sunlight outside seems yellow as egg yolk, the sea blue like smoke. Ignacio's son Fidel gives me my own wooden doll to take home. I realize I had forgotten that the ceremony was all about my rash; it felt like something more important.

It is an arduous two-day task to find boats back to Chichimen. I sit soaked in dugouts for long hours, propelled in turn by paddle, engine, and sail. I learn to let the rocking of the waves lull me like a hammock, no longer telling time by my watch but by the sun.

A glorious silver evening floods the lagoon between Chichimen and its neighbor when I return. The coconut palms look wet, the sea green like fresh paint.

Don Ramón emerges from his hut. Then his entourage all appears, grinning broadly and laughing with delight when I step from the canoe straight into a deep wave.

Buna and Eulogio pull up the cuffs of my shirt and crow over my arms: rash all gone, skin smoother then ever. I feel like a lizard, a snake, a cricket risen from its old husk. In my sunstruck state I seem to be back among close friends. I would live here forever, I think, watching my shoulders grow brown on an island lying outside history's stream.

Born in Oxford, England, Henry Shukman is a regular contributor to GQ, Condé Nast Traveler, *and* Islands *magazines. He is the author of three books, including* Savage Pilgrims: On the Road to Santa Fe *and* Travels with My Trombone: A Caribbean Journey. *He lives in Las Cruces, New Mexico.*

Recommended Reading

Arvigo, Rosita, with Nadine Epstein and Marilyn Yaquinto. *Sastun: My Apprenticeship with a Maya Healer.* San Francisco: HarperSanFrancisco, 1994.

Benz, Stephen. *Green Dreams: Travels in Central America.* Victoria, Australia: Lonely Planet Publications, 1998.

Benz, Stephen. *Guatemalan Journey*. Austin: University of Texas Press, 1996.

Cahill, Tim. *Pass the Butterworms: Remote Journeys Oddly Rendered.* New York: Vintage Departures, 1997.

Cahill, Tim. *Pecked to Death By Ducks*. New York: Vintage Departures, 1994.

Cahill, Tim. *Road Fever: A High Speed Travelogue*. New York: Vintage Departures, 1992.

Canby, Peter. *The Heart of the Sky: Travels Among the Maya*. New York: HarperCollins, 1992.

Coe, Michael. *Breaking the Maya Code*. New York: Thames & Hudson, 1993.

Danner, Mark. *The Massacre at El Mozote: A Parable of the Cold War.* New York: Vintage Books, 1993.

Didion, Joan. *Salvador*. New York: Simon & Schuster, 1983.

Ferlinghetti, Lawrence. *Seven Days in Nicaragua Libre*. San Francisco: City Light Books, 1984.

Freidel, David, Linda Schele, and Joy Parker. *Maya Cosmos: Three Thousand Years on the Shaman's Path.* New York: William Morrow, 1995.

Galeano, Eduardo, Judith Brister (translator). *Days and Nights of Love and War.* New York: Monthly Review Press, 2000.

Guillermoprieto, Alma. *The Heart That Bleeds: Latin America Now*. New York: Vintage Books, 1994.

Harbury, Jennifer K. *Searching for Everardo: A Story of Love, War, and the CIA in Guatemala*. New York: Warner Books, 1997.

Hiestand, Emily. *The Very Rich Hours: Travels in Orkney, Belize, the Everglades, and Greece*. Boston: Beacon Press, 1992.

Krich, John. *El Béisbol: Travels Through the Pan-American Pastime*. Englewood Cliffs, NJ: Prentice Hall Press, 1989.

Kruckewitt, Joan. *The Death of Ben Linder: The Story of a North American in Sandinista Nicaragua*. New York: Seven Stories Press, 1999.

Maslow, Jonathan Evan. *Bird of Life, Bird of Death: A Naturalist's Journey Through a Land of Political Turmoil*. New York: Simon & Schuster, 1986.

Menchú, Rigoberta, Ann Wright (translator). *Crossing Borders*. London: Verso, 1998.

Menchú, Rigoberta, Ann Wright (translator). *I...Rigoberta Menchú: An Indian Woman in Guatemala*. London: Verso, 1983.

McCauley, Lucy. *Women in the Wild: True Stories of Adventure and Connection*. San Francisco: Travelers' Tales, 1998.

Prechtel, Martin. *Secrets of the Talking Jaguar: A Mayan Shaman's Journey to the Heart of the Indigenous Soul*. New York: Jeremy P. Tarcher, 1998.

Rabinowitz, Alan. *Jaguar: Struggle and Triumph in the Jungles of Belize*. New York: Arbor House, 1986.

Rushdie, Salman. *The Jaguar Smile: A Nicaraguan Journey*. New York: Henry Holt, 1997.

Schele, Linda, and Peter Mathews. *The Code of Kings: The Language of Seven Sacred Maya Temples and Tombs. New* York: Scribner, 1998.

Shaw, Christopher. *Sacred Monkey River: A Canoe Trip with the Gods*. New York: W. W. Norton, 2000.

Stephens, John Lloyd. *Incidents of Travel in Central America, Chiapas, and Yucatán*. Washington, DC: Smithsonian Institution Press, 1993.

Theroux, Paul. *The Old Patagonian Express: By Train Through the Americas*. New York: Houghton Mifflin Company, 1979.

Weisbecker, Allan C. *In Search of Captain Zero: A Surfer's Road Trip Beyond the End of the Road*. New York: Jeremy P. Tarcher, 2001.

White, Randy Wayne. *The Sharks of Lake Nicaragua: True Tales of Adventure, Travel, and Fishing*. New York: The Lyons Press, 1999.

Wright, Ronald. *Time Among the Maya: Travels in Belize, Guatemala, and Mexico*. New York: Owl Books, 1991.

Index

Index of Contributors

Acknowledgments

I would like to give special thanks to coeditor Natanya Pearlman, whose perceptive critical eye, unfailing enthusiasm, keen skill with words and stories, and true friendship made this project a pleasure from start to finish. Thanks also to my friends and family for their usual forbearance while I am putting a book together, and to James, Sean, Tim, and Wenda O'Reilly, Susan Brady, Krista Holmstrom, Kathy Meengs, Christine Nielsen, Mija Riedel, Tara Austen Weaver, Desiree Earl, Patty Holden, Judy Johnson, and Michele Wetherbee for their support and contributions to the book.

—Larry Habegger

I could not have hoped for a more thoughtful collaborator than I was blessed with in Larry Habegger—a wonderful editor, colleague, and friend, as well as a rare individual who always keeps life's priorities in good order. Larry, simply, thank you. To James O'Reilly, I also give my true thanks, for many things, including dreaming and believing (again and again), and especially for enthusiasm and kindness. As for the rest of the gang at Travelers' Tales—and what a gang it is!—I have been endlessly inspired, entertained, moved, and fed by my years in their company. Thank you, all of you: Lisa Bach, Susan Brady, Desiree Earl, Deborah Greco, Krista Holmstrom, Jennifer Leo, Kathy Meengs, Christine Nielsen, and Tara Weaver—you've made the past three years a pleasure. Heartfelt gratitude to Mija Riedel, for the hours she gave to this book, as well as for her generous, buoyant spirit, and thanks to Wenda O'Reilly, Sean O'Reilly, and Tim O'Reilly, for their years of dedication to Travelers' Tales. To Marybeth Bond and Pamela Michael, warm and celebratory appreciation for, years ago, beginning my Travelers' Tales journey in the best of all possible ways. Many thanks also to Michele Wetherbee, Judy Johnson, and Patty Holden, for committed, excellent work. I am indebted to Jane Anne Staw and my writer's group (all incarnations) for a steady supply of creative community and education—consistently some of the best hours. And, finally, to my ever-supportive friends and family—

particularly my parents, Dan and Cinda Pearlman, and my *compañero* in love and adventure, Grant Reading—thank you, thank you, thank you.

—Natanya Pearlman

"The Moon and Danzel Cabral" by Bucky McMahon reprinted from the March 1999 issue of *Esquire*. Copyright © 1999 by Bucky McMahon. Reprinted by permission of the author.

"The Lone Ranger" by Tim Cahill excerpted from *Pass the Butterworms: Remote Journeys Oddly Rendered* by Tim Cahill. Copyright © 1997 by Tim Cahill. Reprinted by permission of Vintage Departures, a division of Random House, Inc., and by permission of Lowenstein Associates.

"At the Station" by Emily Hiestand excerpted from *The Very Rich Hours: Travels in Orkney, Belize, the Everglades, and Greece* by Emily Hiestand. Copyright © 1992 by Emily Hiestand. Reprinted by permission of Beacon Press.

"Am I Glad to See You!" by Paul Theroux excerpted from *The Old Patagonian Express: By Train Through the Americas* by Paul Theroux. Copyright © 1979 by Cape Cod Scriveners Company. Reprinted by permission of Houghton Mifflin Company and Penguin UK.

"Exploring the Place of Fright" by David Roberts reprinted from the July/August 2001 issue of *National Geographic Adventure*. Copyright © 2001 by David Roberts. Reprinted by permission of the author.

"On Guatemala's Gringo Circuit" by Doug Fine first appeared in SALON.com, at http://www.salon.com. Copyright © 1998 by Doug Fine. Reprinted by permission of the author.

"A Garífuna Awakening" by Natanya Pearlman published with permission from the author. Copyright © 2002 by Natanya Pearlman.

"In Search of Ben Linder's Killers" by Paul Berman reprinted from the September 25, 1996 issue of *The New Yorker*. Copyright © 1996 by Paul Berman. Reprinted by permission of the author.

"Corn Island and the Festival of Crabs" by Jason Wilson first appeared in SALON.com, at http://www.salon.com. Copyright © 2000 by Jason Wilson. Reprinted by permission of the author.

"Bones and Heads with Hussein" by Tom Joseph published with permission from the author. Copyright © 2002 by Tom Joseph.

"In Search of Blue Butterflies" by Sue Hubbell reprinted from the May 15, 1994 issue of *The Sophisticated Traveler*. Copyright © 1994 by Sue Hubbell. Reprinted by permission of Darhansoff, Verrill, Feldman Literary Agents.

"The Last Penal Colony" by Scott Anderson reprinted from the May 2000 issue of *Esquire*. Copyright © 2000 by Scott Anderson. Reprinted by permission of the author.

"Surfing La Libertad" by Kevin Naughton reprinted from the Fall 2001 issue of *The Surfer's Journal*. Copyright © 2001 by Kevin Naughton. Reprinted by permission of the author.

"Pacaya!" by Steve Wilson published with permission from the author. Copyright © 2002 by Steve Wilson.

"*Viva* Sandino Koufax!" by John Krich excerpted from *El Béisbol: Travels Through the Pan-American Pastime* by John Krich. Copyright © 1989 by John Krich.

Reprinted by permission of the author.

"In Search of Zen" by Lea Aschkenas published with permission from the author. Copyright © 2002 by Lea Aschkenas.

"The Rainbow Special" by Cara Tabachnick published with permission from the author. Copyright © 2000 by Cara Tabachnick.

"An Evening with the Croc Poachers" by Randy Wayne White excerpted from *The Sharks of Lake Nicaragua: True Tales of Adventure, Travel, and Fishing* by Randy Wayne White. Copyright © 1999 by Randy Wayne Wright. Reprinted by permission of The Lyons Press.

"Dancing for Centavos" and "I Hear Voices" by Martin Mitchinson published with permission from the author. Copyright © 2002 by Martin Mitchinson.

"The Lady Who Lassoed Jaguars" by Joseph Diedrich published with permission from the author. Copyright © 2002 by Joseph Diedrich.

"When Water Bends" by Victoria Schlesinger published with permission from the author. Copyright © 2002 by Victoria Schlesinger.

"Everardo" by Jennifer K. Harbury excerpted from *Searching for Everardo: A Story of Love, War, and the CIA in Guatemala* by Jennifer K. Harbury. Copyright © 1997 by The Everardo Foundation. Reprinted by permission of Warner Books, Inc. and The Everardo Foundation.

"Deceptive Moonrise" by Yael Flusberg published with permission from the author. Copyright © 2002 by Yael Flusberg.

"Return to Laj Chimel" by Rigoberta Menchú excerpted from *Crossing Borders* by Rigoberta Menchú, translated and edited by Ann Wright. Copyright © 1998 by Verso, translation copyright © 1998 by Ann Wright, worldwide rights copyright © Giunti Gruppo Editoriale, S.p.A. Reprinted by permission of Verso.

"In the Land of the Cunas" by Henry Shukman reprinted from the May/June 1998 issue of *Islands*. Copyright © 1998 by Islands Publishing Company. Reprinted by permission of Islands Publishing Company.

Additional Credits (arranged alphabetically by title)

Selection from "Belize It or Not" by Tony Perrottet published with permission from the author. Copyright © 2002 by Tony Perrottet.

Selection from "Belize: Music, Tin Roofs, and Progress" by Archie Satterfield published with permission from the author. Copyright © 2002 by Archie Satterfield.

Selection from "*Cara a Cara*, September 2, 1982" by Mija Riedel published with permission from the author. Copyright © 2002 by Mija Riedel.

Selections from *The Death of Ben Linder: The Story of a North American in Sandinista Nicaragua* by Joan Kruckewitt. Copyright © 1999 by Joan Kruckewitt. Reprinted by permission of Seven Stories Press.

Selection from "Earthquake" by Isabelle Selby published with permission from the author. Copyright © 2002 by Isabelle Selby.

Selections from "Easy in the Cayes" by Doug Peacock reprinted from the March/April 1999 issue of *Islands*. Copyright © 1999 by Islands Publishing Company. Reprinted by permission of Islands Publishing Company.

Selection from "A Family, A Plan, A Canal" by Kimberly Brown Seely first appeared in the Fall/Winter 2000 issue of *Travel & Leisure Family*. Copyright © 2000 by Kimberly Brown Seely. Reprinted by permission of the author.

Selection from *The Fearless Shopper: How to Get the Best Deals on the Planet* by Kathy Borrus copyright ©1999 by Kathy Borrus. Reprinted by permission of Travelers' Tales, Inc.

Selection from *Femme d'Adventure: Travel Tales from Inner Montana to Outer Mongolia* by Jessica Maxwell copyright © 1997 by Jessica Maxwell. Reprinted by permission of the author.

Selection from "The Forgotten Highway," by Benjamin Ryder Howe reprinted from the March 2001 issue of *The Atlantic Monthly*. Copyright © 2001.

Selection from "The Golden Time of the Cuna" by David Yeadon published with permission from the author. Copyright © 2002 by David Yeadon.

Selection from *Green Dreams: Travels in Central America* by Stephen Benz copyright © 1998 by Stephen Benz. Reprinted by permission of Lonely Planet Publications.

Selection excerpted from *The Heart of the Sky: Travels Among the Maya* by Peter Canby copyright © 1992 by Peter Canby. Reprinted by permission of HarperCollins Publishers, Inc.

Selection from *The Heart That Bleeds: Latin America Now* by Alma Guillermoprieto copyright © 1994 by Alma Guillermoprieto. Reprinted by permission of Alfred A. Knopf, a division of Random House, Inc.

Selection from "Honduran Heat" by Lani Wright published with permission from the author. Copyright © 2002 by Lani Wright.

Selection from *In Search of Captain Zero: A Surfer's Road Trip Beyond the End of the Road* by Allan C. Weisbecker copyright © 2001 by Allan C. Weisbecker.

Selection from "In Search of Guatemala's Resplendent Quetzal" by Michael Shapiro published with permission from the author. Copyright © 2002 by Michael Shapiro.

Selections from *Incidents of Travel in Central America, Chiapas, and Yucatán* by John Lloyd Stephens published by Smithsonian Institution Press. Copyright © 1993 by Karl Ackerman.

Selection from "Living Wisdom of the Painted Men" by Ryan A. Murdock published with permission from the author. Copyright © 2002 by Ryan A. Murdock.

Selection from *The Massacre at El Mozote: A Parable of the Cold War* by Mark Danner copyright © 1993 by Mark Danner. Reprinted by permission of Vintage Books, a division of Random House, Inc.

Selections from "Paul and Ray's Exceptional Adventure" by Paul Haeder published with permission from the author. Copyright © 2002 by Paul Haeder.

Selection from "Playing with Fire" by Doug Lansky published with permission from the author. Copyright © 2002 by Doug Lansky.

Selection from "A Pyramid Scheme" by Ronald Wright published with permission from the author. Copyright © 2002 by Ronald Wright.

Selection from *Sacred Monkey River: A Canoe Trip with the Gods* by Christopher Shaw copyright © 2000 by Christopher Shaw. Reprinted by permission of W.W. Norton & Company.

Selection from *Salvador* by Joan Didion copyright © 1983 by Joan Didion. Reprinted by permission of Simon & Schuster, Inc.

Selection from "Salvadoran Vignettes" by Marguerite Watson published with permission from the author. Copyright © 2002 by Marguerite Watson.

Selection from *Sastun: My Apprenticeship with a Maya Healer* by Rosita Arvigo with Nadine Epstein and Marilyn Yaquinto. Copyright © 1994 by Rosita Arvigo with Nadine Epstein. Reprinted by permission of HarperCollins Publishers, Inc.

Selections from *The Sharks of Lake Nicaragua: True Tales of Adventure, Travel, and Fishing* by Randy Wayne White copyright © 1999 by Randy Wayne Wright. Reprinted by permission of The Lyons Press.

Selection from "Snapshots" by Judith Nolan published with permission from the author. Copyright © 2002 by Judith Nolan.

Selection from "Up the Volcano" by Lucy McCauley excerpted from *Women in the Wild,* edited by Lucy McCauley. Copyright © 1998 by Lucy McCauley. Reprinted by permission of the author.

Selections from "We Are All Refugees" by Paul Haeder published with permission from the author. Copyright © 2002 by Paul Haeder.

About the Editors

Larry Habegger has been writing about travel since 1980. He has visited almost fifty countries and six of the seven continents, traveling from the frozen arctic to equatorial rain forest, the high Himalayas to the Dead Sea. With coauthor James O'Reilly he wrote a serialized mystery novel and several short stories for the *San Francisco Examiner* in the early 1980s, and since 1985 their syndicated column, "World Travel Watch," has appeared in newspapers in five countries and on Internet-based information centers. He was a founding editor of Travelers' Tales and currently serves as executive editor. He was born and raised in Minnesota and lives with his family on Telegraph Hill in San Francisco.

Natanya Pearlman first traveled in Central America at age seventeen on a trip to Guatemala—a country whose combination of extraordinary beauty and struggle left a lasting impression. Since then, she's returned to Central America multiple times, including once to build a school in the mountains of Nicaragua, where she lived for four months. Natanya is a freelance editor and writer, and lives in Berkeley, CA.

TRAVELERS' TALES

THE SOUL OF TRAVEL

Footsteps Series

THE FIRE NEVER DIES
One Man's Raucous Romp Down the Road of Food, Passion, and Adventure
By Richard Sterling
ISBN 1-885-211-70-8
$14.95
"Sterling's writing is like spitfire, foursquare and jazzy with crackle...."
—*Kirkus Reviews*

LAST TROUT IN VENICE
The Far-Flung Escapades of an Accidental Adventurer
By Doug Lansky
ISBN 1-885-211-63-5
$14.95
"Traveling with Doug Lansky might result in a considerably shortened life expectancy...but what a way to go." —Tony Wheeler, Lonely Planet Publications

ONE YEAR OFF
Leaving It All Behind for a Round-the-World Journey with Our Children
By David Elliot Cohen
ISBN 1-885-211-65-1
$14.95
A once-in-a-lifetime adventure generously shared.

THE WAY OF THE WANDERER
Discover Your True Self Through Travel
By David Yeadon
ISBN 1-885-211-60-0
$14.95
Experience transformation through travel with this delightful, illustrated collection by award-winning author David Yeadon.

TAKE ME WITH YOU
A Round-the-World Journey to Invite a Stranger Home
By Brad Newsham
ISBN 1-885-211-51-1
$24.00 (cloth)
"Newsham is an ideal guide. His journey, at heart, is into humanity." —Pico Iyer, author of *Video Night in Kathmandu*

KITE STRINGS OF THE SOUTHERN CROSS
A Woman's Travel Odyssey
By Laurie Gough
ISBN 1-885-211-54-6
$14.95

★★★

ForeWord Silver Medal Winner
—Travel Book of the Year

THE SWORD OF HEAVEN
A Five Continent Odyssey to Save the World
By Mikkel Aaland
ISBN 1-885-211-44-9
$24.00 (cloth)
"Few books capture the soul of the road like *The Sword of Heaven*, a sharp-edged, beautifully rendered memoir that will inspire anyone." —Phil Cousineau, author of *The Art of Pilgrimage*

STORM
A Motorcycle Journey of Love, Endurance, and Transformation
By Allen Noren
ISBN 1-885-211-45-7
$24.00 (cloth)

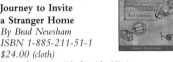

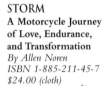

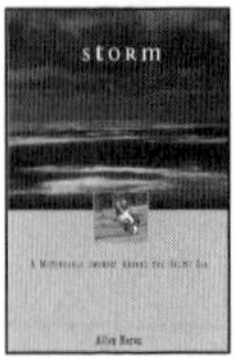

★★★

ForeWord Gold Medal Winner
—Travel Book of the Year

Travelers' Tales Classics

COAST TO COAST
A Journey Across 1950s America
By Jan Morris
ISBN 1-885-211-79-1
$16.95
After reporting on the first Everest ascent in 1953, Morris spent a year journeying by car, train, ship, and aircraft across the United States. In her brilliant prose, Morris records with exuberance and curiosity a time of innocence in the U.S.

TRADER HORN
A Young Man's Astounding Adventures in 19th Century Equatorial Africa
By Alfred Aloysius Horn
ISBN 1-885-211-81-3
$16.95
Here is the stuff of legends—tale of thrills and danger, wild beasts, serpents, and savages. An unforgettable and vivid portrait of a vanished late-19th century Africa.

THE ROYAL ROAD TO ROMANCE
By Richard Halliburton
ISBN 1-885-211-53-8
$14.95
"Laughing at hardships, dreaming of beauty, ardent for adventure, Halliburton has managed to sing into the pages of this glorious book his own exultant spirit of youth and freedom."
—*Chicago Post*

UNBEATEN TRACKS IN JAPAN
By Isabella L. Bird
ISBN 1-885-211-57-0
$14.95
Isabella Bird was one of the most adventurous women travelers of the 19th century with journeys to Tibet, Canada, Korea, Turkey, Hawaii, and Japan. A fascinating read for anyone interested in women's travel, spirituality, and Asian culture.

THE RIVERS RAN EAST
By Leonard Clark
ISBN 1-885-211-66-X
$16.95
Clark is the original Indiana Jones, relaying a breathtaking account of his search for the legendary El Dorado gold in the Amazon.

Travel Humor

NOT SO FUNNY WHEN IT HAPPENED
The Best of Travel Humor and Misadventure
Edited by Tim Cahill
ISBN 1-885-211-55-4
$12.95
Laugh with Bill Bryson, Dave Barry, Anne Lamott, Adair Lara, and many more.

THERE'S NO TOILET PAPER... ON THE ROAD LESS TRAVELED
The Best of Travel Humor and Misadventure
Edited by Doug Lansky
ISBN 1-885-211-27-9
$12.95

Humor Book of the Year —Independent Publisher's Book Award

ForeWord Gold Medal Winner—Humor Book of the Year

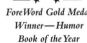

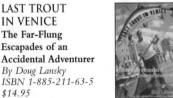

LAST TROUT IN VENICE
The Far-Flung Escapades of an Accidental Adventurer
By Doug Lansky
ISBN 1-885-211-63-5
$14.95
"Traveling with Doug Lansky might result in a considerably shortened life expectancy...but what a way to go."
—Tony Wheeler, Lonely Planet Publications

Women's Travel

A WOMAN'S PASSION FOR TRAVEL

More True Stories from A Woman's World

Edited by Marybeth Bond & Pamela Michael

ISBN 1-885-211-36-8

$17.95

"A diverse and gripping series of stories!" —Arlene Blum, author of *Annapurna: A Woman's Place*

A WOMAN'S WORLD

True Stories of Life on the Road

Edited by Marybeth Bond

Introduction by Dervla Murphy

ISBN 1-885-211-06-6

$17.95

Winner of the Lowell Thomas Award for Best Travel Book— Society of American Travel Writers

WOMEN IN THE WILD

True Stories of Adventure and Connection

Edited by Lucy McCauley

ISBN 1-885-211-21-X

$17.95

"A spiritual, moving, and totally female book to take you around the world and back." —*Mademoiselle*

A MOTHER'S WORLD

Journeys of the Heart

Edited by Marybeth Bond & Pamela Michael

ISBN 1-885-211-26-0

$14.95

"These stories remind us that motherhood is one of the great unifying forces in the world" —*San Francisco Examiner*

Food

ADVENTURES IN WINE

True Stories of Vineyards and Vintages around the World

Edited by Thom Elkjer

ISBN 1-885-211-80-5

$17.95

Humanity, community, and brotherhood comprise the marvelous virtues of the wine world. This collection toasts the warmth and wonders of this large, extended family in stories by travelers who are wine novices and experts alike.

FOOD (Updated)

A Taste of the Road

Edited by Richard Sterling

Introduction by Margo True

ISBN 1-885-211-77-5

$18.95

Silver Medal Winner of the Lowell Thomas Award for Best Travel Book—Society of American Travel Writers

HER FORK IN THE ROAD

Women Celebrate Food and Travel

Edited by Lisa Bach

ISBN 1-885-211-71-6

$16.95

A savory sampling of stories by some of the best writers in and out of the food and travel fields.

THE ADVENTURE OF FOOD

True Stories of Eating Everything

Edited by Richard Sterling

ISBN 1-885-211-37-6

$17.95

"These stories are bound to whet appetites for more than food."

—*Publishers Weekly*

Spiritual Travel

THE SPIRITUAL GIFTS OF TRAVEL
The Best of Travelers' Tales
Edited by James O'Reilly and Sean O'Reilly
ISBN 1-885-211-69-4
$16.95

A collection of favorite stories of transformation on the road from our award-winning Travelers' Tales series that shows the myriad ways travel indelibly alters our inner landscapes.

THE WAY OF THE WANDERER
Discover Your True Self Through Travel
By David Yeadon
ISBN 1-885-211-60-0
$14.95

Experience transformation through travel with this delightful, illustrated collection by award-winning author David Yeadon.

PILGRIMAGE
Adventures of the Spirit
Edited by Sean O'Reilly & James O'Reilly
Introduction by Phil Cousineau
ISBN 1-885-211-56-2
$16.95

—★★★—

ForeWord Silver Medal Winner — Travel Book of the Year

A WOMAN'S PATH
Women's Best Spiritual Travel Writing
Edited by Lucy McCauley, Amy G. Carlson & Jennifer Leo
ISBN 1-885-211-48-1
$16.95

"A sensitive exploration of women's lives that have been unexpectedly and spiritually touched by travel experiences.... Highly recommended."
—*Library Journal*

THE ROAD WITHIN
True Stories of Transformation and the Soul
Edited by Sean O'Reilly, James O'Reilly & Tim O'Reilly
ISBN 1-885-211-19-8
$17.95

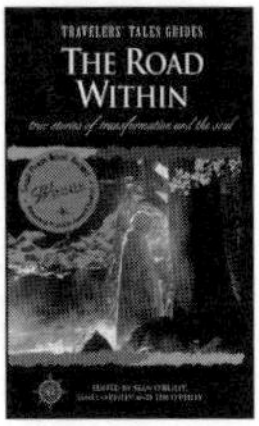

—★★★—

Best Spiritual Book—Independent Publisher's Book Award

THE ULTIMATE JOURNEY
Inspiring Stories of Living and Dying
James O'Reilly, Sean O'Reilly & Richard Sterling
ISBN 1-885-211-38-4
$17.95

"A glorious collection of writings about the ultimate adventure. A book to keep by one's bedside—and close to one's heart." —Philip Zaleski, editor, *The Best Spiritual Writing series*

Adventure

TESTOSTERONE PLANET
True Stories from a Man's World
Edited by Sean O'Reilly, Larry Habegger & James O'Reilly
ISBN 1-885-211-43-0
$17.95

Thrills and laughter with some of today's best writers: Sebastian Junger, Tim Cahill, Bill Bryson, and Jon Krakauer.

DANGER!
True Stories of Trouble and Survival
Edited by James O'Reilly, Larry Habegger & Sean O'Reilly
ISBN 1-885-211-32-5
$17.95

"Exciting...for those who enjoy living on the edge or prefer to read the survival stories of others, this is a good pick."
—*Library Journal*

Special Interest

365 TRAVEL
A Daily Book of Journeys, Meditations, and Adventures
Edited by Lisa Bach
ISBN 1-885-211-67-8
$14.95

An illuminating collection of travel wisdom and adventures that reminds us all of the lessons we learn while on the road.

THE GIFT OF RIVERS
True Stories of Life on the Water
Edited by Pamela Michael
Introduction by Robert Hass
ISBN 1-885-211-42-2
$14.95

"*The Gift of Rivers* is a soulful compendium of wonderful stories that illuminate, educate, inspire, and delight."
—David Brower, Chairman of Earth Island Institute

FAMILY TRAVEL
The Farther You Go, the Closer You Get
Edited by Laura Manske
ISBN 1-885-211-33-3
$17.95

"This is family travel at its finest." —*Working Mother*

LOVE & ROMANCE
True Stories of Passion on the Road
Edited by Judith Babcock Wylie
ISBN 1-885-211-18-X
$17.95

"A wonderful book to read by a crackling fire."
—*Romantic Traveling*

THE GIFT OF BIRDS
True Encounters with Avian Spirits
Edited by Larry Habegger & Amy G. Carlson
ISBN 1-885-211-41-4
$17.95

"These are all wonderful, entertaining stories offering a *bird's-eye view!* of our avian friends."
—*Booklist*

A DOG'S WORLD
True Stories of Man's Best Friend on the Road
Edited by Christine Hunsicker
ISBN 1-885-211-23-6
$12.95

This extraordinary collection includes stories by John Steinbeck, Helen Thayer, James Herriot, Pico Iyer, and many others.

THE GIFT OF TRAVEL
The Best of Travelers' Tales
Edited by Larry Habegger, James O'Reilly & Sean O'Reilly
ISBN 1-885-211-25-2
$14.95

"Like gourmet chefs in a French market, the editors of Travelers' Tales pick, sift, and prod their way through the weighty shelves of contemporary travel writing, creaming off the very best."
—William Dalrymple, author of *City of Djinns*

Travel Advice

SHITTING PRETTY
How to Stay Clean and Healthy While Traveling
By Dr. Jane Wilson-Howarth
ISBN 1-885-211-47-3
$12.95

A light-hearted book about a serious subject for millions of travelers—staying healthy on the road—written by international health expert, Dr. Jane Wilson-Howarth.

THE FEARLESS SHOPPER
How to Get the Best Deals on the Planet
By Kathy Borrus
ISBN 1-885-211-39-2
$14.95

"Anyone who reads *The Fearless Shopper* will come away a smarter, more responsible shopper and a more curious, culturally attuned traveler."

—Jo Mancuso, *The Shopologist*

GUTSY WOMEN
More Travel Tips and Wisdom for the Road
By Marybeth Bond
ISBN 1-885-211-61-9
$12.95

Second Edition—Packed with funny, instructive, and inspiring advice for women heading out to see the world.

SAFETY AND SECURITY FOR WOMEN WHO TRAVEL
By Sheila Swan & Peter Laufer
ISBN 1-885-211-29-5
$12.95

A must for every woman traveler!

THE FEARLESS DINER
Travel Tips and Wisdom for Eating around the World
By Richard Sterling
ISBN 1-885-211-22-8
$7.95

Combines practical advice on foodstuffs, habits, and etiquette, with hilarious accounts of others' eating adventures.

THE PENNY PINCHER'S PASSPORT TO LUXURY TRAVEL
The Art of Cultivating Preferred Customer Status
By Joel L. Widzer
ISBN 1-885-211-31-7
$12.95

Proven techniques on how to travel first class at discount prices, even if you're not a frequent flyer.

GUTSY MAMAS
Travel Tips and Wisdom for Mothers on the Road
By Marybeth Bond
ISBN 1-885-211-20-1
$7.95

A delightful guide for mothers traveling with their children—or without them!

Destination Titles:
True Stories of Life on the Road

AMERICA
Edited by Fred Setterberg
ISBN 1-885-211-28-7
$19.95

AMERICAN SOUTHWEST
Edited by Sean O'Reilly & James O'Reilly
ISBN 1-885-211-58-9
$17.95

AUSTRALIA
Edited by Larry Habegger
ISBN 1-885-211-40-6
$17.95

BRAZIL
Edited by Annette Haddad & Scott Doggett
Introduction by Alex Shoumatoff
ISBN 1-885-211-11-2
$17.95

CENTRAL AMERICA
Edited by Larry Habegger & Natanya Pearlman
ISBN 1-885-211-74-0
$17.95

CUBA
Edited by Tom Miller
ISBN 1-885-211-62-7
$17.95

FRANCE (**Updated**)
Edited by James O'Reilly, Larry Habegger & Sean O'Reilly
ISBN 1-885-211-73-2
$18.95

GRAND CANYON
Edited by Sean O'Reilly, James O'Reilly & Larry Habegger
ISBN 1-885-211-34-1
$17.95

GREECE
Edited by Larry Habegger, Sean O'Reilly & Brian Alexander
ISBN 1-885-211-52-X
$17.95

HAWAI'I
Edited by Rick & Marcie Carroll
ISBN 1-885-211-35-X
$17.95

HONG KONG
Edited by James O'Reilly, Larry Habegger & Sean O'Reilly
ISBN 1-885-211-03-1
$17.95

INDIA
Edited by James O'Reilly & Larry Habegger
ISBN 1-885-211-01-5
$17.95

IRELAND
Edited by James O'Reilly,
Larry Habegger &
Sean O'Reilly
ISBN 1-885-211-46-5
$17.95

ITALY (Updated)
Edited by Anne Calcagno
Introduction by Jan Morris
ISBN 1-885-211-72-4
$18.95

JAPAN
Edited by Donald W. George
& Amy G. Carlson
ISBN 1-885-211-04-X
$17.95

MEXICO (Updated)
Edited by James O'Reilly
& Larry Habegger
ISBN 1-885-211-59-7
$17.95

NEPAL
Edited by Rajendra
S. Khadka
ISBN 1-885-211-14-7
$17.95

PARIS
Edited by James O'Reilly,
Larry Habegger &
Sean O'Reilly
ISBN 1-885-211-10-4
$17.95

SAN FRANCISCO
Edited by James O'Reilly,
Larry Habegger &
Sean O'Reilly
ISBN 1-885-211-08-2
$17.95

SPAIN (Updated)
Edited by Lucy McCauley
ISBN 1-885-211-78-3
$19.95

THAILAND (Updated)
Edited by James O'Reilly
& Larry Habegger
ISBN 1-885-211-75-9
$18.95

TIBET
Edited by James O'Reilly,
Larry Habegger &
Kim Morris
ISBN 1-885-211-76-7
$18.95

TUSCANY
Edited by James O'Reilly
& Tara Austen Weaver
ISBN 1-885-211-68-6
$16.95